VOLU[...]

WORLD'S GREATEST COLLECTION OF

BIBLE
Word Games

BARBOUR BOOKS
An Imprint of Barbour Publishing, Inc.

Print ISBN 978-1-63409-651-5

Published by Barbour Books, an imprint of Barbour Publishing, Inc., P.O. Box 719, Uhrichsville, Ohio 44683, www.barbourbooks.com

Our mission is to publish and distribute inspirational products offering exceptional value and biblical encouragement to the masses.

Member of the
Evangelical Christian
Publishers Association

Welcome to the
World's Greatest Collection
of Bible Word Games

So you love the Bible? Enjoy word puzzles? Then this is the book for you!
   Scattered throughout the pages of this book are eleven types of fun,
challenging, and educational puzzles, all based on the world's greatest Book—
the Bible. Exercise your knowledge of scripture and your puzzle-solving abilities
as you work your way through the following puzzles:

Drop Twos (see page 5): Remove two letters from each seven-letter word in the
left-hand column to create a new five-letter word (you may need to rearrange the
remaining letters). Put the two dropped letters into the spaces to the right of the
blanks. Then use these letters to spell out a phrase or sentence from the Bible.

Acrostics (see page 6): Read the definition in the left-hand column and write the
word it describes in the right-hand column. Then place the coded letters from the
right-hand column in the puzzle form following to spell out the verse indicated.

Word Searches (see page 8): Find and circle the search words in the puzzle
grid—words may run forward, backward, up, down, and on the diagonal. When
a scripture passage is given, find the words highlighted in **bold type**.

Cryptoscriptures (see page 10): Each of the cryptoscriptures is a Bible verse in
substitution code. For example, JEHOVAH might become M P X S T Q X if M is
substituted for J, P for E, X for H, and so on. One way to break the code is to look
for repeated letters: E, T, A, O, N, R, and I are the most often used. A single letter
is usually A or I. OF, IT, and IS are common two-letter words. Try THE and AND
for a three-letter group. The code is different for each cryptoscripture. (There are
two cryptoscriptures per page.)

Bible Sudoku (see page 11): Each 9 x 9 grid includes "givens," as with
traditional sudoku puzzles. In this case, the givens are nine unique letters—
which will spell out a biblical word or phrase. The nine-letter word or phrase
is determined from the scripture printed below the puzzle. Solving the puzzle
involves placing the nine letters in each row, column, and 3 x 3 minigrid (the
white and shaded areas) so that no letter is duplicated in a row, column, or
minigrid. Use your skills of deduction!

Crosswords (see page 12): Fill in the puzzle grid by starting answers in the appropriately-numbered boxes, and continuing either across to the right or down. Capitalized clues have answers that relate to the theme of the puzzle.

Scrambled Circles (see page 18): Unscramble the words from the list provided, placing the corrected words in the blanks corresponding with the numbers. Then use the circled letters to answer the question that follows.

Anagrams (see page 19): Unscramble the letters of the word or phrase given to create another word or phrase from the Bible.

Spotty Headlines (see page 24): Fill in the missing letters of each "headline," which relates to a Bible story. Then unscramble the letters you've added to the headline to form a name, which is the subject of the headline.

Telephone Scrambles (see page 25): Each set of telephone push-buttons contains a hidden Bible word—and you'll need to determine which letter of each combination is part of the word.

Bible Quotations (see page 30): Place the letters in each column into the puzzle grid preceding to form words. The letters may or may not fit into the grid in the same order in which they're given; black spaces indicate the ends of words. When a letter has been used, cross it off and do not use it again. When the grid has been properly filled in, you'll be able to read a Bible verse by scanning the lines of the grid from left to right.

Most clues are direct quotations are taken from the King James Version of the Bible, though some newer translations have also been referenced for variety. Puzzle answers begin on page 315.

One of a Kind
DANIEL 2:48

God makes mysteries known to His own unique people. Solve this puzzle to find out how an Old Testament hero benefited from accurately interpreting a Babylonian ruler's dream.

LANTERN	Memorize	_____	1. ___ ___
HOLIEST	Shoulder covering	_____	2. ___ ___
ENDWISE	Weaves	_____	3. ___ ___
KESTREL	Oak and maple	_____	4. ___ ___
AMIABLE	Easy walk	_____	5. ___ ___
GRANTED	Scored	_____	6. ___ ___
GURGLED	Stuck	_____	7. ___ ___
MENACED	Beat	_____	8. ___ ___
ABALONE	Aristocrat	_____	9. ___ ___
BLASTED	Apathetic	_____	10. ___ ___
MACHINE	Dishes	_____	11. ___ ___
INVADES	Grape plants	_____	12. ___ ___
AVENGER	Brink	_____	13. ___ ___

___ ___ ___ ___ ___ ___ ___ ___ ___ ___ ___ ___ ___

___ ___ ___ ___ ___ ___ ___ ___ ___ ___ ___ ___ ___
 1   2   3   4   5   6   7   8   9   10 11 12 13

A Brotherly Brother

Sibling rivalry can be the pits, yet sometimes in dire circumstances, older brothers can really deliver. Solve this puzzle to learn about one such brother who rose to the challenge.

Jacob's fourth son

$\overline{15}$ $\overline{35}$ $\overline{21}$ $\overline{3}$ $\overline{26}$

Meaning "brothers"

$\overline{22}$ $\overline{4}$ $\overline{36}$ $\overline{14}$ $\overline{33}$ $\overline{25}$ $\overline{5}$ $\overline{38}$

Groups of sheep

$\overline{31}$ $\overline{16}$ $\overline{37}$ $\overline{1}$ $\overline{34}$ $\overline{20}$

Joseph was _____ in the field while looking for his brothers (Genesis 37:15)

$\overline{7}$ $\overline{23}$ $\overline{19}$ $\overline{32}$ $\overline{12}$ $\overline{29}$ $\overline{6}$ $\overline{24}$ $\overline{8}$

His father feared Joseph had been rent into _____ (Genesis 37:33)

$\overline{9}$ $\overline{13}$ $\overline{30}$ $\overline{18}$ $\overline{10}$ $\overline{28}$

The coat of _____ colors

$\overline{11}$ $\overline{27}$ $\overline{2}$ $\overline{17}$

29-10-35-22-36-19   20-3-13-32   35-19-14-37

14-26-12-11,   28-33-30-21   24-37   22-16-37-37-21,

22-35-14   18-23-28-14   26-6-11   13-2-14-37

14-33-6-20   9-13-14   14-26-3-14   6-28   13-19   14-26-5

7-13-16-21-12-4-2-30-20-28,   3-2-21   16-27-17

2-37   26-23-24-21   35-9-37-38   33-6-11.

GENESIS 37:22

Word Search
by N. Teri Grottke

The Prodigal Son
LUKE 15:11–32

BELLY
CERTAIN
CITIZEN
COUNTRY
DIVIDED
FAIN
FALLETH
FAR
FATHER
FEED
FIELDS
FILLED
GATHERED
GIVE
GOODS
HUSKS

JOURNEY
LIVING
MIGHTY
PORTION
RIOTOUS
SONS
SPENT
SUBSTANCE
SWINE
TOGETHER
TOOK
TWO
WANT
WASTED
YOUNGER

```
J  P  Y  P  E  C  N  A  T  S  B  U  S  W  F
O  G  O  O  T  I  G  Y  R  D  Z  E  R  D  A
U  O  U  R  P  T  Y  T  D  E  M  A  L  B  I
R  O  N  T  F  I  T  H  L  D  F  S  D  L  N
N  D  G  I  W  Z  O  G  R  I  R  U  E  J  Y
E  S  E  O  N  E  O  I  Z  V  J  O  R  H  R
Y  Z  R  N  R  N  K  M  Q  I  T  T  E  A  E
E  S  D  L  E  I  F  C  W  D  G  O  H  O  H
N  U  I  A  S  X  O  A  E  N  M  I  T  E  T
I  O  U  K  O  U  S  L  I  F  L  R  A  V  E
W  L  S  S  N  T  L  V  G  A  A  L  G  I  G
S  U  O  T  E  I  I  S  P  E  N  T  A  G  O
H  N  R  D  F  L  F  A  L  L  E  T  H  F  T
S  Y  S  T  N  A  W  I  F  D  E  E  F  E  F
C  E  R  T  A  I  N  R  O  W  T  N  R  B  R
```

Cryptoscripture

by Sharon Y. Brown and David Austin

Biblical Battlers

Some biblical characters were formidable opponents. Crack the crypstoscripture codes below to find the names of two such warriors who stood head and shoulders above the rest in strength and stature.

NSK FWJ CRTNS MNOJ N GRS, NSK LNUUJK

WXG SNTJ GNTGRS: NSK FWJ LWXUK HOJC,

NSK FWJ UROK MUJGGJK WXT.

UAO KBTLT ITAK CDK U QBUWYNCA CDK CR

KBT QUWY CR KBT YBNSNEKNATE, AUWTO

JCSNUKB, CR JUKB, IBCET BTNJBK IUE ENH

QDGNKE UAO U EYUA.

God's Favored

MEDIUM

	A	B	C	D	E	F	G	H	I
1		S	I	O	T	U		E	R
2			U					T	I
3		O		R				U	
4	I			E		G			H
5		E		U	S		I		
6					H			S	E
7		U	H	S	G		T		
8	S	R					E		
9				H	U		G	R	

Hint: Column I

God saw Noah was this before Him _____ (Genesis 7:1).

Crossword
by David K. Shortess

"Simon, Simon"

Jesus had a brother named Simon. "Is this not the carpenter, the son of Mary, the brother of James, and Joses, and of Juda, and Simon?" (Mark 6:3). However, he is not found in this puzzle.

ACROSS

1 An early city of the tribe of Judah (Joshua 15:26)
5 "Behold the ____ of God!" (John 1:36)
9 A SIMON WHO HAD AN INFAMOUS SON NAMED ____ (John 13:26)
14 *Nothing* in Nogales
15 A grandson of Esau (Genesis 36:10–11)
16 "We spend our years as ____ that is told" (Psalm 90:9) (2 words)
17 "____ with joy receiveth it" (Matthew 13:20)
18 "Change my ____, because I am perplexed" (Galatians 4:20 NIV)
19 Faux silk
20 A SIMON FROM SAMARIA WHO PRACTICED ____ (Acts 8:9, 11 NIV)
22 Ukrainian capital
24 "____ God blessed them" (Genesis 1:22)
25 Short literary pieces
27 A SIMON, ONE OF THE TWELVE, CALLED ____ (Luke 6:15)
30 Canadian First Nation member
32 City in Harar province, Ethiopia
33 "Stand in ____, and sin not" (Psalm 4:4)
36 "They may ____ whole month" (Numbers 11:21) (2 words)
38 "O God, do not ____ my plea" (Psalm 55:1 NIV)
42 A SIMON AS JESUS ADDRESSED HIM (John 21:15) (4 words)
45 Artist's workplace
46 Lute, harp, and piano ensemble
47 "Neither hath the ____ seen" (Isaiah 64:4)
48 "____ my Father are one" (John 10:30) (2 words)
50 "Keep a tight ____ on his tongue" (James 1:26 NIV)

52 A SIMON WHO LIVED BY THE SEA AND WAS ____ (Acts 10:6) (2 words)
55 Epitomes of slowness
59 "____ his son" (1 Chronicles 7:27)
60 "Some would even ____ to die" (Romans 5:7)
63 One of the first seven deacons (Acts 6:5)
64 Dizzy with joy
67 "God ____ the increase" (1 Corinthians 3:6)
69 Bathe
70 "Death will ____ them" (Revelation 9:6 NIV)
71 "An ____ for every man" (Exodus 16:16)
72 "Had no ____ who it was" (John 5:13 NIV)
73 A SIMON LIVING IN BETHANY WHO WAS A ____ (Matthew 26:6)
74 "Where are the ____?" (Luke 17:17)
75 Social misfit

DOWN

1 "He had ____ written" (Revelation 19:12) (2 words)
2 "I said, Should such a ____ I flee?" (Nehemiah 6:11) (2 words)
3 "Am I ____ head" (2 Samuel 3:8) (2 words)
4 "The inspired man a ____" (Hosea 9:7 NIV)
5 "From the ____ of our inheritance" (Numbers 36:3)
6 "Sallu, ____, Hilkiah" (Nehemiah 12:7)
7 "What a wretched ____ am I!" (Romans 7:24 NIV) (2 words)
8 "A passing ____ that does not return" (Psalm 78:39 NIV)

12

9 "With her _____ on her shoulder" (Genesis 24:45 NIV)

10 Actress Hagen

11 "Then the same _____ evening" (John 20:19) (2 words)

12 "He _____ on the land" (Mark 6:47)

13 "He _____ you abundant showers" (Joel 2:23 NIV)

21 A SIMON WHO BORE THE CROSS FOR JESUS AND WAS A _____ (Mark 15:21)

23 Substantiates

26 "Wherewith shall it be _____?" (Luke 14:34)

28 Knee (2 words)

29 "Whether he be a sinner _____, I know not" (John 9:25) (2 words)

31 Arena where 65 Down commanded (abbr.)

33 "The foal of an _____" (Matthew 21:5)

34 "To _____, Israel" (Nehemiah 11:3)

35 Australian big bird

37 "Go to the _____, thou sluggard" (Proverbs 6:6)

39 "Love _____ another" (1 John 3:23)

40 "Without a _____ of brightness?" (Amos 5:20 NIV)

41 NNE + 90 degrees

43 Viking's Zeus

44 Hockey's Bobby

49 "Wounded the _____?" (Isaiah 51:9)

51 "To give us a _____ his holy place" (Ezra 9:8) (2 words)

52 "It is his _____" (Acts 12:15)

53 Sheer fabric

54 "On to Daberath _____ to Japhia" (Joshua 19:12 NIV) (2 words)

56 "Which _____ before Titus" (2 Corinthians 7:14) (2 words)

57 "A _____ of good men" (Titus 1:8)

58 Golfer Sammy

61 "The two-horned _____ had seen" (Daniel 8:6 NIV) (2 words)

62 "And, behold, I, _____ I" (Genesis 6:17)

65 WWII general (initials)

66 "Your" to a hillbilly

68 "_____ the lamp of God went out" (1 Samuel 3:3)

Acrostic
by Suzanne Stepp

A Burning Sentence

No matter how hot the fires we face, there is another who walks with us among the flames. Crack this code to discover more about this miraculous burning issue.

The people were forced to worship the ____ of the king (Daniel 3:5)

$$\overline{}\ \overline{}\ \overline{}\ \overline{}\ \overline{}$$
18 5 26 7 23

Nebuchadnezzar was angry and "full of ____" (Daniel 3:19)

$$\overline{}\ \overline{}\ \overline{}\ \overline{}$$
22 30 19 3

Nebuchadnezzar's title: ____ of Babylon

$$\overline{}\ \overline{}\ \overline{}\ \overline{}$$
32 6 24 11

An order of the king (Daniel 3:29)

$$\overline{}\ \overline{}\ \overline{}\ \overline{}\ \overline{}\ \overline{}$$
9 31 12 28 1 15

Shadrach, Meshach, and Abednego were ____ before the king (Daniel 3:13)

$$\overline{}\ \overline{}\ \overline{}\ \overline{}\ \overline{}\ \overline{}\ \overline{}$$
16 2 33 20 8 25 13

A form of religious practice

$$\overline{}\ \overline{}\ \overline{}\ \overline{}\ \overline{}\ \overline{}\ \overline{}$$
21 10 27 17 4 29 14

25-1   12-10-5-5-26-24-9-23-9   13-4-15   5-33-17-13

5-6-8-4-13-3   5-31-24   13-25-26-13   21-23-19-1

6-24   4-29-17   26-2-5-3   13-33   16-6-24-9

17-4-26-9-28-26-12-25,   5-23-17-25-26-12-4,   26-24-9

26-16-15-9-24-1-11-10,   26-24-9   13-33   12-26-17-13

13-4-23-5   6-24-13-10   13-4-31   16-30-2-24-18-24-7

22-18-15-27-3   22-20-2-24-26-12-1.

DANIEL 3:20

Zacchaeus
Luke 19:1–10

And **Jesus entered** and **passed** through **Jericho**. And, behold, there was a **man named Zacchaeus**, which was the chief **among** the **publicans**, and he was **rich**. And he **sought** to see Jesus who he was; and could not for the **press**, because he was **little** of **stature**. And he ran before, and **climbed** up into a **sycomore tree** to see him: for he was to **pass** that **way**. And when Jesus came to the place, he looked up, and saw him, and said unto him, Zacchaeus, make **haste**, and come down; for to day I must **abide** at thy **house**. And he made haste, and came down, and received him **joyfully**. And when they saw it, they all **murmured**, saying, That he was gone to be guest with a man that is a **sinner**. And Zacchaeus stood, and said unto the **Lord**: **Behold**, Lord, the **half** of my **goods** I **give** to the **poor**; and if I have taken any thing from any man by **false accusation**, I restore him **fourfold**. And Jesus said unto him, This day is **salvation** come to this house, forsomuch as he also is a **son** of Abraham. For the Son of man is **come** to **seek** and to **save** that which was **lost**.

```
S  S  A  P  G  J  O  Y  F  U  L  L  Y  G  N
S  Y  C  O  M  O  R  E  S  Z  D  R  O  L  O
H  A  L  F  Y  N  O  I  T  A  V  L  A  S  I
O  H  C  I  R  A  N  D  R  C  P  E  P  Y  T
U  M  V  W  E  N  W  O  S  C  P  N  U  D  A
S  T  U  S  E  L  O  B  N  H  R  T  B  L  S
E  O  L  R  I  P  N  K  A  A  E  E  L  O  U
K  A  U  T  M  O  J  E  M  E  S  R  I  F  C
F  C  T  G  S  U  S  E  J  U  S  E  C  R  C
D  L  I  P  H  A  R  S  R  S  T  D  A  U  A
E  I  E  A  C  T  V  E  V  I  G  I  N  O  E
M  M  T  S  P  O  E  E  D  I  C  N  S  F  D
A  B  S  S  L  R  M  L  V  G  C  H  O  L  I
N  E  A  E  T  O  B  E  H  O  L  D  O  M  B
H  D  H  D  S  S  T  A  T  U  R  E  V  G  A
```

Scrambled Circle
by Suzanne Stepp

Questioning the Master

Although we may be shy with Jesus in the beginning of our faith, we would do well to proclaim Him publicly in the end.

1. AVEHEYLN

2. GILTH

3. EICEVER

4. EOVDL

5. ARTYELH

6. TSAREM

7. ERLRU

8. RISEPH

He had some serious questions for Jesus.

1. _ _ _ _ _◯_ _

2. _◯_ _ _

3. _ _◯_ _ _ _

4. _◯_ _◯

5. ◯_ _ _ _ _ _

6. ◯_ _ _ _ _

7. _◯_ _ _

8. _ _ _ _◯_

Answer: _ _ _ _ _ _ _ _ _

Anagram
by Paul Kent

Bad Guys

This puzzle emphasizes the sinners, rather than the saints, of the Bible. Can you reorganize these words into the names of three bad guys? Hint: The first two are from the Gospels, the last one from the Old Testament prophets.

Into apple suit

_ _ _ _ _ _ _   _ _ _ _ _

I joust as I card

_ _ _ _ _   _ _ _ _ _ _ _

Race hen and buzz

_ _ _ _ _ _ _ _ _ _ _ _

Crossword
by David K. Shortess

A Pinwheel of Prophets

Jesus is the scarlet thread that is woven throughout the tapestry of God's
word. Work this puzzle to patch together the names of prophets who spoke
of Christ before He "materialized."

*And beginning at Moses and all the prophets, he expounded
unto them in all the scriptures the things concerning himself.*
LUKE 24:27

ACROSS

1 Alcohol abuse program
5 Mentalist's claim
8 Word found 71 times in the Psalms
13 Away from the weather
14 "And pass _____ Zin"
   (Numbers 34:4) (2 words)
15 Muse of lyric poetry
16 BIBLICAL PROPHET
17 "They shall _____ their swords into"
   (Isaiah 2:4)
18 BIBLICAL PROPHET
19 "Let come _____ what will"
   (Job 13:13) (2 words)
20 Meg and Beth's sis
21 "I have covered my bed with
   colored _____ from Egypt" (Proverbs
   7:16 NIV)
22 Scrutinize again
24 "_____ we find such a one as this is"
   (Genesis 41:38)
25 Samuel's mentor (1 Samuel 3:1)
26 BIBLICAL PROPHET
31 "Precious stones, wood, _____,
   stubble" (1 Corinthians 3:12)
34 City in Georgia
36 He played Superman
37 Baseball family
39 "He delighteth not in the
   strength of the _____"
   (Psalm 147:10)
41 "For with _____ and with malice"
   (Ezekiel 36:5 NIV)
42 Wet thoroughly
44 Kosher unleavened bread

46 "In a _____ it shall be made with oil"
   (Leviticus 6:21)
47 BIBLICAL PROPHET
49 Baseball statistic (abbr.)
51 Question response (abbr.)
52 Comedian Red
56 "Some fell among _____" (Matthew
   13:7)
60 He said, "Float like a butterfly, sting
   like a bee"
61 "Never _____ of doing what is right"
   (2 Thessalonians 3:13 NIV)
62 BIBLICAL PROPHET
63 General Robert (2 words)
64 BIBLICAL PROPHET
65 "Rise _____ us go" (Mark 14:42)
   (2 words)
66 Two-person contest
67 "The _____ is made worse"
   (Mark 2:21)
68 Two-element electron tube
69 Baseball official (abbr.)
70 Lyric poems

DOWN

1 "Every fortified city and every
   _____ town" (2 Kings 3:19 NIV)
2 "Neither pray I for these _____" (John
   17:20)
3 Has an opinion
4 Frequently used computer key
5 "Still the _____ and the avenger"
   (Psalm 8:2)
6 "None can _____ his hand" (Daniel
   4:35)

7 "The fining _____ is for silver" (Proverbs 17:3)
8 Conference
9 The Emerald Isle
10 "With a _____ of blue" (Exodus 28:28)
11 "_____ hour when he is not aware" (Luke 12:46) (2 words)
12 Coastal Washington tribal members
14 BIBLICAL PROPHET
21 Test site, for short
23 City on the Danube
24 "Jesus said unto him, If thou _____ believe" (Mark 9:23)
26 Israeli folk dance (var.)
27 A hundred pounds of nails
28 Large brown alga
29 Eye layer
30 "Was found to have a _____ mind" (Daniel 5:12 NIV)
31 Islamic pilgrimage
32 Medicinal plant
33 "Love ye _____ enemies" (Luke 6:35)

35 Traumatic periods of unconsciousness
38 "That _____ their tongues, and say" (Jeremiah 23:31)
40 BIBLICAL PROPHET
43 Give off
45 Metal-bearing mineral mass that can be profitably mined
48 _____ and outs
50 "So will I compass thine _____ LORD" (Psalm 26:6) (2 words)
52 "I _____, but my heart waketh" (Song of Solomon 5:2)
53 Clocked
54 "Jeremias, _____ of the prophets" (Matthew 16:14) (2 words)
55 "Where the birds make their _____" (Psalm 104:17)
56 Dull sound
57 Arizona tribe
58 European capital
59 "A _____ shaken with the wind?" (Matthew 11:7)
60 Grad
63 Prof's e-mail suffix, perhaps

21

Acrostic
by Suzanne Stepp

A Criminal or a King

In our attempt to please men instead of God, we may find ourselves making an indecent proposal. Decode these encrypted verses to discover one man-pleasing ruler's offer to a malicious mob.

The thirty pieces of silver was the price of ____
(Matthew 27:6)

__ __ __ __ __
34 41 16 22 5

Pilate sat on the ____ seat (Matthew 27:19)

__ __ __ __ __ __ __ __
17 30 6 24 1 19 35 10

The multitude was ____ to destroy Jesus (Matthew 27:20)

__ __ __ __ __ __ __ __ __
31 3 36 18 11 29 43 25 8

Pilate ____ his hands of the matter

__ __ __ __ __ __
4 26 40 14 37 21

Soldiers were mocking Jesus when ____ He was the King of the Jews (Matthew 27:29)

__ __ __ __ __ __
28 7 32 20 38 13

Two thieves were ____ with Jesus

__ __ __ __ __ __ __ __ __
23 9 42 12 39 33 2 27 15

(continued)

10-14-37-32   14-7-15   10-14-25-38   26

35-16-10-29-34-41-19   31-36-20-28-22-38-3-9,

12-29-41-41-27-5   34-26-9-7-34-34-29-40.

10-14-3-36-25-33-16-9-3   4-14-19-35 10-14-37-32

4-27-36-19   24-7-10-14-37-9-3-43   10-22-13-25-10-14-37-9,

31-2-41-26-10-25   40-7-39-6   42-38-10-16   10-14-27-1,

4-14-22-1   4-2-41-41   32-25   10-14-26-10   20   9-19-41-

37-29-18-27   11-35-10-22   32-16-30?

34-7-36-29-34-34-26-28,   22-36   17-25-18-30-28?
MATTHEW 27:16—17

Do Something Amazing

Ordinary people did some extraordinary things in the pages of scripture. Try to solve these spotty headlines to find three New Testament men who did some amazing things.

B●AV● MAN ATTEM●TS
●O WALK ON WAT●R

— — — — —

EVANGE●●ST DISA●●EARS,
S●OWS UP M●LES AWAY

— — — — — —

A●RONS ●SED TO HE●L SICK PEOP●E

— — — —

Those Who Judged

Before Israel had kings, judges ruled the twelve tribes. Can you crack these telephone codes to identify the names of some Old Testament adjudicators?

| MNO 6 | MNO 6 | PRS 7 | DEF 3 | PRS 7 |

| JKL 5 | MNO 6 | DEF 3 | JKL 5 |

| MNO 6 | TUV 8 | GHI 4 | MNO 6 | GHI 4 | DEF 3 | JKL 5 |

| PRS 7 | GHI 4 | ABC 2 | MNO 6 | GHI 4 | ABC 2 | PRS 7 |

| GHI 4 | GHI 4 | DEF 3 | DEF 3 | MNO 6 | MNO 6 |

| JKL 5 | DEF 3 | PRS 7 | GHI 4 | TUV 8 | GHI 4 | ABC 2 | GHI 4 |

| PRS 7 | ABC 2 | MNO 6 | PRS 7 | MNO 6 | MNO 6 |

| DEF 3 | JKL 5 | MNO 6 | MNO 6 |

Jewish Mother, Greek Father
Acts 16:1–2

Then came he to **Derbe** and Lystra: and, **behold**, a certain **disciple** was **there**, **named Timotheus**, the son of a **certain woman**, which was a **Jewess**, and **believed**; but his **father** was a **Greek**: **which** was **well reported** of by the **brethren that were** at **Lystra** and **Iconium**.

```
L V H S H E Y X O L M X B X J
C L W J R E B D K W U L R M E
S S E W E J P Y E B I A F P P
K U R W W I T B B Q N L N E H
A R E H T A F C E O O L F R N
R D I H H O L E G L C D G T R
R C E T T F N R O R I D N H X
H Y O T A O O T E S E E Z E G
L Y S T R A M A C M R E V R H
Z C H R E O K I A H Y L K E M
S E A I B N P N T G S O K Y D
N V U M R L A E H P U S O Z T
Y Z D O E U R M R Q P R M H L
X O U A D B E H O L D X P T T
C S C C D R P G E W C M X H I
```

Crossword
by David K. Shortess

Biblical Warriors

God is the one who gives us strength to win battles. Solve this puzzle and complete three verses regarding Old Testament warriors who were a force to be reckoned with.

There were giants in the earth in those days. . .the same became mighty men which were of old, men of renown.
GENESIS 6:4

ACROSS

1 San ____, Italian resort city
5 "Eli ____ unto her" (1 Samuel 1:14)
9 "This man is a ____" (Acts 22:26)
14 Famous cookie
15 Madrid paintings
16 "To ____ harnessed" (Song of Songs 1:9 NIV) (2 words)
17 "AT THAT DAY SHALL THE HEART OF THE ____ BE AS THE HEART OF A WOMAN IN HER PANGS" (Jeremiah 49:22) (4 words)
20 City SW of Honshu, Japan
21 "They ____ my path" (Job 30:13)
22 Decorate again
23 This creature should be the sluggard's role model (Proverbs 6:6)
25 "Eat not of it ____" (Exodus 12:9)
27 "WAKE UP ____ ALL THE MEN OF WAR DRAW NEAR" (Joel 3:9) (4 words)
36 "Lest he ____ thee to the judge" (Luke 12:58)
37 "____, I have no man" (John 5:7)
38 Amoz's son (2 Kings 20:1)
39 Blue pencils
41 Old horse
43 Lowest deck of seats in a stadium
44 Where Jethro lived (Exodus 3:1)
46 Spanish sun
48 "I cast my ____ against them" (Acts 26:10 NIV)
49 "HE HAD SLAIN GEDALIAH THE SON OF AHIKAM, ____ WAR" (Jeremiah 41:16) (4 words)
52 "One beka ____ person" (Exodus 38:26 NIV)

53 "I am as ____ mocked" (Job 12:4)
54 "Passeth through the paths of the ____" (Psalm 8:8)
58 "To a point below Beth ____" (1 Samuel 7:11 NIV)
60 "Thou didst ____ the earth with rivers" (Habbakuk 3:9)
65 "PASS BEFORE YOUR BRETHREN ARMED, ____ OF VALOUR" (Joshua 1:14) (4 words)
68 Proportion
69 Sit for an artist
70 "____ your heart, and not your garments" (Joel 2:13)
71 Inactive
72 "I will give him the morning ____" (Revelation 2:28)
73 Cainan's father (Genesis 5:9)

DOWN

1 Tomato variety
2 Composer Satie
3 Vast
4 ____ and aahs
5 "Their dark ____" (Proverbs 1:6)
6 "As a seal upon thine ____" (Song of Solomon 8:6)
7 Object
8 Tenfold
9 U.K. fliers (abbr.)
10 "An ____ for every man" (Exodus 16:16)
11 "All things were ____ by him" (John 1:3)
12 "It became ____ in his hand" (Exodus 4:4) (2 words)
13 Captain of the Nautilus

18 Formerly Siamese
19 "_____ trying to please men?" (Galatians 1:10 NIV) (3 words)
24 "Behold, seven _____ ears and blasted" (Genesis 41:6)
26 "This shall be your _____ border" (Numbers 34:6)
27 Student paper
28 If Ovid had II eggs for breakfast and Nero had II, together they _____ (2 "words")
29 Skip or slur over a syllable, as "ma'am"
30 "The law might be fully _____ us" (Romans 8:4 NIV) (2 words)
31 Worthless stuff
32 "They deceive the minds of _____ people" (Romans 16:18 NIV)
33 "The camps that _____ the east" (Numbers 10:5) (2 words)
34 "Give _____ my words" (Psalm 5:1) (2 words)
35 "The _____ cometh in" (Hosea 7:1)
40 Cornmeal mush in New England

42 "_____ the pool of Siloam" (John 9:11) (2 words)
45 Dinah, to Esau (Genesis 25:25–26 and Genesis 34:1)
47 Illegal hangman
50 Daddy's dad
51 "Our hearts did _____" (Joshua 2:11)
54 Rani's gown
55 Enthusiasm
56 Old ones (Ger.)
57 "Grievous words _____ up anger" (Proverbs 15:1)
59 "Children not accused of _____ or unruly" (Titus 1:6)
61 Jane _____
62 "These things saith the _____" (Revelation 3:14)
63 Prefix meaning ein
64 "The four _____ of the grate of brass" (Exodus 38:5)
66 "When it is _____" (Job 6:17)
67 Organization founded by Juliette Gordon Low (abbr.)

29

Bible Quotation
by G. Rebecca Shodin

Follow Him
JOHN 14:6

As long as we're following Christ, we're heading in the right direction. Solve this puzzle to find a verse by which to navigate your course.

H	W	I	Y	I	S	H	T	N	O
R	U	A	H	U	T	N	E	E	T
T	F	B	L	N	M	O	T	B	U
H	J	E	N	H	T	E	M	A	I
T	E	A	T	A	A	O	D	H	T
M	U	U	S	T	F	R	S	H	T
	M	T	U		C	E		H	E
	H	A	Y		O				E
			N		E				
					M				

Paul in Prison
ACTS 16:28

God rewards us when we pray and praise Him, especially when we're in dire straits. Solve this puzzle to find out what Paul did after the prison doors flew open and his chains fell away.

Word	Clue		
BOATING	Dance	_____	1. ___ ___
TEARFUL	Signal	_____	2. ___ ___
HOLSTER	Failure	_____	3. ___ ___
ADAPTER	Valued	_____	4. ___ ___
AIRLESS	Begets	_____	5. ___ ___
OCELLUS	Prison rooms	_____	6. ___ ___
LAUNDRY	Lecherous	_____	7. ___ ___
CLAMPED	Enough	_____	8. ___ ___
REVERIE	Mysterious	_____	9. ___ ___
ISOLATE	Blackboard	_____	10. ___ ___
IDEALLY	Dawdle	_____	11. ___ ___
DIARCHY	Not bald	_____	12. ___ ___
WITLESS	Narrow openings	_____	13. ___ ___

___ ___ ___ ___ ___ ___ ___ ___ ___ ___ ___ ___ ___

1 2 3 4 5 6 7 8 9 10 11 12 13

Word Search
by John Hudson Tiner

Paul's Fellow Helper
2 CORINTHIANS 7:6–7; 8:23

Nevertheless God, that **comforteth those** that are **cast down**, comforted us by the coming of **Titus**; and not by his **coming only**, but by the **consolation wherewith** he was **comforted** in you, **when** he **told** us your **earnest desire**, your **mourning**, **your fervent mind toward** me; so that I **rejoiced** the **more**. . . . **Whether** any do enquire of Titus, he is my **partner** and **fellowhelper concerning** you: or our **brethren** be **enquired** of, **they** are the **messengers** of the **churches**, and the **glory** of **Christ**.

Word Search
by John Hudson Tiner
(continued)

```
S Y W H E R E W I T H Y R T F
R S S U T I T I F S V R H N E
E X E R H E R D E C I O J E R
G T U L E D T S L N S L F R V
N O U C E H E R L E Y G C H E
E W E S O H T E O G R O C T N
S A I N C N T E W F N O U E T
S R Q R Q S S R H C M I M R V
E D U O E U E O E W H O M B P
M H H N X N I R L V Y R C O W
C H R A T T N R P A E R I T C
P A Y R O I W H E N T N H S L
E X A L N W O D R D N I M A T
Z P D G L D E T R O F M O C C
C T H E Y U W M O U R N I N G
```

Acrostic
by Suzanne Stepp

A Right-Hand Man

There's nothing like a good "company" representative. Solve this acrostic to learn how significant one good right-hand man can be.

Pharaoh imposed many _____ on the Israelites (Exodus 5:4)

$\overline{10}$ $\overline{45}$ $\overline{27}$ $\overline{19}$ $\overline{31}$ $\overline{1}$ $\overline{53}$

Where the Israelites wandered

$\overline{20}$ $\overline{36}$ $\overline{51}$ $\overline{11}$ $\overline{44}$ $\overline{30}$ $\overline{17}$ $\overline{3}$ $\overline{49}$ $\overline{25}$

God had seen the _____ of the Israelites (Exodus 3:7)

$\overline{24}$ $\overline{16}$ $\overline{40}$ $\overline{2}$ $\overline{52}$ $\overline{21}$ $\overline{35}$ $\overline{8}$ $\overline{28}$ $\overline{46}$

The elders were _____ together (Exodus 4:29)

$\overline{7}$ $\overline{29}$ $\overline{43}$ $\overline{18}$ $\overline{34}$ $\overline{4}$ $\overline{23}$ $\overline{12}$

The people bowed their heads to _____ the Lord (Exodus 4:31)

$\overline{33}$ $\overline{5}$ $\overline{48}$ $\overline{39}$ $\overline{22}$ $\overline{41}$ $\overline{15}$

Pharaoh's servants who gave work orders to the Israelites (Exodus 5:6)

$\overline{37}$ $\overline{9}$ $\overline{42}$ $\overline{26}$ $\overline{14}$ $\overline{32}$ $\overline{50}$ $\overline{6}$ $\overline{47}$ $\overline{38}$ $\overline{13}$

29-32-48-5-17   49-15-24-26-34   9-2-51   6-18-44

33-28-4-12-39   20-22-36-21-18   37-22-31   2-28-38-11

18-32-19   42-15-5-26-23-46   45-1-6-5   14-28-25-47-13,

24-1-11   12-52-11   35-18-31   39-8-7-17-53

41-46   43-18-3   50-36-7-22-37   28-40   6-22-47

15-44-5-15-2-34.

EXODUS 4:30

Sudoku
by Sara Stoker

The Perfect One

MEDIUM

	A	B	C	D	E	F	G	H	I
1	D	E	F			W	O		
2					D	N		F	
3	R		L						U
4	N			E			D		
5		D		R	F	O	U		
6		U		N	W			L	R
7		O				R			L
8	F		E		U		N	W	
9		L				F	R	E	

Hint: Row 7

A name Isaiah foretold Jesus would have: _____
(Isaiah 9:6).

36

Surprise!

When Jesus is around, you never know what's going to happen, as this leper discovered.

1. DLEBSES

2. RIPSIT

3. UNORM

4. DFAOBRE

5. LPEINCAN

He threw a party for Jesus but was not prepared for the woman with the perfume.

1. _ _ _○_ _ _ _

2. _ _○_ _ _ _

3. ○_ _ _ _ _

4. _○_ _ _ _ _ _

5. _ _ _○_ _ _ _

Answer: _ _ _ _ _ _

Crossword
by Sarah Lagerquist Simmons

Fathers-in-Law

The Bible's numerous father-in-laws are hidden among the begats and prolific Bible stories. In order to solve this puzzle, you'll have to shake some men out of their fruitful family trees. Good luck with this *relatively* mind-boggling challenge!

And unto Enoch was born Irad: and Irad begat Mehujael: and Mehujael begat Methusael: and Methusael begat Lamech.
GENESIS 4:18

ACROSS

1 Monk
6 "God said to Moses, 'Reach out and ____ it by the tail' " (Exodus 4:4 MSG)
10 "Their lungs breathe out poison ____" (Psalm 5:9 MSG)
13 Cain's occupation
15 Roman emperor
16 "Lest being present I should ____ sharpness" (2 Corinthians 13:10)
17 Turkey's capital
18 U.S. state
19 Type of engineering (abbr.)
20 TOHU'S FATHER (1 Samuel 1:1)
22 REBEKAH'S FATHER-IN-LAW
24 "____ began men to call upon the name of the Lord" (Genesis 4:26)
26 Rowing poles
28 TAMAR COVERED HERSELF WITH A ____ TO DECEIVE HER FATHER-IN-LAW (Genesis 38:14 NIV)
29 "Maintain good works for necessary ____" (Titus 3:14)
30 Soured milk includes this
31 "Wherefore look ye so ____ today?" (Genesis 40:7)
32 "Neither shalt thou ____ the corners of thy beard" (Leviticus 19:27)
33 "The king. . .stands at the parting of the road, at the ____ of the two roads" (Ezekiel 21:21 NKJV)
34 Pallid
35 "I make mention of you always in my ____" (Romans 1:9)
37 Brutish
41 Large North American deer
42 British nobleman
43 Microprocessor (abbr.)
44 Relating to the nose
47 DAVID CUT OFF THE SKIRT OF HIS FATHER-IN-LAW'S ____ (1 Samuel 24:4)
48 "The services of. . .worship were conducted daily, which was the ____ for Israel" (1 Chronicles 16:37 MSG)
49 Middle Eastern official
50 Table
51 SHUAH'S FATHER-IN-LAW MADE A COAT OF ____ COLORS (Genesis 37:3)
52 Plaster of paris preparations
54 "They. . .must keep their hair trimmed and ____" (Ezekiel 44:20 MSG)
56 Change (abbr.)
57 Cursive (abbr.)
59 33rd U.S. President
63 "____ them about thy neck" (Proverbs 6:21)
64 ASENATH'S FATHER-IN-LAW WAS THIS MAN'S FATHER (Genesis 41:45)
65 Brook
66 "Bow down thine ____" (2 Kings 19:16)
67 Thin strip of wood
68 Country in South Arabia

DOWN

1 Costs no one anything (abbr.)
2 REBEKAH ____ TO DRAW WATER FOR HER FUTURE FATHER-IN-LAW'S SERVANT AND CAMELS (Genesis 24:20)

3 Nettle

4 Surprises

5 Play it again

6 Wildebeest

7 Delay

8 Descendants of Abraham

9 Danish physicist

10 "He smote the rock, that the waters _____ out" (Psalm 78:20)

11 "The terrors of death _____ me" (Psalm 55:4 NIV)

12 "Delight is not _____ for a fool" (Proverbs 19:10)

14 Tap

21 "Are there not twelve _____ in the day?" (John 11:9)

23 Front of an army

24 Russian ruler (alt.)

25 Zeus's sister

27 It held the Ten Commandments

29 Baseball official (abbr.)

30 "They lost all control of the ship. It was a _____ in the storm" (Acts 27:13 MSG)

31 DAVID'S FATHER-IN-LAW

33 "His countenance _____" (Genesis 4:5)

34 THE FATHER-IN-LAW OF SOLOMON'S MANY WIVES _____ A LINEN EPHOD (1 Chronicles 15:27 NIV)

36 JACOB WORKED A TOTAL OF FOURTEEN _____ TO EARN HIS BRIDE FROM HIS FATHER-IN-LAW

37 JACOB'S FATHER-IN-LAW

38 Portrait

39 Agile

40 Buzz

42 Greek goddess of the dawn

44 Nullify

45 Famed female flyer Earhart

46 LEAH AND HER _____ SHARED THE SAME FATHER-IN-LAW

47 River in central Serbia

48 "Doth not even _____ itself teach you" (1 Corinthians 11:14)

50 Blizzard (Rus.)

51 "Children of this world _____, and are given in marriage" (Luke 20:34)

53 "Fine _____ have been poured upon me" (Psalm 92:10 NIV)

55 Conjectured time of appearance (abbr.)

58 "He _____ the lamps before the LORD" (Exodus 40:25 NKJV)

60 BOAZ'S _____ HAD NAASSON AS A FATHER-IN-LAW (Matthew 1:4–5)

61 Yes

62 Negation of a word (prefix)

Evangelists
ACTS 6:5; 8:5–6

And the **saying pleased** the **whole multitude**: and they **chose Stephen**, a man **full** of **faith** and of the **Holy Ghost**, and Philip, and **Prochorus**, and **Nicanor**, and **Timon**, and **Parmenas**, and **Nicolas** a **proselyte** of **Antioch**. . . . Then Philip **went down** to the **city** of **Samaria**, and **preached Christ** unto them. And the **people** with one **accord gave heed** unto **those things** which **Philip spake**, **hearing** and **seeing** the **miracles** which he did.

Word Search
by John Hudson Tiner
(continued)

A	T	I	M	O	N	V	W	E	Y	F	K	A	J	U
I	S	D	V	U	C	W	D	H	Z	U	J	L	Z	G
R	O	G	G	H	M	U	O	C	O	L	S	K	O	Q
A	H	C	O	I	T	N	A	D	H	L	E	U	I	D
M	G	S	N	I	C	O	L	A	S	R	E	V	A	G
A	E	S	T	E	P	H	E	N	Y	T	I	C	G	D
S	W	L	G	S	S	P	A	K	E	L	N	S	R	E
D	U	Q	Y	N	M	R	A	O	P	W	G	O	T	S
M	H	R	H	T	I	A	F	R	E	I	C	Y	A	A
V	E	E	O	Y	R	H	E	N	M	C	L	Y	U	E
V	A	S	D	H	A	A	T	Y	A	E	I	I	L	L
A	R	O	N	A	C	I	N	L	S	N	N	P	H	P
K	I	H	Y	H	L	O	E	O	G	L	O	A	P	P
V	N	T	E	X	E	T	R	H	E	E	D	L	S	V
I	G	D	I	E	S	P	E	P	P	F	X	I	I	V

Telephone Scramble
by Connie Troyer

Unexpected Good Guys

God can do anything, including prompting nefarious men to do something decent. Can you uncover a few men of position and power who changed their ways?

ABC 2	ABC 2	JKL 5	ABC 2	ABC 2	MNO 6

ABC 2	GHI 4	GHI 4	JKL 5	ABC 2	MNO 6

WXY 9	ABC 2	ABC 2	ABC 2	GHI 4	ABC 2	DEF 3	TUV 8	PRS 7

ABC 2	GHI 4	ABC 2	PRS 7	TUV 8	DEF 3	PRS 7	TUV 8	PRS 7

GHI 4	ABC 2	MNO 6	ABC 2	JKL 5	GHI 4	DEF 3	JKL 5

ABC 2	MNO 6	PRS 7	MNO 6	DEF 3	JKL 5	GHI 4	TUV 8	PRS 7

TUV 8	GHI 4	PRS 7	GHI 4	ABC 2	JKL 5	ABC 2	GHI 4

Taking a Stand

When the battle lines were drawn against Jesus, several people made last ditch efforts to save Him, either by proclaiming His innocence or by means of physical force. Solve the puzzles below to discover two men who tried to take a stand between Jesus and His accusers.

OB SWWP JNSBF, NKE JNYOBE OLY ONKEY

DBXWFB SOB TZCSLSZEB, YNHLKU, L NT

LKKWGBKS WX SOB DCWWE WX SOLY IZYS

ABFYWK.

YBJ BY SISNZ JPG WHEDL NZJE PNW YFSQA:

MED SFF JPAG JPSJ JSVA JPA WHEDL WPSFF

YADNWP HNJP JPA WHEDL.

Crossword
by David K. Shortess

Fathers and Sons

Just as our loving fathers disciplined us, so does our Lord—to make us strong, teachable, pliant, and obedient godly people, able to carry out His commands. Solve this puzzle to find four famous father-and-son pairings from the Old Testament.

The LORD disciplines those he loves, as a father the son he delights in.
PROVERBS 3:12 NIV

ACROSS

1 "To the _____ ye shall give the less" (Numbers 33:54)
6 Philippine knife
10 "Ye should walk _____" (2 John 1:6) (2 words)
14 Split to wed
15 _____ Bator
16 Massachusetts colonial governor
17 BIBLICAL FATHER AND SON FOUND IN 1 KINGS 1 (3 words)
20 "There is but a _____ between me and death" (1 Samuel 20:3)
21 "These going before tarried for _____ Troas" (Acts 20:5) (2 words)
22 "They shall see _____ eye" (Isaiah 52:8) (2 words)
23 "The camel, and the _____, and the coney" (Deuteronomy 14:7)
25 Old Greek markets
26 BIBLICAL FATHER AND SON FOUND IN GENESIS 27 (3 words)
31 "My maids, _____ me for a stranger" (Job 19:15)
32 "I will fear no _____" (Psalm 23:4)
33 "Make bare the _____" (Isaiah 47:2)
36 "The LORD's chosen _____" (Isaiah 48:14 NIV)
37 Sups
39 Marco _____
40 Land east of Eden (Genesis 4:16)
41 "They are all _____ dogs" (Isaiah 56:10 NIV)
42 _____ and aahed
43 BIBLICAL FATHER AND SON FOUND IN GENESIS 29 (3 words)
46 Hard, volcanic rock
49 Computer network terminal
50 "Their laying _____ was known to Saul" (Acts 9:24)
51 Post-WWII alliance (abbr.)
53 "Publish ye, praise ye, and _____ LORD" (Jeremiah 31:7) (2 words)
57 BIBLICAL FATHER AND SON FOUND IN 1 SAMUEL 14 (3 words)
60 Contemporary of Agatha
61 "_____ old lion" (Genesis 49:9) (2 words)
62 "Call me not _____" (Ruth 1:20)
63 "Be ye therefore followers of God, as _____ children" (Ephesians 5:1)
64 "Go up, and _____ thy father" (Genesis 50:6)
65 Clandestine date

DOWN

1 G-men
2 Israeli Red Sea port
3 "Where the women _____ hangings" (2 Kings 23:7)
4 Celebration of the Magi's visit
5 "_____ skins of rams" (Exodus 35:23)
6 Lab burner inventor
7 "Wax not _____ treasure" (Luke 12:33) (2 words)
8 "I will raise him up at the _____ day" (John 6:44)
9 "Lead _____ Benjamin" (Hosea 5:8 NIV) (2 words)
10 "Where _____ cannot come" (John 8:21 NIV) (3 words)
11 Christener
12 "_____ girdle" (Jeremiah 13:2) (3 words)
13 A Cyclades isle
18 Emanation

19 "Is it _____ for you to flog a Roman" (Acts 22:25 NIV)
24 "In the very _____" (John 8:4)
25 "Such _____ common to man" (1 Corinthians 10:13) (2 words)
26 "_____ do all things" (Philippians 4:13) (2 words)
27 By oneself
28 _____ lang syne
29 Brightest star in Cygnus
30 "Adam knew _____" (Genesis 4:1)
33 "For, _____ that formeth the mountains" (Amos 4:13) (2 words)
34 Elevation (abbr.)
35 "In _____ will praise his word" (Psalm 56:4) (2 words)
37 Type of tape
38 "Now come _____ thee" (John 17:13) (2 words)
39 Polaris
41 "The island was called _____" (Acts 28:1 NIV)
42 "Wherewith the _____ number of them" (Numbers 3:48)
43 "The _____ was commanded to guard them" (Acts 16:23 NIV)

44 A Paris suburb
45 "Let us go up at _____" (Jeremiah 6:4)
46 "The law is not _____ on faith" (Galatians 3:12 NIV)
47 "Or ever I was _____" (Song of Solomon 6:12)
48 "There was of the house of _____ servant" (2 Samuel 9:2) (2 words)
51 Fargo school (abbr.)
52 "Take _____ and put an omer" (Exodus 16:33 NIV) (2 words)
54 Nautical greeting
55 Edible roots
56 "Fire was _____ by night" (Exodus 40:38) (2 words)
58 Collar
59 "Go to the _____" (Proverbs 6:6)

45

A Serious Misstep

Sometimes haste makes waste. Crack this puzzle's code to discover how one woman's rush to deliver resulted in an unsteady future for her charge.

A signifier: "of the _____ of Israel"

‾‾ ‾‾ ‾‾ ‾‾ ‾‾
13 19 10 4   25

Saul was Jonathan's ____

‾‾ ‾‾ ‾‾ ‾‾ ‾‾ ‾‾
9   21 1   26 17 6

Counted or considered as

‾‾ ‾‾ ‾‾ ‾‾ ‾‾ ‾‾ ‾‾ ‾‾
18 30 16 33 2   23 14 8

Middle

‾‾ ‾‾ ‾‾ ‾‾ ‾‾
5   24 34 12 31

God's mighty ____ (2 Samuel 22:33)

‾‾ ‾‾ ‾‾ ‾‾ ‾‾
28 7   32 22 35

"____, we are thy bone and thy flesh" (2 Samuel 5:1)

‾‾ ‾‾ ‾‾ ‾‾ ‾‾ ‾‾
11 27 20 15 3   29

Acrostic

by Suzanne Stepp

(continued)

26-24-4   23-10-6-12-14   31-2-15-33   13-24-5   10-28,

21-23-8   9-3-30-29:   21-23-34   24-1   16-21-5-22   31-19

28-21-12-4,   21-4   12-13-25   5-21-34-27   20-21-4-31-14

1-7   9-3-17-25,   31-26-21-1   20-25   9-27-3-3,   21-23-29

11-14-16-21-5-17   3-21-5-30.   21-23-34   26-24-12

23-21-5-22   32-21-4   5-30-28-20-24-11-19-12-26-17-1-13.
2 SAMUEL 4:4

by Suzanne Stepp

Finding Someone Special
ACTS 13:22

God loves steadfast men who are in line with His will. Work this puzzle to
discover the man God chose to lead His people.

H	I	E	A	N	Y	O	E	F	L	J	M
S	U	R	S	I	A	O	I	H	A	A	E
T	E	N	D	I	M	A	N	E	W	M	N
O	S	E	V	I	D	N	V	O	N	B	F
A	P	M	U	M	N	V	O	N	B	G	E
T	D	D	E	T	A	E	T	E	G	E	T
U	T	E	W	R	H	N	N	T	E	D	S
T	H	A	R	I	A	K	V	E	D	E	F
	O	H	E	O	M	T	S	D	D	S	O
	I	H	N	D	V	A	I	D			S
	E		O	R		A	A				
	H		G	N		I					

Old Testament Prophets

They spoke directly for God—and were often ignored. Can you solve these spotty headlines to uncover three great prophets of the Old Testament?

WEEPING, NOT JOY, CHARACTERIZES YOUNG MALE PROPHET

— — — — — — — —

GOVERNMENT LEADER IN TROUBLE FOR PRAYING TO GOD

— — — — — —

GOD'S PROPHET MARRIES PROSTITUTE

— — — — —

Faithful Father of Nations
GENESIS 17:5–7

Neither shall thy name any **more** be **called Abram**, but thy **name** shall be **Abraham**; for a **father** of **many** nations **have** I **made** thee. And I will make thee **exceeding fruitful**, and I will **make nations** of thee, and **kings shall come** out of thee. And I **will establish** my covenant **between** me and thee and thy seed after thee in **their generations** for an **everlasting covenant**, to be a God **unto** thee, and to thy **seed after thee**.

```
Q R X R G W M U M J Q M P E R
C E E F K A S G F P N A U O O
H E B T R S N O I T A N O A K
D N Q B F W K I N G S Y F I Y
E F A B R A H A M F S A E Y V
L V E M L G N D R N T D P E G
L X E Z E N U O H A V E M L
A D M R V S I I E M P I A L W
C H O O L T T R D X L K I E Q
U E C F F A T E N E E W T E B
O T N U R B S H R D E E S H W
I J L E G L H T E O F C V T C
W C N B Z I A I I I M F X I T
O E O M U S L E I N R I R E U
G C B P N H L N J D G I N S Z
```

Crossword
by David K. Shortess

What's His Line?

Whether or not you are seeking God's call on your life, He has called each of us to faithfully serve in the tasks assigned us. Can you discover the occupation of each person named in caps?

The labourer is worthy of his hire.
LUKE 10:7

ACROSS

1 Asner and Ames
4 "____ in a poke" (2 words)
8 ESAU (Genesis 25:27)
14 "Fifteen in a ____" (1 Kings 7:3)
15 1947 biochemistry Nobel laureate
16 Gunsmoke actor James
17 Hophni's father (1 Samuel 1:3)
18 Shades
19 Fifth part of an act in a Roman play (2 words)
20 ALEXANDER (2 Timothy 4:14)
23 Pile driver head
24 "Nor on any ____" (Revelation 7:1)
25 School founded by Henry VI
26 Doctrinal ending (suffix)
28 "There is a ____ here" (John 6:9)
30 To wind in and out
34 "If you have ____ with men on foot" (Jeremiah 12:5 NIV)
37 Basic bread spread
39 Just barely got by
40 Good Judean king (1 Kings 15:9, 11)
41 MALCHUS (John 18:10)
44 "Sir, come down ____ my child die" (John 4:49)
45 "Neither shall they learn war any ____" (Isaiah 2:4)
47 "Waters to ____ in" (Ezekiel 47:5)
48 Island of western Scotland
50 "But a wise man will ____ it" (Proverbs 16:14 NIV)
52 "Blessed ____. . ." (Matthew 5:3–11)
53 "Firm unto the ____" (Hebrews 3:6)
54 "And I saw when the ____ opened one of the seals" (Revelation 6:1)
57 "The open ____ between the side rooms" (Ezekiel 41:9 NIV)
61 "Then Gideon took ____ men of his servants" (Judges 6:27)
63 DEMETRIUS (Acts 19:24)
66 Choose (2 words)
68 ____ vera
69 "Was ____ unto him" (Matthew 18:34)
70 ____ Nevadas
71 "The ____ of the scornful" (Psalm 1:1)
72 Harem room
73 EZRA (Nehemiah 8:1)
74 Spreads hay
75 "I have ____ you with milk" (1 Corinthians 3:2)

DOWN

1 "And do not ____ a sacred stone" (Deuteronomy 16:22 NIV)
2 Sorrow
3 Filch
4 "Even in laughter the heart may ____" (Proverbs 14:13 NIV)
5 "His fury is ____ out like fire" (Nahum 1:6)
6 "I was not in safety, neither had ____" (Job 3:26) (2 words)
7 Gadget (var.)
8 "____ thou eaten of the tree" (Genesis 3:11)
9 Street youngster
10 Compass point between N and NE
11 AQUILA (Acts 18:2–3)
12 "But ____ have I hated" (Romans 9:13)

13 Request for a formal answer (abbr.)
21 Soccer great
22 Pant leg length
27 "And if any man will ____ thee at the law" (Matthew 5:40)
29 Classifieds
31 H+ or OH–
32 Trillion (prefix)
33 "On the east of ____" (Genesis 4:16)
34 "With the ____ third of a hin" (Numbers 28:14 NIV) (2 words)
35 "He it is, to whom I shall give ____" (John 13:26) (2 words)
36 JESUS (Mark 6:3–4)
37 1984 author
38 CXII ÷ II
42 Follows heir- or host-
43 "Of stone, and ____ for mortar" (Genesis 11:3 NIV)
46 Follows hallow- or eight-
49 Enlarge a hole
51 Accumulate on a surface

52 "Now when this was noised ____" (Acts 2:6)
55 Nautical halt
56 Brawl
58 "Houses may be ____ the frogs" (Exodus 8:9 NIV) (2 words)
59 Piece for the piano
60 "My messenger ____ of you" (Mark 1:2 NIV)
61 "Waves thereof ____ themselves" (Jeremiah 5:22)
62 Heroic narrative
64 "Dies ____" (Latin hymn of mourning)
65 "So if the Son ____ you free" (John 8:36 NIV)
67 Day before Saturday (abbr.)

Acrostic
by Suzanne Stepp

A Special Friend

> There is no tie closer than that of two men whose souls, minds, and spirits are simpatico. Solve this acrostic to uncover the names of the first true "soul brothers."

David and Jonathan made a _____ (1 Samuel 18:3)

__34__ __5__ __24__ __12__ __42__ __1__ __19__ __30__

A _____ and arrow

__4__ __25__ __40__

Saul's weapon against David (1 Samuel 18:11)

__29__ __14__ __3__ __38__ __33__ __21__ __9__

An offering to God

__20__ __31__ __8__ __26__ __41__ __13__ __43__ __18__ __37__

Listened or gave heed (1 Samuel 19:6)

__6__ __35__ __27__ __11__ __39__ __23__ __7__ __32__ __16__

Jonathan said he would _____ with Saul about David
(1 Samuel 19:3)

__15__ __22__ __10__ __36__ __17__ __2__ __28__

30-6-37   20-22-17-33   25-13   29-5-7-31-30-6-27-2

40-1-20   39-9-21-30   40-41-30-6   30-6-23   20-25-17-33

22-13   16-27-3-21-16,   31-42-16   29-25-19-27-30-6-1-9

33-5-24-35-16   6-43-10   14-20   6-21-20   22-40-7

20-5-17-33.

1 SAMUEL 18:1

Improper Names

No, we're not saying they're "bad" names. . .they're just not "proper" names.
Can you determine these three Bible men known by descriptive titles? Note:
None of these exact names is found in the King James Version, but you'll
definitely know them and their stories.

This tin car

— — — — — — — — — —

Go Martian soda

— — — —   — — — — — — — —

A gold prison

— — — — — — — —   — — —

Check Your Hearing
1 Samuel 3:9

Sometimes when God speaks, we need others to clarify His message.
Solve this puzzle to discover what a receptive young prophet did upon the
guidance of his godly mentor.

BLASTED	Wire-bound	_____	1. ___ ___
ADENOSE	Crowded	_____	2. ___
AMNESTY	Heavily fleshed	_____	3. ___
AMASSED	Joined edges	_____	4. ___
MISDEAL	Apart	_____	5. ___
ASSUAGE	Wise men	_____	6. ___
BEASTLY	Explosion	_____	7. ___
LODGING	Proceeding	_____	8. ___
WHERETO	At that place	_____	9. ___
WEAKEST	Tent peg	_____	10. ___
MEANING	Likeness	_____	11. ___ ___

___ ___ ___ ___ ___ ___ ___ ___ ___ ___ ___

‾1‾ ‾2‾ ‾3‾ ‾4‾ ‾5‾ ‾6‾ ‾7‾ ‾8‾ ‾9‾ ‾10‾ ‾11‾

Job

ACCEPTED	MESSENGER
ACQUAINTANCE	MOURN
ALMIGHTY	OXEN
BILDAD	PERFECT
BRETHREN	SATAN
CAMELS	SEVEN
COUNSEL	SHEEP
DAUGHTERS	SISTERS
ELIHU	SONS
ELIPHAZ	THREE
FOUNDATIONS	UPRIGHT
HOUSEHOLD	UZ
JUSTIFIED	WHIRLWIND
KNOWLEDGE	WRATH
LORD	ZOPHAR

```
M S M M F E G D E L W O N K A
M E J B O J S H E E P W M R C
H V J B U P R I G H T H S S Q
T E J Q N R U O M Z C I T T U
A N U U D A U G H T E R S Z A
R Y S T A L Z Z Z F F L I N I
W T T N T O O X E N R W S E N
R H I C I R T H R E E I T R T
A G F Z O D Z M E J P N E H A
H I I R N N A T A S Z D R T N
P M E S S E N G E R U R S E C
O L D H P M L E S N U O C R E
Z A H P I L E R R R N M H B M
H H U H I L E H H S L E M A C
H D E T P E C C A D A D L I B
```

Crossword
by David K. Shortess

King After King

When we truly accept Christ and are obedient to His Word, we gain a new heart and a new nature. What a privilege God has granted us through Christ! Solve this puzzle to discover eight Old Testament kings of Israel who lived before Christ—some with a godly heart, some with an evil nature.

Therefore if any man be in Christ, he is a new creature:
old things are passed away; behold, all things are become new.
2 CORINTHIANS 5:17

ACROSS

1 "Is it _____ for you to flog a Roman" (Acts 22:25 NIV)
6 "And the third beast had _____ as a man" (Revelation 4:7) (2 words)
11 "Sir, come down _____ my child die" (John 4:49)
14 "To _____ for wickedness" (Daniel 9:24 NIV)
15 Soft drinks
16 "When anyone went to a wine _____ to draw" (Haggai 2:16 NIV)
17 "Go _____ possess the land" (Deuteronomy 1:8) (2 words)
18 Lock
19 Kin to Ltd. (abbr.)
20 THREE SUCCESSIVE EVIL KINGS OF ISRAEL (1 Kings 15:25–16:14) (3 words)
23 Over there
24 So long
25 "The proud have _____ snare for me" (Psalm 140:5) (2 words)
29 "Giving all diligence, _____ your faith virtue" (2 Peter 1:5) (2 words)
32 "Let thy servant abide instead of the _____ bondman to my lord" (Genesis 44:33) (2 words)
36 "An _____ pleasing to the LORD" (Leviticus 1:13 NIV)
38 "_____ that my words were now written! _____ that they were printed in a book" (Job 19:23) (2 words)
40 Its, in Paris
41 TWO SUCCESSIVE EVIL KINGS OF ISRAEL (2 Kings 15:17–26) (2 words)
45 _____ Arbor, Michigan
46 Away from the wind
47 Walk like a crab

48 "The Lord hath _____ of them" (Matthew 21:3)
50 Where Saul's medium lived (1 Samuel 28:7)
53 Hardy heroine
54 "The. . .child shall play on the hole of the _____" (Isaiah 11:8)
56 "I tell you, _____" (Luke 13:3)
58 THREE SUCCESSIVE KINGS OF ISRAEL (1 Kings 16:16–22:53) (3 words)
67 Snow, English, or split
68 "No _____ shall come on his head" (Judges 13:5)
69 "He. . .cannot _____ much" (Leviticus 14:21) (2 words)
70 Work unit
71 Something taboo (2 words)
72 Very angry
73 "We. . .passed to the _____ of Cyprus" (Acts 27:4 NIV)
74 Spread about
75 "My _____ for me" (1 Chronicles 22:7) (2 words)

DOWN

1 "Where the body of Jesus had _____" (John 20:12)
2 Sicilian volcano
3 "Shamgar. . .slew six hundred men with an ox _____" (Judges 3:31)
4 "There was one _____, a prophetess" (Luke 2:36)
5 "Being _____ the hand of them. . ., I came into Damascus" (Acts 22:11) (2 words)
6 "Instead, he puts it on _____" (Luke 8:16 NIV) (2 words)
7 "Not seeing the sun _____ season" (Acts 13:11) (2 words)

8 Summer drinks
9 Ledger, at times
10 English 101 paper
11 "Ye thought _____ against me" (Genesis 50:20)
12 American bullfrog genus
13 What acid does on glass
21 Python, for example
22 Snaky fish
25 "So they hanged _____ on the gallows" (Esther 7:10)
26 Actress Dunne
27 He wrote, "No man is an island"
28 "I _____ poor man" (1 Samuel 18:23) (2 words)
30 Lacquered the cloth on an airplane's skin
31 "_____ Lord is at hand" (Philippians 4:5)
33 "They are all gone _____" (Psalm 14:3)
34 "Two tenth _____ unto one ram" (Numbers 28:28)
35 "And he sat down among the _____" (Job 2:8)
37 "_____! I am warm" (Isaiah 44:16 NIV)
39 "My heart _____ turned to wax" (Psalm 22:14 NIV)

42 Proboscidean pachyderm
43 "Blessed are ye, when _____ shall revile you" (Matthew 5:11)
44 "And the archers _____ him" (1 Chronicles 10:3)
49 Southeast Asia language group
51 "Set them in two rows, six _____" (Leviticus 24:6) (3 words)
52 Cry at the stadium
55 The woman named in Hebrews 11:11 and her namesakes (var.)
57 Horizontal, multi-element antennas
58 German auto
59 "You, a _____ man" (John 10:33 NIV)
60 "I know. . .thy _____ against me" (Isaiah 37:28)
61 "_____ begat Sadoc" (Matthew 1:14)
62 "A _____ of a man" (Numbers 19:16)
63 Not a one
64 "Make _____ oil" (Exodus 30:25) (2 words)
65 Pooch in The Thin Man
66 Cultivates, at times

61

Scrambled Circle

by Ken Save

Rome Rules

Men-pleasers often restrict the godly from their mission.

1. SHLEF   5. TECUXEE   9. TIDEESP

2. NARENM   6. NALELF   10. RUNOM

3. LETAD   7. CHRETST   11. DASHEW

4. HISERP   8. RIDEES

Paul was kept under arrest for two years by these two Roman governors.

1. ⦿ _ _ _ _

2. _ _ _ _ ⦿ _

3. _ _ _ ⦿ _

4. _ _ _ ⦿ _ _

5. _ ⦿ _ _ _ _

6. ⦿ _ _ _ _ _

7. _ _ _ ⦿ _ _ _

8. _ _ ⦿ _ _ _

9. _ _ _ _ _ ⦿ _

10. _ _ ⦿ _ _

11. _ _ ⦿ _ _ _

Answer: _ _ _ _ _ and _ _ _ _ _ _

Old Testament Deceit

We have been warned—our sins will find us out (Numbers 32:23). Solve this puzzle to find the names of Old Testament men who lied and suffered because of it.

| PRS 7 | MNO 6 | TUV 8 | GHI 4 | PRS 7 | GHI 4 | ABC 2 | PRS 7 |

| JKL 5 | ABC 2 | ABC 2 | MNO 6 | ABC 2 |

| ABC 2 | ABC 2 | GHI 4 | ABC 2 | MNO 6 |

| DEF 3 | GHI 4 | TUV 8 | DEF 3 |

| DEF 3 | ABC 2 | TUV 8 | GHI 4 | DEF 3 |

| PRS 7 | ABC 2 | MNO 6 | ABC 2 | ABC 2 | JKL 5 | JKL 5 | ABC 2 | TUV 8 |

| DEF 3 | ABC 2 | PRS 7 | GHI 4 | TUV 8 | PRS 7 |

| JKL 5 | ABC 2 | ABC 2 | ABC 2 | MNO 6 |

by Suzanne Stepp

A True Blessing

> We do indeed reap what we sow. Solve this acrostic to glean what was sown by a gracious man whose actions ultimately reaped a grateful woman.

Ruth _____ grain in Boaz's field (Ruth 2:7–8)

‾‾	‾‾	‾‾	‾‾	‾‾	‾‾	‾‾	‾‾
32	9	16	41	20	1	30	15

Ruth was _____ for her kindness to Naomi (Ruth 3:10)

‾‾	‾‾	‾‾	‾‾	‾‾	‾‾	‾‾
22	13	46	39	3	43	27

Containers (Ruth 2:9)

‾‾	‾‾	‾‾	‾‾	‾‾	‾‾	‾‾
26	10	33	21	49	4	51

Shared in suffering or grief

‾‾	‾‾	‾‾	‾‾	‾‾	‾‾	‾‾	‾‾	‾‾	‾‾	‾‾
17	29	8	34	23	45	6	37	18	31	11

Ruth ate with Boaz and was _____ (Ruth 2:14)

‾‾	‾‾	‾‾	‾‾	‾‾	‾‾	‾‾	‾‾
36	24	38	5	47	12	42	28

A return for something done (Ruth 2:12)

‾‾	‾‾	‾‾	‾‾	‾‾	‾‾	‾‾	‾‾	‾‾	‾‾
40	2	25	44	14	50	35	19	7	48

22-44-9-18   25-44-8-14-23-19-28-42-11   41-47-36

29-44-24-19-32   8-20-19,   7-9-29-37-19-32,   4-49-16

6-43-1   32-13-35-23-19   48-26-2-19   9-14-44-19-32

45-41-31   17-6-10-23-26-49-33,   9-19-27

40-46-50-1-44-23-12-6   41-30-40   19-44-16:   23-19-15

13-42-45   38-9-13-4   23-13-21-44   39-44-8-43

44-5   45-6-31   6-23-19-28-38-24-4-51   44-5

50-24-40-34-44-3-49   38-44-1   41-46-1.

RUTH 2:15–16

The Brothers Boanerges

DIFFICULT

	A	B	C	D	E	F	G	H	I
1	T			F	H			E	O
2	D	N			T	R			F
3			H	U					T
4	E		D	N			R	T	
5		H			D				U
6	R	O					F		
7				O	F	U			D
8	U	D			R	T	O		
9			F			E			R

Hint: Column I

James and John were known as the sons _____ _____
(Mark 3:17).

Bible Quotation
by Suzanne Stepp

Visiting with God
GENESIS 6:9

Work this Bible quotation puzzle to find a man whom God lifted above a world deluged with trouble.

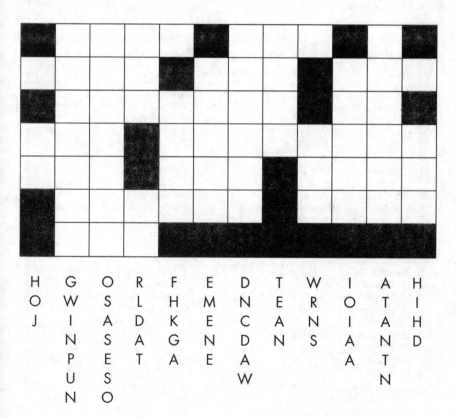

Crossword
by Sarah Lagerquist Simmons

Brothers-in-Law

In the days of the patriarchs, it was not uncommon for a man to have more than one wife—nor to marry a cousin, half-sister, or sister-in-law. This made for a somewhat complicated family tree. Solve this puzzle and a few Old Testament marital mazes by uncovering the names of some well-known brothers-in-law.

And Abraham said of Sarah his wife, She is my sister. . . . She is the daughter of my father, but not the daughter of my mother; and she became my wife.
GENESIS 20:2, 12

ACROSS

1 Group that organizes Great American Smokeout (abbr.)
4 LEAH'S BROTHER-IN-LAW
9 Jonah was ____ when he fell asleep during a storm (2 words)
14 "There was no harm in the ____" (2 Kings 4:41)
15 Tuft of small stiff feathers
16 Decides fate of defendant
17 "Into your hand ____ they delivered" (Genesis 9:2)
18 Proofreading symbol
19 Group of desirable people
20 Squeaks
22 Hailed mode of transportation
24 "Soldiers led him. . .into the ____" (Mark 15:16)
25 Plant part
27 Soldiers suffer from this (abbr.)
31 "There is none ____ beside him" (Deuteronomy 4:35)
32 Decrease
33 "____, she is broken that was the gates" (Ezekiel 26:2)
34 "They are drenched by mountain ____" (Job 24:8 NIV)
36 ZIPPORAH'S BROTHER-IN-LAW
38 Gushed
40 Jeered
42 Ditch
43 16 dry quarts is equal to 2 of these
44 Legislation to protect our water (abbr.)
45 Paul sailed to this country (Acts 27)
47 Projection

51 Graduate (abbr.)
53 Geek
54 Whit
55 "God hath spoken ____; twice have I heard this" (Psalm 62:11)
57 Famed broadcast journalist Cronkite
59 "Ye shall ____ your enemies" (Leviticus 26:7)
62 FATHER OF RACHEL'S BROTHER-IN-LAW
65 Sea eagle
66 Sand hills
67 "Our enemies totally lost their ____" (Nehemiah 6:15 MSG)
68 Direction (abbr.)
69 Secret meeting
70 "Fools waste their lives in fun and ____" (Ecclesiastes 7:4 MSG)
71 Small amount

DOWN

1 Type of helicopter
2 "They dragged her out to the palace's horse ____" (2 Kings 11:15 MSG)
3 Metals
4 "____ of all trades"
5 "____, my brother!" (1 Kings 13:30)
6 "Nabal and every ____ in his misbegotten brood" (1 Samuel 25:21 MSG)
7 Cry of triumph (Sp.)
8 DAVID LOST HIS BROTHER-IN-LAW AND FATHER-IN-LAW IN ONE ____ (2 Samuel 1:4)

9 Mythical Greek hero
10 Type of flower
11 This neutral country's international communication system (abbr.)
12 Greek goddess of the dawn
13 "Thou _____ a fair woman to look upon" (Genesis 12:11)
21 Warnings
23 Realtor accreditation (abbr.)
25 "There went with him a _____ of men" (1 Samuel 10:26)
26 Package carrier company (abbr.)
28 "The king arose, and _____ his garments, and lay on the earth" (2 Samuel 13:31)
29 "Feet _____ with the preparation of the gospel of peace" (Ephesians 6:15)
30 ASENATH'S BROTHER-IN-LAW
32 "_____ the kine to the cart" (1 Samuel 6:7)
35 JUDITH'S BROTHER-IN-LAW SOLD HER HUSBAND POTTAGE, WHICH HE _____
36 "She moved him to _____ of her father a field" (Joshua 15:18)
37 "The Pharisees began to _____ Him vehemently" (Luke 11:53 NKJV)
38 Lower jaw
39 LEAH'S OTHER BROTHER-IN-LAW
40 "And Jacob _____ his peace" (Genesis 34:5)

41 "Who can withstand his _____ blast?" (Psalm 147:17 NIV)
42 Help for agricultural businesses (abbr.)
43 "The down-and-out on a _____ with the high-and-mighty" (Isaiah 5:11 MSG)
45 Enlargement (abbr.)
46 Beginning in golf: _____ off
48 "They will come upon you. . .in spite of your many sorceries and all your _____ spells" (Isaiah 47:9 NIV)
49 Breastbones
50 " 'Master, your mina has _____ ten minas' " (Luke 19:16 NKJV)
52 ELISHEBA'S BROTHER-IN-LAW
56 "Thou puttest thy _____ in a rock" (Numbers 24:21)
57 "The priest shall _____ the offering before the LORD" (Numbers 5:25)
58 High cards
59 Time in the Midwest (abbr.)
60 One of Caleb's descendants (1 Chronicles 2:50)
61 "I will not take _____ thing that is thine" (Genesis 14:23)
63 Israelites crossed the Red _____
64 "_____ some of yourselves unto the war" (Numbers 31:3)

Fifteen Years Added to His Life
ISAIAH 38:2–5

Then **Hezekiah turned** his **face toward** the **wall,** and **prayed** unto the LORD, and **said, Remember** now, O LORD, I **beseech** thee, how I have **walked** before thee in **truth** and with a **perfect heart,** and have **done** that which is **good** in thy **sight.** And Hezekiah **wept sore. Then came** the **word** of the LORD to **Isaiah, saying,** . . .I have **heard** thy **prayer,** I **have seen** thy **tears: behold,** I **will** add unto thy **days fifteen years.**

```
B L R G D Q B Q Q F E H A Q H
M S T H E N P R A Y E D G A L
Y A R S C N N C E S A Y I N G
D I M A B E E Y C M R K Y T T
N D F T E P E T D O E E Y H J
J L C T H Y Y S E Z Y M T A D
X B F U O G M H E A A U B A P
Y I L R L L I H D B R Q Y E N
F O I N D B L S R T P S R E R
W H L E E H A I A S I F D P H
J P E D E E Y P W D E K L A W
R Z R A S N S F O C M L V I O
V O R E R O S Y T Z A E T U R
L T G O O D T P E W C I I L D
Z W E O S N L V Z Y G H A W U
```

Cryptoscripture

by Sharon Y. Brown and David Austin

Great Love

> Two New Testament men demonstrated great love for our Lord and Savior. Can you crack these alphabet codes to discover the names of these saintly fellows?

KIPR QMTW MRBXPZPL, XIMK HPMR FP KC XPPQ

MRL KC DZPME HSRP IPMZK? ACZ S MH ZPMLF

RCK KC DP DCTRL CRWF, DTK MWBC KC LSP

MK NPZTBMWPH ACZ KIP RMHP CA KIP WCZL

NPBTB.

IZBQN LSCZ LSIL IMC EBMQ BJ DBZCQ LSCMC

SILS QBL MTFCQ I NMCILCM LSIQ HBSQ LSC

EIOLTFL.

Lesser-Known Men
of the New Testament

Peter, Paul, John. . .some New Testament men are very familiar to us. But can you solve these spotty headlines to uncover three lesser-known guys of the Christian era?

R●NAWAY ●LAV●
BEC●●ES A CHRI●T●A●

— — — — — — —

A●ROGAN● ●OMINE●RING MAN
REJ●CT● A●OST●LIC AUT●OR●TY

— — — — — — — —

H●MBLE MAN WR●TES DOWN ●VERY WORD
OF ●OMANS WHILE APO●●LE DIC●ATES

— — — — — —

Acrostic
by Connie Troyer

Beloved Brother

Benjamin was Joseph's favorite brother. Solve the acrostic to discover how this preferred status richly suited Jacob's youngest son.

Joseph's brother Benjamin was born nearest this place
(Genesis 35:16–17)

$$\overline{18} \quad \overline{1} \quad \overline{31} \quad \overline{25} \quad \overline{39} \quad \overline{15}$$

Benjamin's original name (Genesis 35:18)

$$\overline{11} \quad \overline{6} \quad \overline{26} \quad \overline{36} \quad \overline{2} \quad \overline{17}$$

Benjamin's brothers were guilty, or this, concerning Joseph

$$\overline{9} \quad \overline{21} \quad \overline{33} \quad \overline{13} \quad \overline{24} \quad \overline{29} \quad \overline{3} \quad \overline{27}$$

Fancied, or a special one

$$\overline{8} \quad \overline{37} \quad \overline{20} \quad \overline{34} \quad \overline{30} \quad \overline{5} \quad \overline{23}$$

The tribe of Benjamin numbered this in relation to the rest
(1 Samuel 9:21)

$$\overline{4} \quad \overline{19} \quad \overline{40} \quad \overline{32} \quad \overline{7} \quad \overline{38} \quad \overline{35} \quad \overline{12}$$

Jacob prophesied that Benjamin's brother Dan would _____ his people (Genesis 49:16)

$$\overline{16} \quad \overline{28} \quad \overline{10} \quad \overline{22} \quad \overline{14}$$

12-36   24-15-32   34-8   12-25-14-19   25-6

22-24-20-6   38-40-9-25   19-24-2   9-25-40-26-22-39-4

34-8   30-37-17-19-27-2-31   18-28-12   12-36

11-27-2-16-40-19-17-26   25-14   22-24-20-38

31-25-30-14-27   25-21-2-10-30-5-23   13-17-5-9-27-4

36-8   4-17-7-20-1-30   37-2-10   8-17-20-38

9-25-37-26-22-6-35   36-8   30-40-17-19-6-2-12.

GENESIS 45:22

Crossword
by David K. Shortess

Biblical Brothers

All sibling rivalry aside, when it gets right down to it, there is nothing greater than a brother—except a friend like Christ, of course. Can you complete this crossword to find four sets of biblical brothers, two pairs from the Old Testament and two pairs from the New?

A man of many companions may come to ruin, but there is a friend who sticks closer than a brother.
PROVERBS 18:24 NIV

ACROSS

1 "Ourselves a _____ for you to follow" (2 Thessalonians 3:9 NIV)
6 "The wrath of the _____" (Revelation 6:16)
10 "And shall put it upon a _____" (Numbers 4:10)
13 Met offering
14 "To preach the word in _____" (Acts 16:6)
15 "_____ an Ithrite" (2 Samuel 23:38)
16 BIBLICAL BROTHERS FOUND IN MATTHEW 4 (3 words)
19 A grandson of Adam (Genesis 4:25–26)
20 "Commanded to _____ peoples" (Daniel 3:4 NIV)
21 "Wherefore _____ Sarah laugh" (Genesis 18:13)
22 Sun Yat-_____ (Chinese leader)
23 _____ Cruces, NM
24 Singer Martha
25 _____ Victor (abbr.)
28 BIBLICAL BROTHERS FOUND IN MATTHEW 17 (3 words)
31 British noblemen
34 Juan's aunt
35 "Suddenly _____ instant" (Isaiah 30:13) (2 words)
36 "Why _____ so fearful?" (Mark 4:40) (2 words)
37 "Followed the _____" (Genesis 24:61)
38 "How right they are to _____ you!" (Song of Songs 1:4 NIV)
39 Wonderful!
40 "And none _____ deliver" (Micah 5:8)
41 Bells and whistles

42 BIBLICAL BROTHERS FOUND IN GENESIS 25 (3 words)
45 The start and end of a Wisconsin city
46 *Summer* in Paris (Fr.)
47 "And bored a hole in the _____ of it" (2 Kings 12:9)
48 "If a man _____, shall he live again?" (Job 14:14)
51 PC alternative
52 Own in Scotland (Scot.)
53 "And counteth the _____" (Luke 14:28)
54 BIBLICAL BROTHERS FOUND IN GENESIS 5 (3 words)
58 "But the name of the wicked shall _____" (Proverbs 10:7)
59 "For I have _____ blameless life" (Psalm 26:1 NIV) (2 words)
60 Wood-shaping tool
61 "And _____ it up" (Revelation 10:10)
62 "From the _____ of the tongue" (Job 5:21 NIV)
63 "The men of the _____ Nebo, fifty and two" (Nehemiah 7:33)

DOWN

1 Jethro's son-in-law (Exodus 3:1)
2 "Wail, _____ tree" (Zechariah 11:2 NIV) (2 words)
3 "He has a _____" (Matthew 11:18 NIV)
4 Greek god of love
5 Ethernet, for example (abbr.)
6 Having woolly hairs
7 "The Gentiles to live _____ the Jews?" (Galatians 2:14) (2 words)
8 May be a POW
9 Head- or neckwear (var.)

10 "Like a _____, without cause" (Lamentations 3:52)

11 "Blessed _____ the meek" (Matthew 5:5)

12 "Or if the _____ flesh turn again" (Leviticus 13:16)

17 "The written account of _____ line" (Genesis 5:1 NIV)

18 "And Rachel _____, and was buried" (Genesis 35:19)

23 Freeway part

24 "Wind without _____" (Proverbs 25:14)

25 Helicopter part

26 "_____ is deceptive, and beauty" (Proverbs 31:30 NIV)

27 Boleyn, et al.

28 "Shout with _____ God, all the earth!" (Psalm 66:1 NIV) (2 words)

29 "Behold, I _____ at the door, and knock" (Revelation 3:20)

30 Fifth son of Nebo (Ezra 10:43)

31 Guitar kin

32 "And towers in the wooded _____" (2 Chronicles 27:4 NIV)

33 "And his head _____ unto the clouds" (Job 20:6)

37 "His neck with a flowing _____?" (Job 39:19 NIV)

38 "There is _____ here" (John 6:9) (2 words)

40 Cry of disapproval

41 "Sin of Sodom, that was overthrown _____ moment" (Lamentations 4:6) (3 words)

43 "And, behold, a _____ is in thine own eye?" (Matthew 7:4)

44 Ravens fed him (1 Kings 17:1–6)

48 "Know what thy right hand _____" (Matthew 6:3)

49 "Now the parable is this: The seed _____ word of God" (Luke 8:11) (2 words)

50 Libnah, and _____, and Ashan" (Joshua 15:42)

51 "And with what measure ye _____, it shall be measured" (Matthew 7:2)

52 "If anyone _____ anything to them" (Revelation 22:18 NIV)

53 Chit's companion

54 Mrs. in Madrid (abbr.)

55 "My heart was _____ within me" (Psalm 39:3)

56 Teachers' organization (abbr.)

57 Arafat's organization (abbr.)

77

Word Search
by John Hudson Tiner

A Prepared Heart
EZRA 7:6, 10

This Ezra went up **from Babylon**; and he was a **ready scribe** in the law of **Moses, which** the LORD God of Israel had **given**: and the **king granted** him all his **request, according** to the **hand** of the LORD his God **upon** him. . . . For Ezra had **prepared** his **heart** to **seek** the law of the **LORD**, and to do it, and to **teach** in **Israel statutes** and **judgments**.

```
Z Q R L E A R S I J O G V T L
D C G F E C A Y D A E R E S S
L O R D M C N T T I V A O T V
K Z W K E O D W S U C N A I A
X G K Z L R R D E H L T E U E
H F J Y B D A F U N U E Q P Q
H L B U U I E P Q T T D H O D
P A K L D N C Z E S A P S N B
B C E H H G U S R R I F A T T
P N E H R G M V G A P H O V C
O N S C R I B E V Z A I T T E
H Q X I Y V T K N O D R B R O
R N K H S E I F T T A R R K V
H T M W W N M O S E S J R K S
X X Z F G V L J H P H V Q Q Y
```

by Connie Troyer

Christ's Purpose

Accepting Christ as Lord is a matter of life and death. Decode this puzzle to shed more light upon this Son that rules our days.

Jesus' birthplace (Matthew 2:1)

‾10‾ ‾27‾ ‾43‾ ‾37‾ ‾16‾ ‾1‾ ‾30‾ ‾44‾ ‾21‾

Jesus' followers

‾14‾ ‾25‾ ‾36‾ ‾20‾ ‾28‾ ‾13‾ ‾7‾ ‾32‾ ‾19‾

One name of Jesus (John 1:49)

‾15‾ ‾40‾ ‾23‾ ‾11‾ ‾45‾ ‾29‾ ‾38‾ ‾4‾

This man first called Him the Messiah (John 1:40–41)

‾2‾ ‾34‾ ‾39‾ ‾22‾ ‾41‾ ‾5‾

Jesus' prayer spot (John 18:1–2)

‾3‾ ‾31‾ ‾17‾ ‾12‾ ‾42‾ ‾6‾

Also known as The Skull (Luke 23:33; John 19:17–18)

‾26‾ ‾8‾ ‾35‾ ‾33‾ ‾18‾ ‾24‾ ‾9‾

45-38-22   43-40   43-30-25-36   44-6-39

20-37-17-28-19-43   10-40-43-37   14-28-41-4,   18-34-14

17-38-15-27,   2-6-14   17-42-33-25-33-1-14,   43-37-8-43

30-32   21-28-29-37-43   10-27   7-11-24-12 . 10-38-43-37

11-45   43-30-1   12-1-31-39   2-23-39   16-28-33-25-23-3.
ROMANS 14:9

Anagram
by Paul Kent

It's a Miracle!

Miraculous stories dot the pages of the Bible. We know the amazing deeds of men like Elijah, Jesus, and Paul—but this puzzle is all about men on the receiving end of the miracles. Can you unscramble these names of men who experienced God's power?

Huey cuts

_ _ _ _ _ _ _ _

A brute aims

_ _ _ _ _ _ _ _ _

As mulch

_ _ _ _ _ _ _

An Engaging Man
MATTHEW 1:19

There are those among us who retain chivalrous hearts in the midst of unexpected circumstances. Solve this puzzle to discover one such gallant man.

```
C   J   N   R   I   V   O   E   M   W   T   L
Y   U   E   T   X   A   H   R   U   A   W   O
A   H   S   B   E   H   D   L   E   K   W   A
G   I   N   D   A   N   O   L   B   L   L   W
L   A   O   S   J   U   S   P   D   A   A   N
H   K   P   R   I   N   T   D   E   A   A   N
    S   A   E   I   E   P   H   M   I   R   E
    P   U   M   P   I   T   B   Y   R   N   N
            G   T   D   Y   B   A   E   I   I
                A   M       B   A   R
                N
```

Crossword
by Marijane Troyer

Jesus, My Rock

The only one who can quench our spiritual thirst is our Savior, Jesus Christ, for He is our water in the midst of an arid place. Whet your spiritual appetite by working this puzzle to find more names referring to a Man who really rocked!

They drank of that spiritual Rock that followed them:
and that Rock was Christ.
1 CORINTHIANS 10:4

ACROSS

1 Kind of exam
4 Take this to fly to the fjords (abbr.)
7 NAME FROM LUKE 22:61
12 Cape Town's country (abbr.)
13 High jinks
15 Balmoral Castle's river
16 "God shall send forth his ____ and his truth" (Psalm 57:3)
18 "Thus saith the LORD, I have ____ these waters" (2 Kings 2:21)
21 Its capital is Pierre (abbr.)
22 Town in northwestern Pennsylvania
24 "That he should still ____ for ever" (Psalm 49:9)
25 Meadow
26 Mode of transportation (abbr.)
27 Make lace
29 Compete
30 "The mouth of the righteous man ____ wisdom" (Psalm 37:30 NIV)
34 State for newlyweds (abbr.)
35 Tree or street
36 Indian currency (abbr.)
38 Hawaiian bird
39 Title Paul gave to other Christians (abbr.)
40 "Why did we ____ leave Egypt" (Numbers 11:20 NIV)
42 "To offer unto the LORD the ____ sacrifice, and his vow" (1 Samuel 1:21)
44 Own (Scot.)
46 "And thou shalt ____ up the tabernacle according to the fashion" (Exodus 26:30)
48 "Thou trustest in the staff of this broken ____" (Isaiah 36:6)
49 ____ mode

50 Calling or greeting
51 Classic car
52 Model Cheryl
53 "And saveth such ____ be of a contrite spirit" (Psalm 34:18)
55 "But if the LORD make a ____ thing" (Numbers 16:30)
58 Certain parchment scroll (var.)
60 Emergency crew (abbr.)
61 "Ten asses ____ with the good things of Egypt" (Genesis 45:23)
64 "And ____ of Rehoboth by the river reigned in his stead" (Genesis 36:37)
66 Cornhusker state (abbr.)
67 Jacob ____ Israel (abbr.)
68 Pharaoh name
70 Sal of songdom was one
72 "Locks with the ____ of the night" (Song of Solomon 5:2 NASB)
74 "The same came for a witness, ____ bear witness of the Light" (John 1:7)
76 What Santa says
77 NAME OF GOD (Exodus 6:3 AMP)
78 NAME FROM 2 SAMUEL 22:3

DOWN

1 Bone
2 "Behold behind him a ____ caught in a thicket" (Genesis 22:13)
3 "You got fat, became obese, a tub of ____" (Deuteronomy 32:15 MSG)
4 Pig's home
5 City in Canaan
6 "It is only a ____ from the burn" (Leviticus 13:28 NIV)
8 Paean
9 "For my flesh is ____ food" (John 6:55 NIV)

10 "THE LORD IS MY ROCK, AND MY FORTRESS, AND MY _____" (2 Samuel 22:2)

11 "FOR I KNOW THAT MY _____ LIVETH" (Job 19:25)

14 Billy Graham's home state (abbr.)

17 Rebekah's son

18 "And God called the firmament _____" (Genesis 1:8)

19 "Some _____ beast hath devoured him" (Genesis 37:20)

20 "Tabernacle shall be sanctified by my _____" (Exodus 29:43)

22 "He who hurries his footsteps _____" (Proverbs 19:2 NASB)

23 European country (abbr.)

26 Concerning (abbr.)

28 Hebrew letter

31 "Then Joshua _____ his clothes and fell facedown" (Joshua 7:6 NIV)

32 "And the servant _____ Isaac all things that he had done" (Genesis 24:66)

33 Trite

37 Dried up

41 "_____ abode at Corinth" (2 Timothy 4:20)

43 Time period (var.)

45 "Othello" role

47 Twelfth month of the Jewish year

49 Irish nobleman

51 NAME FROM 2 SAMUEL 22:3

54 "PRAISE BE TO MY ROCK! EXALTED BE GOD MY _____" (Psalm 18:46 NIV)

56 Certain railway, familiarly

57 Famed pianist Landowska

59 Spanish cheer

62 "And the _____ beast shall be his" (Exodus 21:34)

63 _____ Valley, California

64 "Moses _____ to judge the people" (Exodus 18:13)

65 Golfer Ernie

69 "Pull me out of _____ net" (Psalm 31:4)

71 Selma's state (abbr.)

73 One who heals (abbr.)

75 First part of the Bible (abbr.)

Word Search
by John Hudson Tiner

Prepare the Way
MATTHEW 3:1–4

In **those days** came **John** the **Baptist**, **preaching** in the **wilderness** of **Judaea**, and saying, **Repent** ye: for the **kingdom** of **heaven** is at **hand**. For this is he that was **spoken** of by the **prophet Esaias**, **saying**, The **voice** of one **crying** in the wilderness, **Prepare** ye the way of the **Lord**, **make** his **paths straight**. And the **same** John had his **raiment** of **camel's hair**, and a **leathern girdle about** his **loins**; and his **meat** was **locusts** and wild **honey**.

```
S  I  K  L  O  I  N  S  V  C  W  V  L  I  B
S  S  Y  A  D  Q  N  R  R  Q  L  O  R  D  A
P  R  E  P  A  R  E  Y  E  S  Z  I  F  X  P
O  N  T  N  E  M  I  A  R  H  I  C  N  R  T
K  M  H  U  R  N  C  Y  M  E  T  E  E  E  I
E  S  C  O  G  E  B  D  K  I  V  A  H  U  S
N  X  T  G  J  U  D  A  E  A  C  P  E  A  T
K  K  N  R  I  F  M  L  E  H  O  M  Y  L  O
S  R  E  O  A  R  O  H  I  R  G  I  E  R  L
H  L  P  E  I  I  D  N  P  W  N  D  N  A  H
T  K  E  Q  S  T  G  L  Q  G  E  X  O  S  T
A  K  R  M  S  A  N  H  E  X  E  S  H  U  Z
P  J  D  Q  A  A  I  S  T  S  U  C  O  L  M
X  D  N  F  M  C  K  A  L  O  Q  B  K  H  S
I  O  M  R  E  V  P  B  S  H  A  I  R  W  T
```

Drop Two
by Dorothy Pryse

Israel's First King
1 SAMUEL 10:12

Under God's power, we are capable of doing extraordinary things. When a new king experienced a change of heart, attitude, and speech, his people put their wonder into words. Solve this drop two puzzle to discover what they said.

BRAINED	Loaf	_____	1. ___ ___
CHASING	Link	_____	2. ___ ___
CHEMIST	Musical sound	_____	3. ___ ___
ASHAMED	Ladies	_____	4. ___ ___
SURFACE	Neckwear	_____	5. ___ ___
LAPPING	Mimicking	_____	6. ___ ___
ARCUATE	Sharp	_____	7. ___ ___
FLORIST	Not last	_____	8. ___ ___
PROMISE	Watered fabric	_____	9. ___ ___
INSHORE	Got up	_____	10. ___ ___
ASCRIBE	Beds	_____	11. ___ ___
MOBSTER	Temperate	_____	12. ___ ___
CASEOUS	Effect	_____	13. ___ ___

___ ___ ___ ___ ___ ___ ___ ___ ___ ___ ___ ___ ___
1   2   3   4   5   6   7   8   9   10   11   12   13

The Wisdom of Kings

From some men, wisdom flows like a fountain. Crack these alphabet codes to discover two kings who used an endless stream of good judgment during their reign.

UFZ WRZ WUDG ORTRNRF QLOZRN UFZ

VFZGKOYUFZLFW GMPGGZLFW NVPX, UFZ

TUKWGFGOO RE XGUKY, GDGF UO YXG OUFZ

YXUY LO RF YXG OGU OXRKG.

AWERBJ ZBE XRPJQ GXBYE WFH ZJXC JX NXPBC

QW YXRPC, BCH JX YXRPCXH RC AXYKEBFXT WCX

BCH QJRYQG GXBYE.

Acrostic
by Suzanne Stepp

Craving Jesus

Sometimes our desire for the Lord outweighs our personal fears. Solve this puzzle to uncover a man who craved Jesus when others rejected Him.

Talking

—— —— —— —— —— —— —— ——
21   8   30 24 16   4   28 11

The _____ began at sundown on Friday

—— —— —— —— —— —— ——
35   3   38 15 32 20   7

_____ ministered to Jesus (Mark 15:40–41)

—— —— —— —— ——
14 29   2   23 10

A title of Jesus: "The King of the _____" (Mark 15:26)

—— —— —— ——
19 34   9 25

The multitude cried out to _____ Jesus (Mark 15:12–14)

—— —— —— —— —— —— ——
27 12 31 17 22   1 36

Jesus was _____ while on the cross (Mark 15:32)

—— —— —— —— —— —— ——
6 37 13 33 26   5 18

19-29-25-30-8-7   29-1   3-6-4-2-24-20-7-32-23-3,   24-28

7-29-28-29-31-12-3-15-26-34   17-29-31-10-35-5-26-26-29-6,

14-7-33-27-7   32-26-25-29   14-3-4-20-37-18   1-29-6

20-7-5   16-22-10-11-18-29-2   29-1   11-29-18,

27-24-2-30,   32-28-18   9-23-10-20   33-28

38-29-26-18-26-36   31-10-20-29   8-4-26-32-20-37,

24-28-18   27-6-3-13-5-18   20-7-34   15-29-18-36   29-1

19-30-25-31-21.

MARK 15:43

Crossword
by David K. Shortess

Joshua's Proclamation

Joshua was a great leader who never retreated when faced with giants, opposing armies, and sin. His strength, faith, and service are prime examples of how we should live our lives. Work this puzzle to uncover the verse describing Joshua's unyielding dedication to God.

Serve the LORD with gladness:
come before his presence with singing.
PSALM 100:2

ACROSS

1 Communication code for the letter *P*
5 Home of the Incas
9 "____ for the widow" (Isaiah 1:17)
14 Stork relative
15 "And Geshem the ____ heard about it" (Nehemiah 2:19 NIV)
16 Leap forward suddenly
17 "I ____; it is sealed" (Isaiah 29:11 NIV)
18 Capital of 5 Across
19 "Ye are not under the law, but ____ grace" (Romans 6:14)
20 BEGINNING OF QUOTE FROM JOSHUA 24:15 (5 words)
23 Biah preceder (see second in Nehemiah 10:12)
24 Talk idly
25 "Out of the ____" (Ezekiel 45:14)
28 Sailing skill
32 "And the night be ____" (Job 7:4)
33 Table scrap
34 "The LORD ____ to me" (Ruth 1:17) (2 words)
35 "And after that also King of ____" (Hebrews 7:2)
36 QUOTE, CONTINUED (3 words)
40 "Judah is a lion's ____" (Genesis 49:9)
42 Large, open wagon
43 "____ their words like deadly arrows" (Psalm 64:3 NIV)
46 "Is any thing too ____ for the LORD" (Genesis 18:14)
47 Reclusive actress of the silents (2 words)
50 GI's duds (abbr.)
51 Language of Laos
52 Maliciously false public statement
53 END OF QUOTE (3 words)
57 "Tell me, art thou a ____" (Acts 22:27)
60 "Or ____ I will come unto thee quickly" (Revelation 2:5)
61 We, at the start, makes it a hot dog
62 "____ all that we ask or think" (Ephesians 3:20)
63 "Let the sea ____" (Psalm 96:11)
64 "Neither ____ you up a standing image" (Leviticus 26:1)
65 Its capital is Lhasa
66 "____, what must I do to be saved?" (Acts 16:30)
67 Common IDs (abbr.)

DOWN

1 Spanish artist
2 Embarrasser
3 Undeveloped plumage (2 words)
4 "As ____ against the wall" (Isaiah 25:4) (2 words)
5 "The ____ tree also" (Joel 1:12)
6 Pennsylvania port
7 "In ____ was there a voice heard" (Matthew 2:18)
8 African lady with stretched lips
9 "Look, I am setting a ____ line among my people Israel" (Amos 7:8 NIV)
10 Crazy (var.)
11 "And keepeth my works unto the ____" (Revelation 2:26)
12 "A child when she was past ____" (Hebrews 11:11)
13 ____ *Rosenkavalier*
21 Research, with *on* (2 words)
22 Skip, as a stone

25 Clavicles
26 "As of many; but as of ____" (Galatians 3:16)
27 Dream indicator (abbr.)
29 Negative votes
30 157.5° from North (abbr.)
31 "And ____ came through the nations" (Deuteronomy 29:16) (2 words)
32 Four quarts (abbr.)
35 "If therefore thine eye be ____" (Matthew 6:22)
37 "Became mighty men which were of ____, men of renown" (Genesis 6:4)
38 "And Moses said, ____ that to day" (Exodus 16:25)
39 Purple Heart recipient, for example (abbr.)
40 "And ____ will go for us" (Isaiah 6:8)
41 "Yea, he ____ power over the angel" (Hosea 12:4)
44 Of Portugal and Spain's peninsula
45 Shapers
47 Needlefish
48 "Like a tree planted by the ____ of water" (Psalm 1:3)

49 Sick people
51 Dogma presented as truth
53 "Lord, ____ me" (Matthew 14:30)
54 A word spoken from the cross (Mark 15:34)
55 Russian emperor
56 "As though they were not ____" (Job 39:16)
57 "The weasel, the ____, any kind" (Leviticus 11:29 NIV)
58 Kimono holder
59 "The ____ will stone them" (Ezekiel 23:47 NIV)

93

Telephone Scramble
by Connie Troyer

Knowing David

David was a great king who knew a great many people. Work this puzzle to discover the names of a few of his friends, relatives, coworkers, and enemies.

| PRS 7 | GHI 4 | GHI 4 | MNO 6 | DEF 3 | GHI 4 |

| MNO 6 | GHI 4 | GHI 4 | GHI 4 | TUV 8 | WXY 9 | MNO 6 | DEF 3 | MNO 6 |

| JKL 5 | MNO 6 | MNO 6 | ABC 2 | TUV 8 | GHI 4 | ABC 2 | MNO 6 |

| JKL 5 | MNO 6 | ABC 2 | ABC 2 |

| MNO 6 | ABC 2 | TUV 8 | GHI 4 | ABC 2 | MNO 6 |

| GHI 4 | MNO 6 | JKL 5 | GHI 4 | ABC 2 | TUV 8 | GHI 4 |

| ABC 2 | GHI 4 | GHI 4 | MNO 6 | DEF 3 | JKL 5 | DEF 3 | ABC 2 | GHI 4 |

| ABC 2 | ABC 2 | GHI 4 | GHI 4 | PRS 7 | GHI 4 |

A Whale of a Story

EASY

	A	B	C	D	E	F	G	H	I
1	H	A					T		
2	E		R			S	A		I
3					H				
4	R		T	F	S		H	A	G
5			G	R	A		S		
6		I	S	H		T	R		
7		F							A
8	G				T		I		H
9		S			E			F	

Hint: Row 8

"Now the LORD had prepared a _____ _____ to swallow up Jonah. And Jonah was in the belly of the fish three days and three nights" (Jonah 1:17).

Faithful Centurion
MATTHEW 8:8–10

The **centurion answered** and said, **Lord**, I am not **worthy** that thou **shouldest** come under my **roof**: but **speak** the **word only**, and my servant **shall** be **healed**. For I am a man under **authority**, **having soldiers under** me: and I say to this man, Go, and he **goeth**; and to **another**, Come, and he **cometh**; and to my **servant**, Do this, and he **doeth** it. **When Jesus heard** it, he **marvelled**, and **said** to **them** that **followed**, **Verily** I say unto you, I **have** not **found** so **great faith**, no, not in **Israel**.

```
C H T I A F Y A L F O U N D M
U P V S G S C T S R O O F E H
E N P R D O H Y I U I Q L H R
Y M D A M A E O L R S X T N G
U J P E M N I T U N O E Z E G
T Z T L R S H T H L O H J H N
Y H T R O W N F H D D V T W I
T N A V R E S Z S E O E O U V
Q Y Z Q C R C O L W M R S U A
W Y Y D O E L L L O D I H T H
H E A L E D E D G L G L A L K
T Z M K I V D R O L A Y V A S
T I W E R I E A N O T H E R V
F X R A A A P E M F S P S C C
W S M S T I A H J R S O E G Y
```

Acrostic

by Connie Troyer

Father of a Great King

Life holds many mysteries, including the destiny that awaits your children.
Crack this acrostic's code to uncover a father who unwittingly sired a king.

Three generations of descent from Boaz as given in Ruth 4:17

__ __ __ __, __ __ __ __ __,
6 41 22 18, 37 32 11 38 47,

__ __ __ __ __ __ __ __ __
26 40 33 19 3 43 25 36 13

The prophet who anointed King David in front of his father and
brothers (1 Samuel 16:13)

__ __ __ __ __ __
4 2 44 34 14 46

David was one of _____ sons (1 Samuel 17:12)

__ __ __ __ __
12 31 17 21 9

What is to grow out of the roots of the stem of Jesse (Isaiah 11:1)?

__ __ __ __ __ __
7 27 15 24 1 30

To prove his ability to Saul, David told of being delivered out of the
_____ of the lion and the bear (1 Samuel 17:37)

__ __ __
45 23 10

David's family was called to this before the anointing
(1 Samuel 16:3–5)

__ __ __ __ __ __ __ __ __
28 39 16 8 42 20 35 29 5

15-24-18   9-30-12   46-6-27-3   28-15-31-13   34-24-

9-6   11-23-44-34-22-46. . .20-35-46-46

9-30-40-24-5   21-6-8-24   10-42-9-21   6-40-46,

2-33-3   17-6,   35   10-31-46-46   38-14-24-18

9-30-47-14   9-6   37-5-4-28-12   9-21-32

7-22-9-21-46-12-30-5-44-36-9-12:   20-6-8   36

30-43-25-12   45-8-6-25-42-3-5-18   44-12   43

26-36-24-17   39-44-6-24-19   30-35-11   28-6-24-38.
                                    1 SAMUEL 16:1

Drop Me a Line

God used particular men to write down the words that became the Bible we know today. Try to solve these spotty headlines to uncover three New Testament authors.

AST●TE DOCTOR WRIT●S TWO BOO●S OF THE BIB●E

— — — —

UND●UNTED ●RISONER CONTIN●ES WRITING ●ETTERS

— — — —

FAV●RITE DISCIPLE SEES ●ARRING E●D TIMES IN ●IS VISION

— — — —

The Substitute

In this instance, "Justus" did not prevail.

1. EATTIMED

2. SAVEW

3. HRTIG

4. ETLRBEM

5. DHIAANMD

6. NIEM

7. TTTSESAU

8. SURCED

He was chosen to replace Judas as one of the twelve apostles.

1. O _ _ _ _ _ _ _

2. _ O _ _ _

3. _ _ _ _ O

4. O _ _ _ _ _ _

5. O _ _ _ _ _ _ _

6. _ O _ _

7. _ _ O _ _ _ _

8. _ _ _ O _ _

Answer: _ _ _ _ _ _ _ _

Crossword
by Sarah Lagerquist Simmons

The "Ahs" Have It

As Shakespeare once said, "What's in a name?" In this case, it's two letters—
ah. Have fun solving this puzzle where the theme is men of the Bible whose
names end in ah.

Ah, so would we have it.
PSALM 35:25

ACROSS

1 First word of a WWII battle site
4 Listlessness
9 "AH" NAME FOR MAN WHO WAS SWALLOWED
14 "Then began _____ to call upon the name of the LORD" (Genesis 4:26)
15 Docks
16 Fleshy tissue hanging in the back of the mouth
17 Time on the West Coast (abbr.)
18 "The children of Israel did eat _____ forty years" (Exodus 16:35)
19 Type of fabric
20 "AH" NAME FOR PROPHET WHO RAN FASTER THAN A CHARIOT
22 Symbol
24 Exhibition (abbr.)
25 " 'If the bright spot remains. . .it is only the _____ of the boil' " (Leviticus 13:23 NASB)
27 "Bring thee a red heifer without _____, wherein is no blemish" (Numbers 19:2)
31 "Then your _____ shall be opened" (Genesis 3:5)
32 Demonstrative
33 Fruit drink
34 Inactive
36 "_____ emotions turn into fist fights" (Proverbs 30:32 MSG)
38 "You will make the camp of Israel _____ to destruction" (Joshua 6:18 NIV)
40 Sea duck
42 Coffee drink
43 Brand of soda pop
44 " 'I have made you a tester of metals and my people the _____' " (Jeremiah 6:27 NIV)
45 "The Leveler _____ the road for the right-living" (Isaiah 26:7 MSG)

47 "_____ not after her beauty in thine heart" (Proverbs 6:25)
51 " 'Always stirring up trouble, always at _____ with his family' " (Genesis 16:9 MSG)
53 JOSIAH IS AN "AH" NAME FOR A BOY WHO BECAME THIS WHEN HE WAS 8 YEARS OLD
54 Member of the Quechuan people living in Peru
55 "It shall bruise thy head, and thou shalt bruise his _____" (Genesis 3:15)
57 Horizontal mark indicating a stressed syllable or long vowel sound
59 South Pacific island group
62 "Be strengthened with might by his Spirit in the _____ man" (Ephesians 3:16)
65 Period of two or more eras
66 Confesses
67 "Joab saw that the _____ of the battle was against him" (2 Samuel 10:9)
68 "I _____ no pleasant bread" (Daniel 10:3)
69 "They received every man a _____" (Matthew 20:9)
70 Ready (arch.)
71 Most insignificant number (abbr.)

DOWN

1 Obstruct
2 Hymn writer Charles
3 Punctual (2 words)
4 Jane Austen novel
5 MAN WITH THIS "AH" NAME OBEYED GOD DESPITE BEING RIDICULED
6 No (Fr.)
7 Type of ornamental vase
8 PROPHET WITH THIS "AH" NAME FORETOLD JESUS' BIRTH AND DEATH

9 Fighting method

10 "The river shall bring forth frogs. . . upon thy people, and into thine _____" (Exodus 8:3)

11 Joshua's father

12 U.S. prizefighter

13 SON OF A FATHER WITH AN "AH" NAME

21 AMON'S SON WHO HAD AN "AH" NAME

23 "The _____ of Sodom and Gomorrah is great" (Genesis 18:20)

25 "The cave that is therein, [was] made _____ unto Abraham" (Genesis 23:20)

26 Time zone (abbr.)

28 "Jacob shall not now be ashamed, neither shall his face now wax _____" (Isaiah 29:22)

29 Central European river

30 Spread grass for drying

32 Glutinous substance

35 Lawyers group (abbr.)

36 "The name of the wicked shall _____" (Proverbs 10:7)

37 Kind of typeface

38 "The _____ God made the earth and the heavens" (Genesis 2:4)

39 "Like a thirsty woman dreaming she's drinking _____ tea and wakes up thirsty" (Isaiah 29:5 MSG)

40 "Paul and Silas prayed, and _____ praises" (Acts 16:25)

41 Brain and spinal cord (abbr.)

42 Cow makes this sound

43 Marsh

45 "He left them in the land of Judah to _____ out a living" (Jeremiah 39:8 MSG)

46 "You dishonor (despise, _____, and scorn) Me" (John 8:49 AMP)

48 "We were like those who dream [it seemed so _____]" (Psalm 126:1 MSG)

49 Hurries

50 "He made a covering for the tent of rams' skins _____ red" (Exodus 36:19 AMP)

52 " 'God has _____ Pharaoh what He is about to do' " (Genesis 41:28 NKJV)

56 "For my yoke is _____, and my burden is light" (Matthew 11:30)

57 Means "God hath numbered thy kingdom. . ." (Daniel 5)

58 Craft

59 "The trees of the LORD are full of _____" (Psalm 104:16)

60 Hail

61 Day after Sunday (abbr.)

63 Right-to-bear-arms lobbyist group

64 "Eat not of it raw, _____ sodden" (Exodus 12:9)

Tax Collector
MATTHEW 9:9–10

And as Jesus **passed forth from thence**, he saw a man, **named Matthew**, **sitting** at the **receipt** of **custom**: and he **saith** unto him, Follow me. And he **arose**, and **followed** him. And it came to pass, as **Jesus** sat at **meat** in the **house, behold, many publicans** and **sinners came** and sat **down** with him and his **disciples**.

```
C H H G M N E N T C D F G M N
W F O R G E A A A G U B A A M
O X L U C A H M E Q G T J N K
C R S R S R E E E N T G Q Y U
X R Y U N E R D I H H R L L W
C X X H S C X T E G T L L W F
E R Z E D E T W F W R D P Y R
T K I I H I J A C K O J U W Y
K I E T S P S I E E F L B H F
J P I M R T X C X M G K L Y Z
P A S S E D T F I Y V A I O N
S C E C N E H T R P R J C E F
H U R W N C B E H O L D A T A
I K O V I E K U S V M E N S I
Z D I B S T I E E M O T S U C
```

Acrostic
by Suzanne Stepp

Goodness Rewarded

Those who are courageous and stand up for what's right are ultimately rewarded. Solve this puzzle to uncover the man whose candle of godliness caused his notoriety to wax greater and greater.

Labored

‾‾‾ ‾‾‾ ‾‾‾ ‾‾‾ ‾‾‾ ‾‾‾
17   9   29   11   22   4

The Jews planned to _____, not retreat (Esther 9:15–16)

‾‾‾ ‾‾‾ ‾‾‾ ‾‾‾ ‾‾‾ ‾‾‾ ‾‾‾
35   2   15   30   8   27   5

Historical accounts of events (Esther 10:2)

‾‾‾ ‾‾‾ ‾‾‾ ‾‾‾ ‾‾‾ ‾‾‾ ‾‾‾ ‾‾‾ ‾‾‾ ‾‾‾
21   7   26   12   37   20   1   24   33   19

Ahasuerus was a powerful and _____ ruler (Esther 10:2)

‾‾‾ ‾‾‾ ‾‾‾ ‾‾‾ ‾‾‾ ‾‾‾
31   23   6   36   28   13

A Jewish remembrance in the month of Adar (Esther 9:28)

‾‾‾ ‾‾‾ ‾‾‾ ‾‾‾ ‾‾‾
10   34   14   25   18

An enemy in war (Esther 9:16)

‾‾‾ ‾‾‾ ‾‾‾
16   3   32

31-3-14-2-33-1-30-25   17-35-19   6-26-32-30-28   23-37

28-36-22   11-20-8-6'-19   7-12-34-19-5,   35-37-4

36-25-19   16-30-18-32   17-33-37-28   9-34-28

28-7-29-9-34-6-36-12-34-28   30-24-24   28-36-32

10-14-3-15-23-37-27-5-19.

ESTHER 9:4

Join the Club

"The more the merrier," an old saying goes. Here are anagrammed names of three groups of Bible men. . .can you unscramble them? Hint: The first two are from the Gospels, the last one from Old Testament history.

Rhine sand

_ _ _ _ _ _ _ _ _

I see harps

_ _ _ _ _ _ _ _ _

Lips shine it

_ _ _ _ _ _ _ _ _ _

Following the Lord

When men immerse themselves in God's Word, they find themselves filled with power, courage, and unwavering fortitude. Crack these cryptoscripture codes to discover two men who, in following wholeheartedly after the Lord, accomplished great things for themselves and their people.

GBV UNVY MYO TVUTYVUO MWH MUYVR RB

HUUZ RMU SYP BG RMU SBVO, YXO RB OB

WR, YXO RB RUYIM WX WHVYUS HRYRJRUH YXO

DJOKFUXRH.

FM QVEXCH ZCK XD Z HXXK BXPEZHM; FM CXV

ZDEZWK, CMWVGME FM VGXP KWQJZNMK:

DXE VGM OXEK VGN HXK WQ UWVG VGMM

UGWVGMEQXMIME VGXP HXMQV.

Crossword

by Sarah Lagerquist Simmons

Men Who Led the Charge

In Old Testament days, many battles were fought and many leaders made. But now we have a new leader—Jesus Christ—the one who will lead us to the Promised Land and the ever-flowing waters! As you solve this puzzle, reflect upon the leaders of old and the One who now has charge over you.

*Behold, I have given him for a witness to the people,
a leader and commander to the people.*

ISAIAH 55:4

ACROSS

1 THIS MAN'S UNCLE LED THE CHARGE AND FOUGHT TO FREE HIM FROM CHEDORLAOMER (Genesis 14)
4 Becloud
9 "He that being ____ reproved hardeneth his neck" (Proverbs 29:1)
14 Displeasure
15 Defense
16 Musical instrument with 88 keys
17 Promos
18 Cold
19 White heron
20 SAUL LED THE MEN OF ISRAEL IN ____ AGAINST THE PHILISTINES (1 Samuel 17:2)
22 "He. . .laid ____ piece one against another" (Genesis 15:10)
24 Stead (arch.)
25 "He's trotting behind her, like a calf led to the butcher ____" (Proverbs 7:21 MSG)
27 Haul
31 "Now shall he be great unto the ____ of the earth" (Micah 5:4)
32 Contaminate
33 ABIMELECH LED MEN INTO SHECHEM, WHILE TWO OTHER COMPANIES ____ UPON THE PEOPLE IN THE FIELD (Judges 9:44)
34 "The focus will ____ from you to God" (Matthew 6:6 MSG)
36 "Thou shalt set ____ unto the LORD all that openeth the matrix" (Exodus 13:12)
38 Join
40 Southwestern stew
42 Melchizedek was king of ____ (Genesis 14:18)

43 ____ COMMANDED JOSHUA TO LEAD THE CHARGE AGAINST AMALEK (Exodus 17:10)
44 "If any man will ____ thee at the law" (Matthew 5:40)
45 High-pitched sound
47 "When he has stood the ____, he will receive the crown of life" (James 1:12 NIV)
51 Dash
53 "Godless nations ____ and rave" (Psalm 46:4 MSG)
54 Winglike
55 Conflict
57 Sausage
59 Small room
62 "____ where it pleaseth thee" (Genesis 20:15)
65 Periodical (abbr.)
66 "Grass dries up, flowers ____" (1 Peter 1:22 MSG)
67 Uncanny
68 MOSES LED THE CHARGE ACROSS THE RED ____
69 Braggarts
70 "Make known his ____ among the people" (1 Chronicles 16:8)
71 Extension

DOWN

1 " 'Whoever commits murder shall be ____ to the court' " (Matthew 5:21 NASB)
2 "I will ____ a place for my people Israel" (1 Chronicles 17:9)
3 "God ____ Abraham" (Genesis 22:1 NIV)
4 GIDEON LED THE CHARGE AND THREW DOWN THE ALTAR OF ____ AS GOD SPOKE (Judges 6:25)
5 River in France

6 "They sewed _____ leaves together, and made themselves aprons" (Genesis 3:7)
7 Sash around a kimono
8 HE LED THE CHARGE AGAINST THE MIDIANITES AFTER SEEKING SIGNS FROM GOD
9 Organization of countries that sell fuel (abbr.)
10 JOSHUA LED THE _____ AGAINST THE AMORITES (Joshua 10)
11 "The Valley of Siddim was full of _____ pits" (Genesis 14:10 NIV)
12 Adversary (abbr.)
13 "God had _____ caused it to rain" (Genesis 2:5)
21 Struggle
23 "Be gentle unto all men, _____ to teach" (2 Timothy 2:24)
25 "Their houses are _____ from fear" (Job 21:9)
26 "Archers _____ him; and he was sore wounded" (1 Samuel 31:3)
28 Spoken
29 "The devil threw him down, and _____ him" (Luke 9:42)
30 Tolkien tree
32 Involuntary contraction
35 "Thou shalt rule over _____" (Genesis 4:7)
36 Trader's organization (abbr.)
37 Pertaining to mail service
38 _____ LED THE CHARGE AGAINST THE AMMONITES (1 Samuel 11:11)

39 "The LORD granted his _____" (Genesis 25:21 NKJV)
40 DAVID, WHO LED THE CHARGE AGAINST THE PHILISTINES, WAS ALSO A _____
41 Slovenian river
42 Grain hoarders exchange (abbr.)
43 JOAB LED THE CHARGE WITH THE CHOICE _____ OF ISRAEL (2 Samuel 10:9)
45 Friend (slang)
46 "We. . .sailed into Syria, and _____ at Tyre" (Acts 21:3)
48 "After he is cleansed, seven days shall _____ for him" (Ezekiel 44:26 NASB)
49 BEFORE ISRAEL HAD A KING, _____ LED THE CHARGE AGAINST THE PHILISTINES (1 Samuel 4:1)
50 AFTER JOSHUA AND HIS MEN ROUTED THE ANAKITES, HE DIVIDED THE LAND ACCORDING TO ISRAEL'S _____ DIVISIONS (Joshua 11:22–23)
52 Powerful person
56 Swindlers
57 "They've. . ._____ back into that same old life again" (2 Peter 2:20 MSG)
58 French town
59 Digital recordings (abbr.)
60 Carafe
61 Exclamation of disapproval
63 Little
64 "And _____ the lamp of God went out" (1 Samuel 3:3)

Word Search
by David Austin

King David

ABSALOM	HIDING
ANOINTED	JERUSALEM
BATHSHEBA	JESSE
BEAR	JONATHAN
BELOVED	LION
BETHLEHEM	MUSICIAN
BRAVE	PSALMS
CAVES	SAMUEL
DAVID	SHEPHERD
GOLIATH	SLING
HARP	WAR
HEART	WATERWAY

```
J  E  V  A  R  B  J  T  B  V  M  S  G
E  A  N  O  I  N  T  E  D  U  H  H  O
R  N  E  B  H  A  T  B  S  S  D  E  L
U  C  A  A  A  H  B  I  E  E  T  P  I
S  C  R  H  L  T  C  S  V  A  W  H  A
A  P  A  E  T  I  H  O  A  A  R  E  T
L  S  H  V  A  A  L  S  R  L  T  R  H
E  E  M  N  E  E  N  P  H  H  O  D  L
M  E  D  K  B  S  L  O  S  E  D  M  E
W  A  T  E  R  W  A  Y  J  A  B  W  U
K  H  I  D  I  N  G  E  V  R  L  A  M
E  J  E  S  S  E  G  I  H  T  O  M  A
G  N  I  L  S  J  D  L  I  O  N  U  S
```

Bible Quotation
by Suzanne Stepp

A Worthy Helper
2 TIMOTHY 4:11

Sometimes, to get by, we need a little help from our friends. Work this puzzle to discover a man who aided Paul while he was imprisoned in Rome.

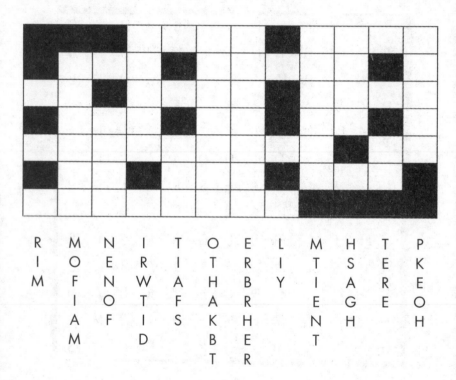

R	M	N	I	T	O	E	L	M	H	T	P
I	O	E	R	I	T	R	I	T	S	E	K
M	F	N	W	A	H	B	Y	I	A	R	E
	I	O	T	F	A	R		E	G	E	O
	A	F	I	S	K	H		N	H		H
	M		D	K	B	E		T			
				B	E						
				T	R						

Prisoners

Several of God's men, including Jesus, were imprisoned because of their faith. Can you solve this puzzle to uncover which other men of the Bible were put behind bars or secreted in dungeons?

GHI	MNO	PRS	GHI	DEF	ABC
4	6	7	4	3	2

JKL	MNO	PRS	DEF	PRS	GHI
5	6	7	3	7	4

PRS	ABC	TUV	JKL
7	2	8	5

PRS	DEF	TUV	DEF	PRS
7	3	8	3	7

PRS	ABC	MNO	PRS	MNO	MNO
7	2	6	7	6	6

PRS	GHI	JKL	ABC	PRS
7	4	5	2	7

PRS	GHI	MNO	DEF	MNO	MNO
7	4	6	3	6	6

Acrostic
by Suzanne Stepp

He Always Loved Him Best

Playing favorites is never a good idea. Solve this puzzle to discover what prompted loving brothers to become colorful turncoats.

He was also called Israel

‾‾ ‾‾ ‾‾ ‾‾ ‾‾
19 35 24 32 5

Jacob had children by two _____ and two handmaids (Genesis 32:22; 35:23–26; 37:2)

‾‾ ‾‾ ‾‾ ‾‾ ‾‾
4   31 36 14 27

Joseph's brothers could not speak _____ to him (Genesis 37:4)

‾‾ ‾‾ ‾‾ ‾‾ ‾‾ ‾‾ ‾‾ ‾‾ ‾‾
21 12 30 26 2   34 17 23 6

Joseph tended the _____ of sheep

‾‾ ‾‾ ‾‾ ‾‾ ‾‾
10 39 28 1   15

When Joseph slept, he was sometimes _____

‾‾ ‾‾ ‾‾ ‾‾ ‾‾ ‾‾ ‾‾ ‾‾
16 37 11 22 3   29 18 9

Joseph's sheaf stood _____ (Genesis 37:7)

‾‾ ‾‾ ‾‾ ‾‾ ‾‾ ‾‾ ‾‾
8   20 33 13 38 7   25

18-32-4   13-27-37-30-2-23   39-28-36-11-16   19-32-27-

14-20-7   3-28-33-2   25-7-35-18   22-39-23   7-29-27

26-7-13-23-16-37-12-18,   5-14-24-34-8-27-11   7-2   4-30-

27   25-7-14   27-28-18   32-10   7-31-27   28-23-16   22-

9-12: 35-18-16   7-12   3-34-16-11   7-13-3   22   24-28-

35-25   32-10   3-30-18-6   1-32-39-28-8-33-27.

GENESIS 37:3

Crossword
by Tonya Vilhauer

Head Honchos

Although there are many head honchos mentioned in the Bible, Christ overrules them all. Pour over this puzzle to discover the names of those leaders who lived before the earthly arrival of the ultimate "reignman"–Jesus.

Esaias saith, There shall be a root of Jesse,
and he that shall rise to reign over the Gentiles.
ROMANS 15:12

ACROSS

1 KING THAT SLEW GOLIATH
6 CA university
10 One of the seven uniformed services of the U.S. (abbr.)
14 Fat
15 Part of speech
16 "Her maidens walked along by the river's _____" (Exodus 2:5)
17 "Of every _____ beast thou shalt take to thee" (Genesis 7:2)
18 Small particle
19 Unknown author (abbr.)
20 Lotion brand
21 "Who sent _____ and wonders into the midst of thee" (Psalm 135:9)
23 Shape of the "bow" in Genesis 9:12
24 Billions of years
26 Salt addition
28 "For that which is _____ esteemed" (Luke 16:15)
31 "Lest he _____ thee to the judge" (Luke 12:58)
32 Predicted time of reaching a destination (abbr.)
33 "For out of it are the _____ of life" (Proverbs 4:23)
36 Shortened form, for short
40 Members of Congress (abbr.)
42 "Thou _____ cursed above all cattle" (Genesis 3:14)
43 Syllables used in songs (2 words)
44 "And the glory, for ever. _____" (Matthew 6:13)
45 Bonnet that protects against UV rays
48 "Whose _____ may reach unto heaven" (Genesis 11:4)
49 Baal was one
51 "He would not _____ her" (Mark 6:26)
53 "For it is the king's _____" (Amos 7:13)
56 Hereditary component
57 "She told her all that the man had done to _____" (Ruth 3:16)
58 Lets down
61 Ark animals went by this
65 Spring flower
67 Jungle
68 Capital of Bangladesh
69 "He that findeth his life shall _____ it" (Matthew 10:39)
70 Vegetable
71 Tapestry
72 "He scorned the _____ of killing only Mordecai" (Esther 3:6 NIV)
73 Tidy
74 Frozen pizza brand

DOWN

1 Pier
2 "Am I not _____ indeed to promote thee to honour?" (Numbers 22:37)
3 Swerve
4 PROPHET WHOSE BOOK COMES BEFORE JEREMIAH'S
5 "Cast him into the _____ of lions" (Daniel 6:16)
6 "He had no _____ with her until she gave birth" (Matthew 1:25 NIV)
7 "Samuel said unto the _____" (1 Samuel 9:23)
8 Stringed instrument found in 1 Samuel 18:6 (NIV)
9 HIGH PRIEST (Acts 23:2)
10 Country of freedom (abbr.)
11 "The LORD came down upon mount _____" (Exodus 19:20)

118

12 "That women _____ themselves in modest apparel" (1 Timothy 2:9)
13 "As a bowing wall shall ye be, and as a tottering _____" (Psalm 62:3)
21 Children's playthings
22 Sun (Sp.)
25 "SAMUEL AROSE AND WENT TO _____" (1 Samuel 3:6)
27 "Who maketh the dumb, or _____, or. . . blind?" (Exodus 4:11)
28 Wife of Zeus
29 Object
30 "They _____ at me and say, 'Aha!' " (Psalm 35:21 NIV)
31 "Canaan begat Sidon. . .and _____" (Genesis 10:15)
34 FIRST KING OF ISRAEL (1 Samuel 15:1)
35 Vase
37 Soak
38 Group of nations
39 Attentive
41 Clip
45 WISE MAN ANOINTED KING (1 Kings 1:39)
46 Greek god of war

47 "Heaven be likened unto _____ virgins" (Matthew 25:1)
50 To cancel (abbr.)
52 PRIEST OF MIDIAN (Exodus 3:1)
53 Texas stew
54 KING OF JUDEA (Luke 1:5)
55 "Her children _____ up, and call her blessed" (Proverbs 31:28)
56 "That we have a _____ high priest" (Hebrews 4:14)
59 "Prepare war, _____ up the mighty men" (Joel 3:9)
60 "AND THEY SPAKE UNTO _____ THE SCRIBE" (Nehemiah 8:1)
62 "Yet if thou _____ the wicked, and he turn not" (Ezekiel 3:19)
63 Yes
64 Talk back
66 "So shall the _____ be calm unto you" (Jonah 1:12)
68 Digital cassette (abbr.)

Wise Men

BETHLEHEM	MARY
EAST	MEN
FOLLOW	MYRRH
GIFTS	MYSTERIOUS
GOLD	PROPHECIES
HEROD	SCHOLARS
INCENSE	SEARCH
INN	STAR
JESUS	TRAVEL
JOSEPH	TREASURES
KINGS	UNKNOWN
MANGER	WISE

```
B  J  T  R  A  V  E  L  T  V  P  H  U
E  I  E  T  R  E  A  S  U  R  E  S  N
T  S  N  M  F  O  L  L  O  W  I  E  K
H  U  R  N  Y  R  J  P  S  N  G  A  N
L  S  C  A  E  S  H  O  C  T  O  R  O
E  E  S  G  L  E  T  E  S  T  L  C  W
H  J  N  M  C  O  N  E  G  E  D  H  N
E  A  M  I  E  S  H  D  R  I  P  D  K
M  E  E  E  E  S  O  C  M  I  F  H  L
N  S  A  W  T  R  K  E  S  Y  O  T  E
G  S  H  A  E  K  I  N  G  S  R  U  S
T  O  R  H  J  U  Q  M  A  R  Y  R  S
J  F  B  Z  F  W  I  S  E  O  A  V  H
```

Sudoku
by Sara Stoker

Gospel Bad Guy

EASY

	A	B	C	D	E	F	G	H	I
1	B			T	I		Y	R	
2	E								
3			Y	R	E	A	M		
4		M			A		B	Y	I
5	A		I		Y	B	R		
6	Y	E	B			R	H		T
7		A			T	Y	I	M	
8			R		H				
9	M				R	I			Y

Hint: Column A

"He spake of Judas Iscariot the son of Simon: for he it was that should _____ _____, being one of the twelve" (John 6:71).

Over the Rainbow
GENESIS 9:1

Sometimes we have to weather the storm before we see the rainbow. This drop two describes what happened after an Old Testament shipbuilder found dry land. Can you solve it?

GOADING	Acting	_____	1. ____ ____
APHONIC	Terror	_____	2. ____ ____
ADVERSE	Poem	_____	3. ____ ____
BLINKED	Admired	_____	4. ____ ____
DATABLE	Lessen	_____	5. ____ ____
ARCHERY	Tote	_____	6. ____ ____
DIARIST	Musical chord	_____	7. ____ ____
DIMNESS	Extracted ore	_____	8. ____ ____
LAWLESS	Enclosures	_____	9. ____ ____
MADONNA	Biblical food	_____	10. ____ ____
NASCENT	Social class	_____	11. ____ ____
SOBERED	Give birth	_____	12. ____ ____

— — — — — — — — — — — —

1 2 3 4 5 6 7 8 9 10 11 12

Acrostic
by Connie Troyer

High Priest of the Jews

> God sometimes uses wicked men to achieve His purpose, as was the case with this malicious yet prophetic high priest. Solve this acrostic to discover the name of the man who tried to silence the Word that still speaks to us today.

Annas was this relation to the high priest (John 18:13)

___ ___ ___ ___ ___ ___   ___ ___   ___ ___ ___
7   22 48 9   40 32   14 29   42 2   51

The high priest gathered with the council to plot Jesus' death after this man was resurrected (John 11)

___ ___ ___ ___ ___ ___ ___
39 10 43 19 1   30 25

Jesus' disciples were "____ sorrowful" once told that one of them would betray Him to the council (Matthew 26:22)

___ ___ ___ ___ ___ ___ ___ ___ ___
12 50 36 20 52 5   44 27 15

A ____ of the high priest lost an ear in the Garden of Gethsemane (John 18:10)

___ ___ ___ ___ ___ ___ ___
3   38 47 21 35 11 26

The high priest said Jesus' testimony was ____ (Matthew 26:65)

___ ___ ___ ___ ___ ___ ___ ___ ___
4   28 49 16 45 23 37 8   33

The high priest also questioned these disciples regarding the healing of the lame man in Acts 4

___ ___ ___ ___ ___   and   ___ ___ ___ ___
17 46 34 6   24   41 13 31 18

27-13-51   36-10-14-49-17-9-2-25   51-10-16   31-6,

51-23-44-36-9   15-35-21-46   36-13-30-27-3-40-39

34-13   26-31-20   41-12-51-3,   26-23-22-48   14-34   51-

19-25   37-50-45-12-5-44-12-11-26   48-31-19-26   13-27-

38   8-2-18   16-23-13-30-42-5   5-44-12   7-13-24   26-

23-52   17-37-13-45-28-40.

JOHN 18:14

Men of Valor

When God gives us an assignment, He also gives us the courage we'll need to accomplish His will. Solve this puzzle to discover nine men who looked up and found the heavenly strength to do earthly deeds.

Joshua chose out thirty thousand mighty men of valour,
and sent them away by night.
JOSHUA 8:3

ACROSS

1 "HE. . .SLEW A THOUSAND MEN" (Judges 15:15)
7 "The angel of God. . .went before the _____" (Exodus 14:19)
11 Annoy like Delilah (Judges 16:16 NIV)
14 Lizard
15 Margarine
16 Wing
17 Not retains, but _____ (John 20:23)
18 Roman emperor
19 "_____ is me for my hurt!" (Jeremiah 10:19)
20 Lazes about
22 "ELIJAH WENT WITH _____ FROM GILGAL" (2 Kings 2:1)
24 Educational cable channel (abbr.)
27 Transport
29 Greenish-blue color
30 Welt
32 "OUR BROTHER _____ IS SET AT LIBERTY" (Hebrews 13:23)
35 Set aflame
37 "I GAVE UNTO _____ MOUNT SEIR" (Joshua 24:4)
38 Agency that investigates child abuse (abbr.)
41 HE WON THE BATTLE WITH THREE HUNDRED MEN (Judges 7:7)
42 "I may _____ unto you some spiritual gift" (Romans 1:11)
44 Pen of animals fed by the prodigal son (Luke 15:15)
45 "Thou shalt have none other _____ before me" (Deuteronomy 5:7)
48 More able
49 DAVID'S FRIEND (1 Samuel 18:3)
51 Self-esteem
52 Coffee
55 "For the _____ that is in the land of Assyria" (Isaiah 7:18)
56 Early form of jazz
57 Defenses
60 "Your descendants will die in the _____ of life" (1 Samuel 2:33 NIV)
64 "He took the _____, and gave thanks" (Luke 22:17)
65 River (Sp.)
67 "WHILE THEY WERE STONING HIM, _____ PRAYED" (Acts 7:59 NIV)
71 Corrida cry
72 Priest's robe
73 Part of a coat
74 "Shut the doors, and _____ them" (Nehemiah 7:3)
75 Brand of cotton swab
76 Belief

DOWN

1 Knight's title
2 "From the _____ of fifty years" (Numbers 8:25)
3 Silent
4 "We should _____ into Italy" (Acts 27:1)
5 "It vomited Jonah _____ dry land" (Jonah 2:10 NKJV)
6 Space agency (abbr.)
7 "This great fire will _____ us" (Deuteronomy 5:25)
8 Nog
9 "Are you not. . .behaving like _____ men?" (1 Corinthians 3:3 NKJV)
10 "Go, wash in the _____ of Siloam" (John 9:7)
11 Gossipy

12 Hawaiian "hello"
13 "To _____ unto the end of barley harvest" (Ruth 2:23)
21 Investigative agency (abbr.)
23 "Who can withstand his _____ blast?" (Psalm 147:17 NIV)
24 "He cropped off the top of his young _____" (Ezekiel 17:4)
25 Legal
26 What trick-or-treaters get
28 Distress call
31 "When he speaketh a _____" (John 8:44)
32 Wooden projection used to build the tabernacle (Exodus 26:17)
33 Language spoken in southeast Asia
34 "We have had _____ fathers who corrected us" (Hebrews 12:9 NKJV)
36 African nation
38 "AND _____ STILLED THE PEOPLE BEFORE MOSES" (Numbers 13:30)
39 Ragu's competition
40 Used to sharpen a razor
43 Used on a sandwich (abbr.)
46 Pat lightly
47 "If my _____ hath turned out of the way" (Job 31:7)

49 First syllable of the river Jacob crossed (Genesis 32:22)
50 "Restore all that was _____" (2 Kings 8:6)
52 ESAU'S BROTHER (Genesis 25:26)
53 Bird's "thumb"
54 "There came a _____ out of the heat" (Acts 28:3)
58 Asian nation
59 River sediment
61 "That which groweth of _____ own accord" (Leviticus 25:5)
62 "The elements shall _____ with fervent heat" (2 Peter 3:10)
63 Fencing sword
66 Japanese sash
68 "As a _____ doth gather her brood" (Luke 13:34)
69 "Adam called his wife's name _____" (Genesis 3:20)
70 "Casting a _____ into the sea" (Matthew 4:18)

127

by Suzanne Stepp

Who Am I?

With the Holy Spirit as inspiration, this man never "doctored" his accounts.

1. IVEDERLED

2. RSTNITUCDE

3. KAMETLCPAER

4. NELEXLCTE

He was a physician and historian.

1. __ __ ◯ __ __ __ __ __ __

2. __ __ __ __ __ ◯ __ __ __ __

3. __ __ __ ◯ __ __ __ __ __ __ __

4. __ __ __ ◯ __ __ __ __ __

Answer: __ __ __ __

Serving Jesus

Ultimately, every Christian serves Jesus. But these spotty headlines describe three men who literally served the Lord at the end of His earthly life. Can you solve each one?

WⓄALTⓄY MAN ⓄROVIDES
HIⓄ OWN TⓄMB FOR ⓄESUS

_ _ _ _ _ _

ⓄIGHTTIⓄE VISⓄTⓄR MIXEⓄ
SPIⓄEⓄ FOR JⓄSⓄS' BODY

_ _ _ _ _ _ _ _ _

ⓄOREⓄGN MAⓄ COⓄPELLED TⓄ CAⓄRY
WEAKⓄⓄED JⓄⓄUS' ⓄROSS TO CALVARⓄ

_ _ _ _ _ _ _ _ _ _ _ _ _

Noah

ANIMALS	HAM
ARARAT	JAPHETH
ARK	MOUNTAIN
BRANCH	NOAH
CANAAN	OBEDIENT
COVENANT	OLIVE
DAYS	PAIRS
DESTROY	RAIN
DOVE	RAINBOW
FAITHFUL	RAVEN
FLOOD	SHEM

```
J  J  A  T  N  V  A  F  O  P  K  D  H
A  R  E  R  I  C  A  N  A  L  E  R  B
P  A  S  C  A  I  O  I  I  S  I  R  A
H  V  T  S  T  R  R  V  T  M  A  V  N
E  E  T  H  N  S  A  R  E  N  A  O  E
T  N  F  R  U  M  O  T  C  N  A  L  E
H  U  D  A  O  Y  K  H  L  H  A  W  S
L  N  K  I  M  O  B  E  D  I  E  N  T
R  A  I  N  B  O  W  D  S  Y  A  D  T
E  A  E  G  H  O  F  L  O  O  D  J  U
Q  N  J  F  B  Z  F  Q  A  V  V  Z  H
J  A  F  K  D  T  M  E  H  S  E  A  B
T  C  U  O  D  I  O  O  V  F  M  X  A
```

by Suzanne Stepp

Master of the World

When Jesus was about to arrive upon the earth, an emperor's decree inadvertently determined His place of birth. Crack this code to uncover what taxing issue this ruler devised to set up the manger scene.

Mary was Joseph's _____ wife (Luke 2:5)

___ ___ ___ ___ ___ ___ ___ ___
45 1   42 14 38 22 7   27

Baby Jesus was wrapped in _____ clothes (Luke 2:7)

___ ___ ___ ___ ___ ___ ___ ___ ___
39 6   28 43 2   18 34 13 44

The city of David (Luke 2:4)

___ ___ ___ ___ ___ ___ ___ ___ ___
31 19 8   35 23 40 5   29 15

Anna spent _____ days in the temple, fasting also (Luke 2:37)

___ ___ ___ ___ ___ ___ ___ ___ ___
9   30 16 25 3   41 37 20 12

Shepherds were abiding in the field in the same _____ (Luke 2:8)

___ ___ ___ ___ ___ ___ ___
21 4   36 17 32 10 26

Jesus would grow and _____ strong in spirit (Luke 2:40)

___ ___ ___
11 33 24

28-17-27   34-8   21-16-15-3   32-14   9-33-39-22   34-13

32-5-4-1-40   43-28-25-39,   8-35-16-32   8-5-45-10-29

11-19-17-32   4-38-8   33   2-7-21-30-7-29   37-41-14-15

21-28-40-22-16-30   33-20-44-36-39-8-38-1,   32-35-28-8

16-23-12   8-35-19   6-4-10-18-2   22-5-14-36-18-43

31-45   32-33-24-3-27.

LUKE 2:1

Anagram
by Paul Kent

New Testament Names

Of the hundreds of male names in the New Testament, we've anagrammed three. Can you figure out which three men these are? Hint: The first two are from the Gospels, the last one from a letter of Paul.

Mice sound

_ _ _ _ _ _ _ _

In more pets

_ _ _ _ _   _ _ _ _ _

Mouse sin

_ _ _ _ _ _ _

Telephone Scramble
by Nancy Bernhard

Deacons

With the miraculous growth of the church came the need for more helpers. Unscramble these telephone codes to discover the names of the men who were appointed deacons.

| MNO 6 | GHI 4 | ABC 2 | ABC 2 | MNO 6 | MNO 6 | PRS 7 | | |

| MNO 6 | GHI 4 | ABC 2 | MNO 6 | JKL 5 | ABC 2 | PRS 7 | | |

| PRS 7 | ABC 2 | PRS 7 | MNO 6 | DEF 3 | MNO 6 | ABC 2 | PRS 7 | |

| PRS 7 | GHI 4 | GHI 4 | JKL 5 | GHI 4 | PRS 7 | | | |

| PRS 7 | PRS 7 | MNO 6 | ABC 2 | GHI 4 | MNO 6 | PRS 7 | TUV 8 | PRS 7 |

| PRS 7 | TUV 8 | DEF 3 | PRS 7 | GHI 4 | DEF 3 | MNO 6 | | |

| TUV 8 | GHI 4 | MNO 6 | MNO 6 | MNO 6 | | | | |

Crossword
by Tonya Vilhauer

Leaders Who Feared God

The guys in charge need all the strength and courage they can get. Work this puzzle to discover just a few of the many God-fearing leaders mentioned in the Bible.

And David said to Solomon his son,
Be strong and of good courage.
1 CHRONICLES 28:20

ACROSS

1 Shock (var.)
6 Sated
11 Greek government
12 "In her mouth was an _____ leaf" (Genesis 8:11)
13 Blood disorder (var.)
15 Pittsburgh player
18 "Thou are neither cold nor _____" (Revelation 3:15)
19 "FATHER OF MANY NATIONS" (Genesis 17:5)
21 Lake in East Asia
22 Allege
24 "So that they will not _____ guilt and die" (Exodus 28:43 NIV)
25 "Thou shalt not _____ by me" (Numbers 20:18)
26 Italian herb
28 Resort
29 "O _____ and see that the LORD is good" (Psalm 34:8)
30 Partner of vigor
32 Urge to attack
33 To bring in from another country (abbr.)
34 Bullfight cheer
35 "AND PHARAOH SAID UNTO _____" (Genesis 41:39)
38 "Hear the sound of marching in the tops of the _____ trees" (2 Samuel 5:24 NIV)
42 Consumers
43 Popular girl's name in the early 1900s (abbr.)
46 Painter Frida
47 Volcanic rock
48 Army unit
50 Green vegetables

51 Stretch to make do
52 "_____ WAS WROTH WITH HIS SERVANTS" (Genesis 41:10)
54 "I _____ no pleasant bread" (Daniel 10:3)
55 Layered fruit and ice cream
57 Splits
59 "The eyes of the wicked will fail, and escape will _____ them" (Job 11:20 NIV)
60 "The _____ that the king rideth upon" (Esther 6:8)
61 "I will make thee _____ over many things" (Matthew 25:21)
62 "A piece of string _____ when it comes close to a flame" (Judges 16:9 NIV)

DOWN

1 Reduces
2 "The Raven" author
3 Wildcat
4 Excuse
5 "Everyone who listens to the Father and _____ from him" (John 6:45 NIV)
6 HE WON THE BATTLE AT JERICHO
7 "Built there an _____" (Judges 21:4)
8 Carpe _____
9 "Adam was first formed, then _____" (1 Timothy 2:13)
10 Greek Ds
13 KING WHO BUILT AN ALTAR FOR BAAL (1 Kings 16:30–32)
14 Model of car made by Chevy
16 "Toward the _____, west, north, and south" (1 Chronicles 9:24)
17 "Nation shall _____ against nation" (Mark 13:8)
20 Professional organization for doctors

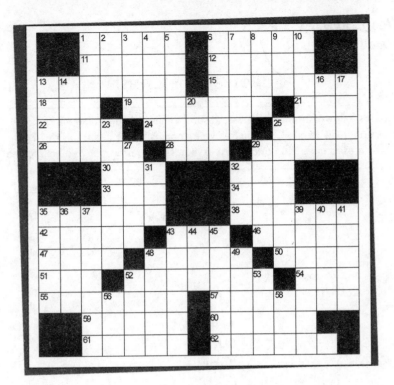

23 Italy's premiere resort
25 First lap of a car race (2 words)
27 What a person with a hurt leg does
29 A Hindu's red dot
31 Car speed (abbr.)
32 To cry like Hagar (Genesis 21:16 NIV)
35 Mint drink
36 Japanese city
37 More austere
39 "Let her glean even among the ____"
   (Ruth 2:15)
40 Having wings
41 "AND HE CALLED FOR ____ AND
   AARON" (Exodus 12:31)
43 Stiff straw hat
44 "A people that do ____" (Psalm
   95:10)
45 SW American Indian tribe
48 "And they did ____ with him sharply"
   (Judges 8:1)
49 One of the Seven Sages of Greece
52 ALSO CALLED SAUL (Acts 13:9)
53 1997 Disney character (abbr.)
56 Virus

58 THIS KING DESTROYED AN IDOL
   ERECTED BY THE QUEEN MOTHER
   (1Kings 15:9–13)

Followers of Christ

Christ's followers went where he did—and continued spreading the good news after His death. Can you follow the names below in this puzzle? Each name is used more than once—but we're not telling how many you might find!

ANDREW
JAMES
JOHN
LUKE
MARK
MATTHEW
PAUL
PETER

```
M  A  R  K  J  T  M  V  H  E  S  A  A
A  L  W  C  M  A  T  T  H  E  W  N  J
T  U  P  E  T  E  R  T  J  K  D  D  A
T  K  S  T  R  K  T  A  J  R  M  R  M
H  E  H  R  R  D  M  E  E  A  D  E  E
E  E  K  A  E  E  N  W  L  M  M  W  S
W  W  M  J  S  T  P  A  N  D  R  E  W
P  K  L  A  O  E  E  J  O  H  N  E  S
E  A  E  U  T  H  G  P  H  H  O  J  U
T  Q  U  E  K  T  N  J  O  L  U  K  E
E  F  R  L  B  E  H  J  L  U  A  P  Z
R  F  Q  A  V  Z  J  E  F  K  D  T  B
T  U  O  D  I  Q  O  V  W  F  X  A  W
```

by David Austin and Sharon Y. Brown

The Patriarchs

> When God told man to be fruitful and multiply, the patriarchs of old obeyed. Solve the cryptoscripture puzzles below to find the "begats" of a shipper and a shepherd.

DTR TBDS GDP CHNK SATRJKR MKDJP BQR: DTR

TBDS EKVDO PSKI, SDI, DTR FDXSKOS.

SAL INR JWQY ZGRU: SAL RYSM USY S

FMAAHAZ NMAIRG, S PSA WB INR BHRXL; SAL

TSFWJ USY S KXSHA PSA, LURXXHAZ HA IRAIY.

Winning God's Approval

MEDIUM

	A	B	C	D	E	F	G	H	I
1			V	Y			R		S
2		Y				V		N	
3			T	S	A		M	Y	V
4	A						Y		
5	S			R	V				M
6		M		A		T	V		
7	V	S			Y	R	N		
8	E		Y		M				A
9	T		M		E		S		

Hint: Row 2

"And the LORD said unto Satan, Hast thou considered _____ _____ Job, that there is none like him in the earth, a perfect and an upright man, one that feareth God, and escheweth evil?" (Job 1:8).

141

Acrostic
by Suzanne Stepp

Saul's Servant

A good king is one who keeps his promises. Crack this code to discover the name of Saul's servant and his encounter with a good king.

David smote this son of Rehob (2 Samuel 8:3)

___ ___ ___ ___ ___ ___ ___ ___ ___
41 10 23 50 46 13 28 35 18

To whatever place (2 Samuel 8:6)

___ ___ ___ ___ ___ ___ ___ ___ ___ ___ ___ ___ ___
19 4 36 40 12 55 3 54 30 48 9 27 56

Held in greater esteem or respect (2 Samuel 7:26)

___ ___ ___ ___ ___ ___ ___ ___ ___
29 14 20 17 44 8 31 47 26

A term used to call attention (2 Samuel 9:4)

___ ___ ___ ___ ___ ___
25 16 51 42 5 34

David showed _____ to Jonathan's son (2 Samuel 9:1)

___ ___ ___ ___ ___ ___ ___ ___
33 43 6 52 21 38 7 15

How often David wanted Mephibosheth to eat at his table
(2 Samuel 9:7)

___ ___ ___ ___ ___ ___ ___ ___ ___ ___ ___
11 37 2 45 39 24 53 32 1 49 22

19-51-47-21   40-4-13-22   12-50-34   11-14-5-49-55-46

51-44-29   53-2-45-37   26-10-9-36-23,   40-12-35

33-44-24-20   7-14-39-52   53-21-40-42   51-31-29,

32-3-45   40-12-30-53   28-36-25-32?   50-6-52   41-27

15-10-31-23,   45-51-22   54-48-56-9-14-17-40   43-7   12-16.
                                          2 SAMUEL 9:2

Crossword
by Tonya Vilhauer

Faithful Ministers

Those who God calls to be prophets and preachers have their work cut out for them. As you solve this puzzle, bring to mind your own minister and pray that God would give him the strength to serve.

I thank Christ Jesus our Lord, who hath enabled me, for that he counted me faithful, putting me into the ministry.
1 TIMOTHY 1:12

ACROSS

1 HE BAPTIZED JESUS (Mark 1:9)
5 "And _____ him, all ye people" (Romans 15:11)
8 "Slew of the Philistines six hundred men with an ox _____" (Judges 3:31)
10 "Fill the _____ sacks with food" (Genesis 44:1)
12 "I am _____ and Omega" (Revelation 1:8)
13 "And when Boaz had _____ and drunk" (Ruth 3:7)
16 Plant used as perfume or in healing (Proverbs 7:17)
18 "JEHOIADA. . .ORDERED THE COMMANDERS OF _____" (2 Kings 11:15 NIV)
20 Display
22 "The woman saith unto him, _____" (John 4:19)
23 PROPHET WHOSE BOOK FOLLOWS JONAH'S
24 Pod vegetable
25 "THEN SIMON _____ HAVING A SWORD DREW IT" (John 18:10)
28 Snakelike fish
29 "He shall be like the _____ in the desert" (Jeremiah 17:6)
31 HE WAS UNDER ELI'S TUTELAGE
33 Shallow areas
35 Chiefly (abbr.)
36 Ship initials used by the navy
37 Governing groups
40 Braces oneself
43 Long-winded
44 "As a _____ gathereth her chickens" (Matthew 23:37)
46 "I will sing _____ of thy mercy in the morning" (Psalm 59:16)

48 Electroencephalograph (abbr.)
49 "AT MIDNIGHT PAUL AND _____ PRAYED" (Acts 16:25)
51 Agency monitoring food and health-related products (abbr.)
52 "Listen to the _____ of my lips" (Job 13:6 NIV)
54 "They are detestable, disobedient and _____ for doing anything good" (Titus 1:16 NIV)
55 Disorder developed after exposure to a terrifying event (abbr.)
56 "He that is surety for a stranger shall _____ for it" (Proverbs 11:15)
58 Eyes
60 Capital of Norway
61 Rice wine
62 "Sent me. . .to _____ out the land" (Joshua 14:7)
63 Note

DOWN

2 Stare
3 Skip
4 HE WAS AN ELKOSHITE AND AN AUTHOR
5 "Can you make a pet of him. . . or put him on a _____?" (Job 41:5 NIV)
6 "Go to the _____, thou sluggard" (Proverbs 6:6)
7 "With their tongues they have _____ deceit" (Romans 3:13)
9 HE HAD A LION PROBLEM
10 "I have made you a tester of _____ and my people the ore" (Jeremiah 6:27 NIV)
11 Fasten
12 Artery

14 Asian country
15 HE WAS TO BUILD AN ARK
17 "He that speaketh _____ shall not escape" (Proverbs 19:5)
19 "He casteth forth his _____ like morsels" (Psalm 147:17)
21 Baseball team
26 To make improvements to or correct
27 Outmoded
29 HE WAS TOLD TO MARRY A PROSTITUTE
30 Painting prop
32 Agency to protect the environment (abbr.)
34 Shack
37 THIS WRITER-PROPHET WAS THE SON OF PETHUEL
38 Spurs
39 Japanese religion
40 Slow, shelled animals
41 Attics
42 Foams
43 Part of the shortest verse in the Bible (John 11:35)

45 Fairy's friend
47 Pops
49 "Nabal. . .was _____ and mean in his dealings" (1 Samuel 25:3 NIV)
50 Vapor
53 HE WAS A HERDSMAN AND PROPHET FROM TEKOA
55 Reserved
57 Poisonous snake found in Isaiah 11:8
59 Archaic adverb meaning "also"

Drop Two
by Dorothy Pryse

A Patient Man
JOB 3:1

As Job came to grips with his losses, his friends sat with him without speaking. Seven days later, something happened to break the silence. Can you solve this drop two puzzle to find out what?

AVARICE	Priest	_____	1. ___ ___
DEFLATE	Make joyful	_____	2. ___ ___
JACINTH	Shackle	_____	3. ___ ___
EROSION	Pine tar	_____	4. ___ ___
BRIQUET	Silent	_____	5. ___ ___
HABITED	Remain	_____	6. ___ ___
HEBRAIC	Clamp	_____	7. ___ ___
IMPULSE	Feather	_____	8. ___ ___
MISDEAL	Perfect	_____	9. ___ ___
GEOLOGY	Spindly stems	_____	10. ___ ___
PLAGUED	Forest space	_____	11. ___ ___
TEACHER	Extend	_____	12. ___ ___
HYDRANT	Late	_____	13. ___ ___

___ ___ ___ ___ ___ ___ ___ ___ ___ ___ ___ ___ ___

1   2   3   4   5   6   7   8   9   10   11   12   13

Bible Quotation
by Suzanne Stepp

Recognizing the Call
1 SAMUEL 3:10

No matter where we are or what we're doing, God can reach us if we're open to His voice. Solve this Bible quotation puzzle to discover whom God called and the response He received.

■				■				■		
		■			■					
■						■				■
		■		■						■
■						■				
			■						■	
		■			■					
		■						■		

T	R	H	M	U	E	S	L	D	N	C	A
A	S	N	D	E	C	L	T	L	H	D	L
M	T	A	E	H	L	R	A	L	U	V	N
E	I	E	T	N	D	P	E	A	K	O	D
N	S	T	N	T	E	O	S	E	R	E	A
O	T	M	H	U	Y	A	E	T	H	S	F
	E		M	S	A	L	S	M	E	R	W
	S		A		S	O	R	H	O		
	R		A					A	E		
	A		E					T			

147

Daniel

ABEDNEGO
BABYLON
CHALDEANS
DELIVER
DEN
DREAM
FOURTH
FRIENDS
FURNACE
INTERPRET

LANGUAGES
LIONS
MESHACH
MYSTERIES
OBEDIENT
PRAYERS
PROPHET
REVELATION
SHADRACH
WALL

```
R  O  B  E  D  I  E  N  T  C  I  J  A
S  E  M  E  S  H  A  C  H  B  N  T  B
V  E  V  H  E  S  C  A  F  A  T  T  E
S  S  I  E  W  A  L  L  O  B  E  F  D
F  P  H  R  L  D  T  M  U  Y  R  U  N
E  R  R  A  E  A  T  D  R  L  P  R  E
S  K  I  A  D  T  T  E  T  O  R  N  G
N  L  N  E  Y  R  S  I  H  N  E  A  O
O  S  W  K  N  E  A  Y  O  P  T  C  E
I  E  G  H  O  D  R  C  M  N  O  E  J
L  D  R  E  A  M  S  S  H  U  D  R  Q
L  A  N  G  U  A  G  E  S  J  F  E  P
B  Z  F  D  E  L  I  V  E  R  O  A  N
```

Acrostic
by Suzanne Stepp

Second-Best but Blessed

> Praying parents receive bountiful blessings for all their children. Crack this code to uncover a gracious God's answer to a famous father's prayer.

God told Abraham to ____ before Him (Genesis 17:1)

$\overline{}$ $\overline{}$ $\overline{}$ $\overline{}$
11   32   21   5

Abraham ____ to think he would have a son at his age (Genesis 17:17)

26   9   13   37   1   20   16

God made a ____ with Isaac (Genesis 17:21)

14   29   8   22   35   3   18   10

To institute an agreement (Genesis 17:19)

7   33   2   36   23   12   39   28   17

Isaac and Ishmael were Abraham's ____ and blood

19   31   4   34   25

Hagar was the ____ of Ishmael

27   15   38   6   30   24

Acrostic

by Suzanne Stepp

(continued)

32-35-16   9-34   19-15-24   39-28-25-27-3-4-12,   39

17-9-8-7   6-20-36-24-16   10-1-7-30:   23-4-17-29-26-16,

39   1-3-8-22   23-12-30-33-34-7-16   25-39-27,

3-18-16   11-39-21-31   27-36-5-4   1-39-27

19-24-13-39-2-19-13-31.

GENESIS 17:20

Crossword
by Sarah Lagerquist Simmons

Delivering the Message

To deliver His message, God uses a myriad of methods: prayer, people, songs, and His Word, just to name a few. Work this puzzle to discover how He has spoken to His children in the past and how He may be speaking to you today.

For this is the message that ye heard from the beginning, that we should love one another.
1 JOHN 3:11

ACROSS

1 And so forth (abbr.)
4 Sleeping
8 "You shall make a ____ for the door of the tabernacle" (Exodus 26:36 NKJV)
14 "Tyrus hath said against Jerusalem, ____, she is broken" (Ezekiel 26:2)
15 "You search and investigate and ____ over the Scriptures" (John 5:39 AMP)
16 Graduates
17 "____ thee out of thy country" (Genesis 12:1)
18 GOD SENT JESUS TO SACRIFICE HIS BLOOD SO THAT OUR SINS CAN BE WHITE AS ____
19 HE DELIVERED A MESSAGE TO SAUL (1 Samuel 10:1)
20 Oil used in wood finishing
22 A sister is this (abbr.)
23 Male name
24 TIMOTHY WAS ____ TO THE THESSALONIANS TO BRING COMFORT (1 Thessalonians 3:2)
27 "No tree in the garden of God could ____ its beauty" (Ezekiel 31:8 NIV)
31 "The women. . .____ goats' hair" (Exodus 35:26)
33 Vex
35 Chit
36 Youth organization promoting agricultural education (abbr.)
38 Roman numeral 12
39 First letter of Arabic alphabet
40 Breakfast food (pl.)
44 "Look after orphans and widows. . .to keep ____ from being polluted by the world" (James 1:27 NIV)
46 Breastplate (var.)
47 Yes (Fr.)
49 Four quarts (abbr.)
50 "Let them have dominion over. . .the fowl of the ____" (Genesis 1:26)
51 "If the LORD make a ____ thing. . .ye shall understand" (Numbers 16:30)
52 Communists
55 "____ it, and make cakes" (Genesis 18:6)
58 "Give her a good ____ of her own medicine!" (Jeremiah 50:11 MSG)
61 "Every man who ____ and drinks sees good in all his labor" (Ecclesiastes 3:13 NASB)
63 "He made the middle ____ to shoot through the boards" (Exodus 36:33)
65 A MAN USED BY GOD TO BRING MESSAGES TO HIS PEOPLE
67 Office of the pope
70 "A man who bears false witness. . .is like a ____, a sword, and a sharp arrow" (Proverbs 25:18 NKJV)
71 "We passed to the ____ of a small island" (Acts 27:16 NIV)
72 THIS PROPHET TOLD HAZAEL HE WOULD BE KING OF ARAM (2 Kings 8:12–13)
73 "Drive and go forward; do not slow down the ____" (2 Kings 4:24 NASB)
74 Fury
75 PROPHET WHO FORETOLD WHO WOULD BUILD THE TEMPLE (2 Samuel 7:1–17)
76 Lawyer (abbr.)
77 Communication option for the deaf (abbr.)

DOWN

1 GOD USED THIS FOWL IN A MESSAGE TO ISRAEL (Ezekiel 17)

2. God told Abram his children would be a "stranger in a land that is not ____" (Genesis 15:13)
3. Herb felines are fond of
4. Projection
5. GOD TOOK EZEKIEL TO A VALLEY FULL OF ____ (Ezekiel 37:1)
6. Wear away
7. GIDEON ASKED GOD FOR A SIGN THAT INCLUDED THE MORNING ____ (Judges 6:39)
8. Talk back
9. "Give up your ____ to what is owed by your brother" (Deuteronomy 15:3 NKJV)
10. Type of dance
11. Ratite
12. Compass direction (abbr.)
13. Nothing
21. Scrapes
25. Veto
26. Group of three
28. "Take thee a ____, and lay it before thee" (Ezekiel 4:1)
29. To form rings or spirals
30. Fit of anger
32. Athletic organization (abbr.)
34. GOD USED PROPHETS TO DELIVER MESSAGES TO THE ____
37. Era (var.)
39. JONAH FELL ____ ON THE SHIP, HAVING REFUSED TO DELIVER GOD'S MESSAGE TO NINEVAH (Jonah 1:5)

40. Samson became ____ when his hair was cut (Judges 16:19)
41. Opposed to (var.)
42. GOD'S WORD WAS LIKE THIS IN THE PROPHET'S BONES (Jeremiah 20:9)
43. "The rich can be ____ for everything they have, but the poor are free of such threats" (Proverbs 13:8 MSG)
45. THE PEOPLE DID NOT GIVE THIS TO GOD'S MESSENGERS (Jeremiah 25:4)
48. Japanese island, ____ Jima
53. Type of flower
54. Turns
56. Embarrass
57. Russian country house
59. Thin strip of wood
60. Belch
62. "The bow of ____ shall strike him" (Job 20:24)
64. Movie: Saving Private ____
66. WHEN GOD COMMANDS, WE SHOULD ____
67. PAUL WAS ABLE TO ____ LETTERS TO THE EARLY CHURCH
68. Cotton State (abbr.)
69. JOSEPH WAS THROWN INTO A ____
70. Number-cruncher (abbr.)

Not an Easy Road

Don't think for a moment that the Christian life is a life of ease—Jesus Himself promised us trouble (John 16:33). Can you solve these spotty headlines to discover three New Testament men who experienced the truth of that promise?

●RIMARY CHRI●TIA● MARTYR
S●ON●D TO D●AT●

— — — — — —

●OUNG ●AN S●RUGGLES T●
PAS●OR FLEDGL●NG C●URCH

— — — — — —

MA●OR CHRISTI●N FIGUR●
●URDERED WITH ●WORD

— — — — —

Family History

In Old Testament times, what gave prophets credibility was not only who they knew, but the family from which they derived.

1. ZAEBITP

2. NWEDOR

3. RCYESRO

4. TYHUO

5. RDCEEAL

6. RNESKTIC

7. LUYMPTIL

8. RAHTE

9. DHNSA

This prophet was the son of Berechiah.

1. _ _ _ _ _ ◯ _

2. _ _ _ _ ◯ _

3. _ _ _ ◯ _ _ _

4. _ _ _ _ ◯

5. _ _ _ _ ◯ _ _

6. _ _ ◯ _ _ _ _ _

7. _ _ _ _ ◯ _ _ _

8. _ ◯ _ _ _

9. ◯ _ _ _ _

Answer: _ _ _ _ _ _ _ _ _

Word Search
by David Austin

Only One

Just as there is only one true, perfect Jesus to follow, there is only one correct spelling of His name in this puzzle. Can you find it among the would-be imposters?

JESUS

```
J  S  E  S  S  J  S  S  J  S  J  S  U
J  J  U  J  S  S  S  S  J  J  E  J  J
S  E  S  S  J  J  E  S  J  S  J  U  S
E  S  E  J  U  J  J  J  E  S  U  J  U
J  S  J  J  J  J  J  J  E  E  J  S  E
E  J  S  U  J  J  J  J  S  S  S  J  J
U  J  J  S  S  E  E  S  S  S  S  S  S
S  S  J  E  J  E  U  E  E  S  J  S  J
J  E  U  J  S  E  J  S  S  J  E  S  S
J  J  J  J  J  U  J  J  J  E  U  J  S
J  U  J  J  J  E  S  J  J  E  J  E  U
U  J  U  J  S  J  S  S  J  E  J  S  J
E  S  J  S  J  S  S  S  J  S  S  E  S
```

Acrostic
by Suzanne Stepp

Strangers on the Road

Whoever said, "Two's company, three's a crowd," must not have known Jesus. Solve this puzzle to uncover a verse regarding a road trip that was stranger than fiction.

Jesus was _____ to death

‾‾ ‾‾ ‾‾ ‾‾ ‾‾ ‾‾ ‾‾ ‾‾ ‾‾
7 33 45 6 39 27 15 35 29

Tomb

‾‾ ‾‾ ‾‾ ‾‾ ‾‾ ‾‾ ‾‾ ‾‾ ‾‾
17 42 3 30 14 21 9 25 18

Amazed

‾‾ ‾‾ ‾‾ ‾‾ ‾‾ ‾‾ ‾‾ ‾‾ ‾‾ ‾‾
23 8 37 31 13 44 4 32 24 16

Scared

‾‾ ‾‾ ‾‾ ‾‾ ‾‾ ‾‾ ‾‾ ‾‾ ‾‾ ‾‾
22 10 36 19 41 2 38 26 11 34

The disciples _____ Jesus (Luke 24:31)

‾‾ ‾‾ ‾‾ ‾‾
12 1 43 20

Happiness

‾‾ ‾‾ ‾‾
40 5 28

(continued)

5-26-35   33-22   2-32-43-27,   20-41-31-4-18

13-23-27-42   20-23-8   7-14-11-33-3-23-17,

23-15-8-20-42-10-36-1-19   4-23-44-29

30-13-2-5   9-36-27,   23-10-37   2-9-33-30

31-1-14-28   23   8-2-25-23-13-19-11-25   44-15

40-38-10-30-17-23-14-18-27,   23-45-6   9-23-4-2

15-5-37   12-26-31-20-1   37-32-24   2-41-36-26-19-4

20-32-44-7-9   23-10-39   21-33-27-35   37-31   3-23-17-8

37-32-38-25-24   36-26   2-9-35-4-24   6-23-28-17?

Luke 24:18

Acrostic
by Donna K. Maltese

An Issue of Faith

No matter what our issues, we, like this woman, can be daring in our faith.
Take comfort in that fact as you solve this puzzle.

After touching Jesus' robe, this woman's issue of blood ____
(Luke 8:44)

$$\overline{}\ \overline{}\ \overline{}\ \overline{}\ \overline{}\ \overline{}\ \overline{}\ \overline{}$$
  6   41   38   16   33   11   26   20

How soon she was healed by Jesus (Mark 5:29)

$$\overline{}\ \overline{}\ \overline{}\ \overline{}\ \overline{}\ \overline{}\ \overline{}\ \overline{}\ \overline{}\ \overline{}\ \overline{}$$
  12   48   23   1   36   19   40   7   31   27   15

At her touch, Jesus felt this leave Him (Mark 5:30)

$$\overline{}\ \overline{}\ \overline{}\ \overline{}\ \overline{}\ \overline{}$$
  28   4   45   42   21   37

After He asked who'd touched Him, this woman fell at
Jesus' feet, fearing and ____ (Mark 5:33)

$$\overline{}\ \overline{}\ \overline{}\ \overline{}\ \overline{}\ \overline{}\ \overline{}\ \overline{}\ \overline{}$$
  30   24   2   49   44   35   13   9   18

What Jesus called this woman (Mark 5:34)

$$\overline{}\ \overline{}\ \overline{}\ \overline{}\ \overline{}\ \overline{}\ \overline{}\ \overline{}$$
  14   25   46   34   3   29   17   10

Jesus told this woman to be of good ____ (Luke 8:48)

$$\overline{}\ \overline{}\ \overline{}\ \overline{}\ \overline{}\ \overline{}\ \overline{}$$
  39   47   8   22   5   32   43

1   31-47-8-27-9,   31-3-36-39-3   31-25-6

14-4-6-2-1-6-2-14   31-4-29-3   1-9   36-6-6-21-26

5-22   44-35-5-5-14   42-31-2-35-28-2   15-2-1-45-12,

39-1-49-26   44-37-40-4-9-14   11-13-49,   38-16-20

43-5-46-33-3-2-14   7-3-2   3-2-49   5-22

11-13-12   18-1-10-8-2-9-30:   22-5-32   6-3-26   6-1-4-14

31-4-48-3-4-9   3-2-24-6-2-35-22,   4-22   4   8-1-15

44-21-41   43-5-46-33-3   11-13-12   19-1-10-8-2-9-30,   4

6-3-1-35-35   44-37   31-3-5-35-26.

MATTHEW 9:20–21

A Surprised Servant-Girl
Acts 12:12–18

AFFIRMED	HOLD
ANGEL	JAMES
ANOTHER	KNEW
ASTONISHED	KNOCKING
BECKONING	MAD
BEFORE	NAMED
BRETHREN	OPENED
BROUGHT	PEACE
CONSTANTLY	PETER
CONTINUED	PLACE
DAMSEL	PRISON
DECLARED	RHODA
DOOR	SHEW
GATE	TOLD
GLADNESS	VOICE
HAND	

```
R H O D A N N N E R H T E R B
A O T E C N Y W B E F O R E R
F L S C D C G B E P O P T H O
F D S L O A G E R H H E N T U
I Q E A O N A I L Q S N W O G
R U N R R Y S U N G U E A N H
M A D E V O T T N C N D M A T
E E A D N E O I A K P D N A H
D O L D V A N L O N E M G I J
A X G O L O I D L O T P W B B
M Z I M K A S X B C E L T E E
S C H C I S H A R K R A Y N O
E L E N A M E D L I E C A E P
L B R A H H D X I N R E T F R
C O N T I N U E D G A T E P E
```

Cryptoscripture
by Sharon Y. Brown

Two Important Women

> Ah, to be a woman who is honored and cherished. Solve these cryptoscripture puzzles to discover two ladies and their encounters with the kings who loved them.

FGZ ZVNF BNQSQ ZPQ JAQNF NPJDX RVN

OAJQR MPX GO RVN ZNNC, VN PHHNPJNM

OAJQR RG EPJX EPUMPDNFN, GSR GO ZVGE VN

VPM LPQR QNTNF MNTADQ.

NLWGZF, EWGK HAE SHBA, UI ZGOL; NLWGZF,

EWGK HAE SHBA; EWGK WHYE FGOLY' LILY

CBEWBQ EWI ZGRJY: EWI WHBA BY HY H SZGRJ

GS DGHEY, EWHE HMMLHA SAGU UGKQE

DBZLHF.

Sarah

MEDIUM

	A	B	C	D	E	F	G	H	I
1	A	P			R				
2	R					U	P	C	S
3		C		S			R		
4			E			D			
5	P	U			H		S	E	
6		A			P		C	U	R
7				D		H		A	U
8		E	C		A				P
9	U	H	A				D	R	

Hint: Row 5

Abraham _____ Ephron's field and cave to bury his late wife, Sarah (Genesis 23:16–17).

Crossword
by David K. Shortess

Esther's People

The book of Esther has some interesting characters. Can you find them in this story of intrigue and courage?

Esther the queen answered and said. . .
Let my life be given me at my petition, and my people at my request.
ESTHER 7:3

ACROSS

1 Edom (Genesis 36:19)
5 Robber to crowd: "Stick 'em up, all ____" (2 words, slang)
9 "Therefore will I change their glory into ____" (Hosea 4:7)
14 Coarse file
15 "Do nothing" in Java cybertalk
16 "Came upon me to ____ my flesh" (Psalm 27:2) (2 words)
17 ESTHER'S KING (Esther 1:1)
19 Allan ____ (Robin Hood's pal)
20 Artist's studio
22 Away from the wind
23 "____ truth shall be established for ever" (Proverbs 12:19) (3 words)
26 Appraise
28 ESTHER'S CHAMBERLAIN (Esther 4:5)
29 "That in the ____ to come" (Ephesians 2:7)
30 "He planteth an ____" (Isaiah 44:14)
31 Moses' brother (Exodus 4:14)
34 "How ____ be quiet" (Jeremiah 47:7) (2 words)
38 "Whatever ____ it is" (Leviticus 11:32 NKJV)
40 ESTHER'S NEMESIS (Esther 3:1)
42 "For the labourer is worthy of his ____" (Luke 10:7)
43 "____ chose for himself the whole plain of the Jordan" (Genesis 13:11 NIV) (2 words)
45 "If that is so, I'll eat ____" (2 words)
47 "And stand in the ____ before me" (Ezekiel 22:30)

48 "That shall he also ____" (Galatians 6:7)
50 AN OLD TESTAMENT QUEEN (Esther 1:9)
52 Marks
55 Called forth
57 "Gather a certain ____ every day" (Exodus 16:4)
58 "Prophesy and say ____" (Ezekiel 38:14) (2 words)
60 Frozen (2 words)
62 ESTHER'S KING'S CHAMBERLAIN (Esther 2:14)
66 Philippine island
67 "Then Daniel ____ in" (Daniel 2:16)
68 "He ____ his clothes" (Genesis 37:29 NIV)
69 American author, Gertrude ____
70 Gaelic
71 "And I will give him the morning ____" (Revelation 2:28)

DOWN

1 "Roaring Twenties," for example
2 African desert (abbr.)
3 Jehoshaphat's dad (1 Kings 22:41)
4 College in New Jersey
5 "Three bullocks, and ____ of flour" (1 Samuel 1:24) (2 words)
6 "____, thou shalt conceive" (Judges 13:5) (2 words)
7 "But I will return again unto ____ God will" (Acts 18:21) (2 words)
8 Cathedral's altar area
9 "And cast out the wheat into the ____" (Acts 27:38)
10 ESTHER'S OTHER NAME (Esther 2:7)

11 "We spend our years as _____ that is told" (Psalm 90:9) (2 words)
12 "He. . .sent. . .riders on _____" (Esther 8:10)
13 Swords
18 City on the Erie Canal
21 Word with doll or time
23 Siamese's, today (poss.)
24 "Fear _____ do with punishment" (1 John 4:18 NIV) (2 words)
25 Singer Waters
27 Short time (abbr.)
29 One of Esau's in-laws (Genesis 36:2)
32 "Build a _____ up to it" (Ezekiel 4:2 NIV)
33 "Bless the Lord, _____ soul" (Psalm 103:1) (2 words)
35 "Nor the pillar of fire by _____" (Exodus 13:22)
36 In a severe pique
37 Another word that might describe the Laodiceans (Revelation 3:14–16)
39 ESTHER'S GUARDIAN (Esther 2:5)

41 Emulate Magellan
44 Golf helper
46 Juan's snacks
49 Tempe school (abbr.)
51 "And fearful _____ and great signs" (Luke 21:11)
52 "For this people's heart is waxed _____" (Matthew 13:15)
53 "And _____ flood stage as before" (Joshua 4:18 NIV) (2 words)
54 "_____ to be born" (Ecclesiastes 3:2) (2 words)
55 "Libnah, and _____, and Ashan" (Joshua 15:42)
56 Things given temporarily
59 Letters on a weather vane
61 Directional suffix
63 "Which he had _____ in the land of Canaan" (Genesis 36:6)
64 One of the three sons of Jether (1 Chronicles 7:38)
65 One of the fenced (fortified) cities of Ziddim (Joshua 19:35)

Acrostic
by Donna K. Maltese

The Girl Who Betrayed the Betrayer

When people pick us out of a crowd, do we deny or proclaim Jesus? Crack the code to discover how one who betrayed Jesus was himself betrayed by a servant girl.

The town in which the betrayer was betrayed

___ ___ ___ ___ ___ ___ ___ ___ ___
34 11 16 25 4 31 36 22 9

The disciple the servant girl betrayed

___ ___ ___ ___ ___
14 20 30 2 35

It seemed the betrayed betrayer had lost his _____ for Jesus

___ ___ ___ ___
24 15 6 33

The betrayer denied Jesus with an _____ (Matthew 26:72)

___ ___ ___ ___
26 10 17 3

Jesus had _____ His disciple's denial in Matthew 26:34

___ ___ ___ ___ ___ ___ ___ ___
23 7 19 28 5 12 37 32

What the cock began doing after the third denial

___ ___ ___ ___ ___ ___ ___
29 8 21 13 27 1 18

31-1-32   13-3-15-1   3-11   13-10-4   18-21-1-20

7-25-17   27-1-30-26   5-3-20   14-7-35-29-3,

31-1-12-5-3-2-19   9-6-27-32   4-6-13   3-27-9,   31-1-32

4-6-27-32   25-1-30-26   5-3-2-9   5-3-6-5   13-2-8-2

5-3-20-8-20,   5-3-27-4   23-28-36-37-7-13   13-10-4

31-33-4-26   13-27-17-3   34-22-4-25-4   26-23

1-6-24-6-16-22-5-3.

MATTHEW 26:71

Word Search
by Janet W. Adkins

Lady Merchant
Acts 16:12–15

ABIDE	PHILIPPI
ATTENDED	PRAYER
BESOUGHT	PURPLE
CERTAIN	RESORTED
CHIEF	RIVER
CITY	SABBATH
COLONY	SAT
CONSTRAINED	SELLER
DAYS	SIDE
HEART	SPAKE
HOUSEHOLD	THITHER
JUDGED	THYATIRA
LYDIA	WOMAN
MACEDONIA	WOMEN
OPENED	WORSHIPPED

```
M I D Y N O L O C R A F T I P
C E R T A I N R Q U E B S H A
O W C N R E S O R T E D I Z T
N I B E S O U G H T K L G D T
S U V M F R Y F T O I O C H E
T I F O E T E L M P D A Y S N
R H E W I Y N H P E X A P L D
A E Y C H P H I T D T L U S E
I A M A C E D O N I A F R E D
N R S O T D R D R S H A P L E
E T L Y D I A A T T E T L L N
D E G D U J R A B H K T E E E
R E Y A R P S A B B A T H R P
D E R W O R S H I P P E D L O
N A M O W D L O H E S U O H S
```

by Suzanne Stepp

Personal Professions

Sometimes God uses our circumstances as examples to others.

1. NAVEGE

2. UEHSO

3. YECMR

4. ESACE

5. WDORS

She was a prostitute married to a prophet.

1. _ _ _ _ O _

2. _ O _ _ _

3. O _ _ _ _

4. _ O _ _ _

5. _ _ _ O _

Answer: _ _ _ _ _

Anagram
by Paul Kent

Mary's Amazing Job

She was young—maybe only a teenager—when God chose her for the most amazing job ever: Give birth to the Savior of the world, Jesus Christ. Can you unscramble these three words or phrases from Mary's story in Luke 1–2?

A hidden man

_ _ _ _ _ _ _ _ _ _

Slight dead clowns

_ _ _ _ _ _ _ _

_ _ _ _ _ _ _

Ah holy events

_ _ _ _ _ _ _ _   _ _ _ _

173

Women of the Bible

The Bible is full of fearless females who served God with courage, strength, obedience, sacrifice, and compassion. Can you find the names of nine of them, scattered throughout this puzzle?

"And many women were there beholding afar off, which followed Jesus from Galilee, ministering unto him."
MATTHEW 27:55

ACROSS

1 "Hitherto have ye _____ nothing in my name" (John 16:24)
6 Singer Fitzgerald
10 Carpet
13 WOMAN OF CENCHREA, WHO WENT TO ROME (Romans 16:1)
14 Advertising gas
15 Used car lot stat. (pl.)
17 Drive back
18 Among
19 "As soon as the sun _____, thou shalt rise early" (Judges 9:33) (2 words)
20 WOMAN FROM EGYPT, WHO WENT TO KADESH (Numbers 20:1)
22 "And he began again to teach by the _____" (Mark 4:1) (2 words)
24 New Deal org.
26 "Caraway is not threshed with a _____" (Isaiah 28:27 NIV)
27 WOMAN OF ROME, WHO WENT TO EPHESUS BY WAY OF CORINTH (Acts 18:1–19)
33 "Guard against all kinds of v" (Luke 12:15 NIV)
34 Soundtracks
35 Hair "ado"
37 "But ye have not so _____ Christ" (Ephesians 4:20)
39 WOMAN OF NAHOR, WHO WENT TO CANAAN (Genesis 24) (var.)
44 New Mexican pueblo
46 Shady spots
47 Greek goddess
51 WOMAN OF JUDAH, WHOSE NAZARENE COUSIN CAME TO VISIT (Luke 1:36–40) (var.)
53 Negatively charged atoms
55 Lyric poem
56 Crucial
58 WOMAN OF JERUSALEM, WHO WENT TO BABYLON (Esther 2:5–7)
63 City on the Oka
64 Singer Horne
66 Ratty residence
68 Fern spore cases
69 South African river
70 "Good night" girl of popular song
71 _____ King Cole
72 Resistance units
73 WOMAN OF UR, WHO WENT TO CANAAN VIA HARAN (Genesis 11:31)

DOWN

1 Spring month (abbr.)
2 Ark passenger (Genesis 7:13)
3 French military cap
4 Shem's great-grandson (Genesis 10:22–24)
5 It's full of bologna
6 Tooth protector
7 Moon buggy
8 WOMAN OF LYSTRA, WHOSE GRANDSON WENT TO MACEDONIA (2 Timothy 1:5)
9 Chilean range
10 "Then shall stand up in his estate a _____ of taxes" (Daniel 11:20)
11 _____ down
12 "_____ not one against another" (James 5:9)
16 Rapidity
21 "If there _____ matter too hard for thee" (Deuteronomy 17:8) (2 words)
23 High school subject

25 "In _____ thy ways" (Proverbs 3:6)
27 Buddy
28 "For ye tithe mint and _____ and all" (Luke 11:42)
29 Mrs. Cantor
30 Dear _____
31 "And his brethren were _____" (Genesis 37:27)
32 "To meet the Lord in the _____" (1 Thessalonians 4:17)
36 Discontinues
38 "Naphtali is a _____ set free" (Genesis 49:21 NIV)
40 Kind of tide
41 Runner Sebastian
42 TV screen, often (abbr.)
43 "And lifts the needy from the _____ heap" (Psalm 113:7 NIV)
45 School zone sign (abbr.)
47 Guitar add-ons
48 "Whose feet they hurt with fetters: he was laid _____" (Psalm 105:18) (2 words)
49 Pitcher Mariano
50 "Pipe down!" (2 words)

52 Standards of excellence
54 Burst of applause
57 WOMAN OF HARAN, WHO WENT TO CANAAN (Genesis 31)
59 Not that
60 Israeli dance
61 At any time
62 California rockfish
65 Site of modern conflict, briefly
67 Oahu wreath

Acrostic
by Donna K. Maltese

The Woman Who Rocked

Although this rock-casting woman is unnamed, she was a hero among her people. Using Judges 9 to help with clues, crack the code to discover who she aimed for and why.

An evil ruler and his men ____ against Thebez

— — — — — — — —
24 6 42 38 34 18 2 13

This woman and her people ____ from their enemy

— — — —
31 5 23 39

The man she mortally wounded was king here

— — — — — — —
9 36 19 41 3 14 26

The wounded king was evil, or ____

— — — — — —
15 4 20 37 29 12

The place from which she flung her rock

— — — — —
8 17 33 27 22

So that it would not be said he was slain by a woman, the king commanded this servant to kill him

— — — — — — — — — — — —
1 16 30 7 35 40 10 21 28 32 11 25

28-6-12   38   42-23-22-8-1-4-6   15-7-34-1-6   41-1-9-8

38   18-4-11-20-11   7-31   38   26-4-5-5-9-8-17-6-24

35-18-7-6   1-10-4-30-2-5-2-20-36-'9   3-14-1-39,

28-6-13   28-5-5   8-7   10-16-1-37-19   3-4-9

9-37-35-5-5.

JUDGES 9:53

Spotty Headline
by Sara Stoker

Strong Women

Sometimes, Bible women excelled in the traditionally male-oriented fields of business and government. These spotty headlines describe three strong women of scripture. Can you solve each one?

TIRE● MISS●ONARIES GRACIOUSL●
HOUSED BY WOM●N SE●LER

— — — — —

COU●AGEOU● QU●EN OU●WITS
●ATEFUL PLOTTING ●NEMY

— — — — — —

L●DY JU●GE ●OOSTS ●ESITANT
A●MY C●MMAND●R

— — — — — —

Telephone Scramble
by Connie Troyer

Ahead of Her Time

Some women of the Bible couldn't help but be progressive. Can you work the clues to discover names of ladies who seemed to be ahead of their time?

| DEF 3 | DEF 3 | ABC 2 | MNO 6 | PRS 7 | ABC 2 | GHI 4 |

| PRS 7 | TUV 8 | TUV 8 | GHI 4 |

| JKL 5 | MNO 6 | ABC 2 | MNO 6 | MNO 6 | ABC 2 |

| ABC 2 | ABC 2 | GHI 4 | GHI 4 | ABC 2 | GHI 4 | JKL 5 |

| PRS 7 | PRS 7 | GHI 4 | PRS 7 | ABC 2 | GHI 4 | JKL 5 | JKL 5 | ABC 2 |

| DEF 3 | ABC 2 | MNO 6 | ABC 2 | PRS 7 | GHI 4 | PRS 7 |

| ABC 2 | GHI 4 | JKL 5 | MNO 6 | DEF 3 |

Lady Deported

Acts 18; Romans 16:3–5; 1 Corinthians 16:19

APOLLOS	JUSTUS
AQUILA	LEAVE
BADE	LEFT
BAPTIZED	PAUL
BELIEVED	PRISCILLA
CHURCH	ROME
CLAUDIUS	SALUTE
CORINTH	SHORN
EPHESUS	SYRIA
GENTILES	TARRIED
GOD	TENTMAKERS
HAVE	TESTIFIED
HELPERS	TOOK
HOUSE	VOW
ITALY	WAY
JEW	WIFE

```
T A J O D A P O L L O S J E W
P R E L X O R E T U L A S N I
A K G E N T I L E S E G H K F
U F O W A Y S J A T M S O Y E
L A O O U U C T F O O T R D Y
K V H L T A I E T I R A N O T
R I O S E T L E A C E R S H E
A Q U I L A L T L B S R S C N
H J S U Q E A A A A E I U R T
T H E Z A T U D R P Y E S U M
N O W V R D E A L T L D E H A
I M E E I L I E H I A B H C K
R J N U I R H Y A Z T A P V E
O E S R Y S D E V E I L E B R
C T E S T I F I E D J M O U S
```

Crossword
by David K. Shortess

Happy Mother's Day!

Wives and mothers are an invaluable resource to be honored and praised. Solve this puzzle to discover a descriptive verse regarding this priceless treasure we call "Mom."

Honor your father and your mother, so that you may live long.
EXODUS 20:12 NIV

ACROSS

1 START OF VERSE APPROPRIATE TO THE THEME DAY (Proverbs 31:10)
4 "____ vanity" (Ecclesiastes 1:2) (2 words)
9 "Arise, and go into the ____ which is called Straight" (Acts 9:11)
15 "That no ____ can come between them" (Job 41:16)
16 "Is like a broken ____" (Proverbs 25:19)
17 "It is time for you ____ LORD" (Psalm 119:126 NIV) (3 words)
18 "Looked out ____ window" (2 Kings 9:30) (2 words)
19 "A whip for the ____" (Proverbs 26:3)
20 Ciphers
21 VERSE, CONTINUED (4 words)
24 "The foal of an ____" (Matthew 21:5)
25 "Their murders, their magic ____" (Revelation 9:21 NIV)
26 "Ye are the ____ of the earth" (Matthew 5:13)
29 "Judah ____ wife for Er, his firstborn" (Genesis 38:6 NIV) (2 words)
31 "____ him, all ye people" (Romans 15:11)
35 Third son of Jether (1 Chronicles 7:38)
36 "Which is the king's ____" (Genesis 14:17)
38 Taos, for example
40 VERSE, CONTINUED (4 words)
44 "On ____ the time I punish him" (Jeremiah 49:8 NIV) (2 words)
45 Sandwich cookie
46 Derivative (abbr.)
47 Newspaper department
48 "Took ____ of him" (Luke 10:34)
50 "They were not ____" (Job 39:16)
51 "God saw ____ it was good" (Genesis 1:10)

53 Fort Worth school (abbr.)
55 END OF VERSE (4 words)
64 On ice
65 Presidential candidate Ralph
66 Cry of surprise
67 State #49
68 "Of Zebulun; ____ the son of Helon" (Numbers 1:9)
69 "____ the sacrifices of the dead" (Psalm 106:28)
70 "There shall be ____ of any man's life among you" (Acts 27:22) (2 words)
71 "Their ____ were evil" (John 3:19)
72 "His eyes were ____" (1 Samuel 4:15)

DOWN

1 Women's corp in WWII (abbr.)
2 "Fighting ____ pregnant woman" (Exodus 21:22 NIV) (2 words)
3 "But though we, ____ angel from heaven" (Galatians 1:8) (2 words)
4 "A woman lay ____ feet" (Ruth 3:8) (2 words)
5 Mournful water fowl
6 "The ____ is King for ever and ever" (Psalm 10:16)
7 "____ ghost" (Matthew 14:26 NIV) (2 words)
8 Fifth Jewish month
9 "Let us ____ rebuilding" (Nehemiah 2:18 NIV)
10 Eagerly promotes
11 Pasta sauce brand
12 "The woodwork will ____ it" (Habbakuk 2:11 NIV)
13 Part of Caesar's last words (2 words)
14 "____ thee like a ball" (Isaiah 22:18)
22 "First seven ____ kine" (Genesis 41:20)
23 "____ the Ithrite" (1 Chronicles 11:40)

26 "They were _____ in two" (Hebrews 11:37 NIV)
27 "I _____ in the night" (Nehemiah 2:12)
28 Tibetan priests
29 Day-_____ dyes
30 "_____ the land of the free"
31 Follows *jugg* or *but*
32 "Her feet _____ not in her house" (Proverbs 7:11)
33 Stress result
34 "Be ye _____ of the word" (James 1:22)
36 Genetic stuff
37 Sternward
38 It means "before" (prefix)
39 "Spring _____ well" (Numbers 21:17) (2 words)
41 Arctic diver
42 "Came unto mount _____" (Numbers 20:22)
43 "_____ the messenger came to him" (2 Kings 6:32)
48 "The fourth part of a _____" (2 Kings 6:25)
49 "Your sin _____ for" (Isaiah 6:7 NIV)
50 Wheel center
51 Arduous journeys

52 "They _____ king over them" (Revelation 9:11 NIV) (2 words)
53 "_____ their winepresses, and suffer thirst" (Job 24:11)
54 Edges of streets
55 "_____ of mine own self do nothing" (John 5:30) (2 words)
56 Sing or fly alone
57 "A colt the _____ of an ass" (Matthew 21:5)
58 "The soldiers _____ mocked him" (Luke 23:36)
59 "The _____ of Siddim was full" (Genesis 14:10)
60 Film star Adams, Ernie Kovacs's wife
61 "Oh that _____ wings like a dove!" (Psalm 55:6) (2 words)
62 "Nothing to _____ was thirsty" (Matthew 25:42 NIV) (2 words)
63 "He shall dwell in the tents of _____" (Genesis 9:27)

Bible Quotation
by Suzanne Stepp

Serve the Servant
ROMANS 16:1–2

Sometimes even helpers need help. Solve this puzzle to find a needful woman who served many, including Paul.

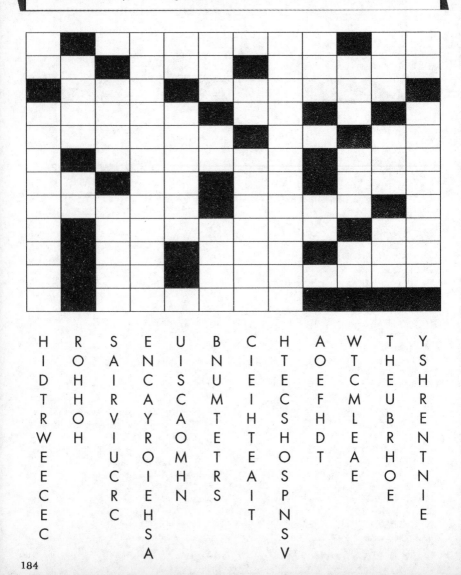

Drop Two
by Dorothy Pryse

Jacob Picks a Wife
GENESIS 29:30

Jacob, himself a deceiver, was once tricked by his father-in-law. After working seven years for one woman, he was given another to wed. Work this drop two to discover how Jacob felt about his second bride.

Word	Clue		#		
SEISMAL	Sticky substance	_____	1.	___	___
NOSTRUM	Play banjo	_____	2.	___	___
REDDEST	Spirited horse	_____	3.	___	___
HAIRNET	Unable to move	_____	4.	___	___
EXACTED	Assessed fees	_____	5.	___	___
HEDDLES	Acts	_____	6.	___	___
OBVERSE	Action words	_____	7.	___	___
LEVYING	Look at	_____	8.	___	___
MAESTRO	Cook in oven	_____	9.	___	___
OVERDID	Urge forward	_____	10.	___	___
RECLAIM	Region	_____	11.	___	___
LEACHED	In pain	_____	12.	___	___

— — — — — — — — — — — —

— — — — — — — — — — — —
1 2 3 4 5 6 7 8 9 10 11 12

Word Search
by Marijane Troyer

King Saul's Daughter

ABNER	HEART
ARK	HE IS SICK
BAHURIM	IMAGE
BED	LOVED
BOLSTER	MERAB
CLOTHED	MESSENGERS
DANCED	MICHAL
DAUGHTER	PHALTI
DAVID	PHILISTINES
DECEIVED ME	PILLOW
DESPISED HIM	RETURN
DOWRY	SAUL
ESCAPED	SLEW
FORESKINS	SNARE
GALLIM	TWAIN
GOAT'S HAIR	WIFE
HAD NO CHILD	WINDOW

```
P  S  R  S  T  E  M  D  E  V  I  E  C  E  D
G  H  N  E  D  E  S  P  I  S  E  D  H  I  M
O  H  I  I  T  L  A  H  P  N  B  I  E  Q  D
A  A  M  L  K  S  B  E  F  R  A  T  I  E  E
T  D  A  A  I  S  L  U  A  U  H  A  S  S  V
S  N  G  D  K  S  E  O  B  T  U  B  S  C  O
H  O  E  A  G  T  T  R  B  E  R  N  I  A  L
A  C  M  N  L  S  W  I  O  R  I  E  C  P  W
I  H  E  C  D  L  N  A  N  F  M  R  K  E  I
R  I  R  E  D  L  I  A  I  E  T  T  E  D  N
S  L  A  D  A  R  K  M  R  N  S  R  O  U  D
L  D  B  H  C  L  O  T  H  E  D  W  A  I  O
E  Q  C  D  A  U  G  H  T  E  R  X  V  E  W
W  I  W  O  L  L  I  P  B  Y  S  A  U  L  H
M  E  S  S  E  N  G  E  R  S  D  E  F  I  W
```

A Showy yet Shallow Woman

Here's a verse about woman very rich in material goods but desperately lacking in spiritual wealth. Crack the code to discover her name and the company she kept.

The name of her brother the king (Acts 25:13)

___ ___ ___ ___ ___ ___ ___
1 42 37 15 34 22 10

The place to which she and her brother came to salute Festus (Acts 25:13)

___ ___ ___ ___ ___ ___ ___ ___
27 33 3 18 43 21 38 12

She sat with the principal _____ of the city

___ ___ ___
44 41 5

At Festus's command, Paul was _____ forth (Acts 25:23)

___ ___ ___ ___ ___ ___ ___
39 13 9 30 25 4 19

Before her and other officials, Paul gave this

___ ___ ___ ___ ___ ___ ___ ___ ___
20 35 7 2 24 31 14 28 17

Festus thought that Paul was afflicted with an _____ mind (Acts 26:24)

___ ___ ___ ___ ___ ___ ___ ___ ___ ___
26 11 32 40 36 29 6 23 16 8

1-28-8   36-4-35-5   4-3   4-43-8   2-4-30-7

18-34-9-23-3-5,   2-4-35   23-15-5-25   37-29-7-32

30-22,   33-28-8   2-4-35   42-14-11-16-21-5-26-6,

33-28-8   39-41-13-5-15-27-41,   1-28-8   2-4-3-17

2-4-10-2   18-12-20   36-24-19-4   2-4-3-31.

Acts 26:30

The Family of Zelophehad

MEDIUM

	A	B	C	D	E	F	G	H	I
1		T	A	D				R	
2					H	T		G	
3	S			U		E		D	
4			R	G		U			H
5	G	U	T					E	
6	H	E	S			R		A	
7	R			E		D		T	S
8		S	D		G			U	
9			U	S	T			H	

Hint: Column D

God allowed the inheritance to go his _____ because Zelophehad had no sons (Numbers 27:7).

That's Some Bath!

Who knows what can happen during our simplest routines—like drawing water!

1. HITCP
2. SRFELEH
3. TAREW
4. SEINRDACE
5. RBNO
6. HICDL
7. MLEIS
8. VIEMSDIW

9. IMDA
10. SEUNR
11. DOLGYO
12. EWBREH
13. RESSIT
14. VRIRE
15. KNIRB

She found more than she expected in the river.

1. ◯ _ _ _ _
2. ◯ _ _ _ _ _ _
3. _ ◯ _ _ ◯
4. _ _ _ _ _ ◯ _ _ _
5. _ ◯ _ _
6. _ ◯ _ _ _
7. ◯ _ _ _ _
8. _ _ ◯ _ _ _ _ _

9. _ ◯ _ _
10. _ ◯ _ _ _
11. ◯ _ _ _ _ _
12. ◯ _ _ _ _ _
13. _ _ _ ◯ _ _
14. _ _ _ ◯ _
15. _ ◯ _ _ _

Answer: _ _ _ _ _ _ _ ' _   _ _ _ _ _ _ _

Crossword
by Sarah Lagerquist Simmons

The "Ahs" Have It

Lots of Old Testament names end in the two letters *ah*. Within this crossword puzzle are a few such denotations belonging to women of the Bible. You'll have an *ah*-ful lot of fun as you embark upon this "appellation" trail!

Ah, so would we have it.
PSALM 35:25

ACROSS

1 Turkish official
6 "AFTER THE SERVANT TOLD ISAAC THE WHOLE STORY OF THE ____, ISAAC TOOK REBEKAH INTO THE TENT OF HIS MOTHER SARAH" (Genesis 24:66 MSG)
10 "The angel of the LORD stood in a ____" (Numbers 22:24)
14 Free from limits
15 THIS WOMAN WAS ORPAH'S SISTER-IN-LAW
16 Award for off-Broadway theater
17 "Make the offering to the LORD to ____ for your lives" (Exodus 30:15 NIV)
18 Ancient Peruvian empire
19 Brass wind instrument
20 "Buy timber and ____ stone to repair the house" (2 Kings 22:6)
21 Froth
23 Pimple (slang)
24 "Agrippa came together with Bernice ____ great pomp" (Acts 25:23 NASB)
26 ZELOPHEHAD'S DAUGHTER WITH AN "AH" ENDING (Joshua 17:3)
28 Card game
31 ANOTHER ONE OF ZELOPHEHAD'S DAUGHTERS WHO ALSO HAD AN "AH" NAME (Joshua 17:3)
32 "Let the ____ land appear" (Genesis 1:9)
33 Ruler of a Muslim country
36 "Receive him not into your house, neither ____ him God speed" (2 John 1:10)
39 Organization (abbr.)
41 Promissory note (abbr.)
42 "The wringing of the ____ bringeth forth blood" (Proverbs 30:33)
43 KETURAH WAS ABRAHAM'S SECOND ____

44 YET ANOTHER ONE OF ZELOPHEHAD'S DAUGHTERS WHO ALSO HAD AN "AH" NAME (Joshua 17:3)
47 Bravo! (Sp.)
48 Bluish green
50 REBEKAH'S SON WAS A ____ (Genesis 25:27)
52 Dances
55 Great dog
56 America (abbr.)
57 Site of the first Islamic mosque in Bahrain
60 New Testament book
64 The sun "rejoiceth as a strong man to run a ____" (Psalm 19:5)
66 South Korean county
67 "Tree, in the which is the ____ of a tree yielding seed" (Genesis 1:29)
68 Distort
69 Egyptian dancer (var.)
70 Metric unit of length
71 "His soul shall dwell at ____" (Psalm 25:13)
72 Section of the Talmud, dealing with the "corner" of produce Jews are to reserve for the poor
73 "They are like the deaf ____ that stoppeth her ear" (Psalm 58:4)

DOWN

1 HEBREW MIDWIFE WITH AN "AH" NAME (Exodus 1:15)
2 Before (Lat.)
3 Boat with a flat bottom
4 BARREN WOMAN WITH AN "AH" NAME (1 Samuel 1:2)
5 Mimic
6 Group of three
7 " 'My clan's the weakest. . .and I'm the ____ of the litter' " (Judges 6:15 MSG)

8 "The LORD will smite thee. . .with the _____" (Deuteronomy 28:27)

9 Light carriage

10 ZIPPORAH'S HUSBAND "SAID UNTO AARON, TAKE A _____, AND PUT AN OMER FULL OF MANNA THEREIN" (Exodus 16:33)

11 Alive with activity

12 Leg bone

13 "For he shall be like the _____ in the desert" (Jeremiah 17:6)

21 Instead of

22 Estuary (Sp.)

25 Wife (abbr.)

27 Factor found in blood

28 Cheese

29 _____ Major

30 Abnormal sac in the body

31 Village in County Dublin, Ireland

34 "The people shall rise up as a great _____" (Numbers 23:24)

35 Coat

36 "Shirts are on and pants buckled, every _____ is spit-polished and tied" (Isaiah 5:25 MSG)

37 "They had gone through the _____ unto Paphos" (Acts 13:6)

38 BILHAH'S SON NAPHTALI IS DESCRIBED BY JACOB AS "A _____ LET LOOSE" (Genesis 49:21 NJKV)

40 REBEKAH PUT GOAT SKINS AROUND HER SON'S _____ (Genesis 27:16)

44 Data structure in computer science

45 Exclamations of triumph

46 Atilla was one

49 Tibetan ox

51 "As he _____ Damascus. . .suddenly a light from heaven flashed around him" (Acts 9:3 NIV)

52 "Let us all have one _____" (Proverbs 1:14)

53 Commercial center of Japan

54 Ties

55 JACOB'S DAUGHTER WHO HAD AN "AH" NAME (Genesis 34:3)

58 Tolkien character

59 ZIPPORAH WAS _____ TO MOSES' CHILDREN (Exodus 2:21)

61 Item in soured milk

62 "In the process of _____ it came to pass" (Genesis 4:3)

63 "Who shall _____ him up?" (Numbers 24:9)

65 "The poor man had nothing, save one little _____ lamb" (2 Samuel 12:3)

67 Tomorrow's agricultural specialists (abbr.)

Word Search
by Janet W. Adkins

David's Warmth
1 KINGS 1–2

ABIATHAR	ISRAEL
ABISHAG	JOAB
ADONIJAH	KINGDOM
BATHSHEBA	LIE
BOSOM	NO HEAT
CHERISHED	PRAY
COASTS	SERVANTS
COVERED	SHUNAMMITE
DAMSEL	SOLOMON
DAVID	SPEAK
ELDER	STRICKEN
FAIR	VIRGIN
FOUND	WIFE
GIVE	ZERUIAH

```
T A R M U H P I R D A V I D B
A B I O I T R D N O H E A T A
N I A S W N H A J I N O D A T
C S H O H I I M C V P Y D S H
O H Z B J L F S E R V A N T S
S A E Y N E M E T N G D U R H
H G R R A A X L K E A W O I E
U R U N I R F A K B R I F C B
N S I X P S P G I V E E D K A
A F A H P I H A N C J L D E C
M G H E Z A T E G I P D O N O
M Y A C S H O U D N G E F X A
I K E E A B N L O P I R A E S
T O N R S O L O M O N M I M T
E C O V E R E D Q U E L R V S
```

Telephone Scramble
by Connie Troyer

Bad Girls

Instead of being the apples of God's eye, these women were rotten to the core. Can you decipher the names of these bad girls?

| GHI 4 | DEF 3 | PRS 7 | MNO 6 | DEF 3 | GHI 4 | ABC 2 | PRS 7 |

| ABC 2 | TUV 8 | GHI 4 | ABC 2 | JKL 5 | GHI 4 | ABC 2 | GHI 4 |

| DEF 3 | DEF 3 | JKL 5 | GHI 4 | JKL 5 | ABC 2 | GHI 4 |

| JKL 5 | DEF 3 | QZ 0 | DEF 3 | ABC 2 | DEF 3 | JKL 5 |

| PRS 7 | ABC 2 | PRS 7 | PRS 7 | GHI 4 | GHI 4 | PRS 7 | ABC 2 |

| MNO 6 | ABC 2 | ABC 2 | ABC 2 | ABC 2 | GHI 4 |

| ABC 2 | MNO 6 | QZ 0 | ABC 2 | GHI 4 |

The Little Maid

Sometimes the least among us show the greatest faith. Such was the case of a lowly little maid who paved the way for an amazing miracle. Can you break the following cryptoscripture codes to discover her awe-inspiring story?

DVI YET PJCFDVP EDI NGVT GMY KJ SGAHDVFTP,

DVI EDI KCGMNEY DQDJ SDHYFZT GMY GW

YET UDVI GW FPCDTU D UFYYUT ADFI; DVI PET

QDFYTI GV VDDADV'P QFWT.

BPK ZQM ZBSK RPWT QMF LSZWFMZZ, JTRIK XTK

LC ITFK JMFM JSWQ WQM VFTVQMW WQBW

SZ SP ZBLBFSB! UTF QM JTRIK FMHTNMF QSL TU

QSZ IMVFTZC.

Crossword

by Sarah Lagerquist Simmons

Mothers of Great Men

It is the child's duty to honor his mother. And nothing honors a mother more than a child who turns out great. Work this puzzle to uncover some honorable biblical mothers of a few great men.

Honour thy father and thy mother: that thy days may be long upon the land which the LORD thy God giveth thee.
EXODUS 20:12

ACROSS

1 Norway's capital
5 SETH'S MOTHER WAS MADE FROM ONE OF HIS FATHER'S ____
9 Tropical tree
14 "Go up, ____ an altar unto the LORD" (2 Samuel 24:18)
15 Brand of cookie
16 Shallot
17 Church niche
18 THIS WOMAN WAS MOTHER TO THE GREATEST MAN OF ALL TIME
19 Pethahiah. . .was the king's ____ in all affairs relating to the people" (Nehemiah 11:24 NIV)
20 AFTER RACHEL TOLD HER SISTER THAT JACOB "SHALL ____ WITH THEE TO NIGHT FOR THY SON'S MANDRAKES" (Genesis 30:15), ISSACHAR WAS CONCEIVED
21 MOTHER TO THE PROPHET WHO LED ISRAEL UNTIL HE ANOINTED A KING FOR THEM (1 Samuel 1)
23 "Joshua discomfited Amalek. . .with the ____ of the sword" (Exodus 17:13)
24 RACHEL WAS ____ FOR MANY YEARS BEFORE GIVING BIRTH TO JOSEPH, WHO BECAME PHARAOH'S SECOND-IN-COMMAND (Genesis 29:31)
26 Snakelike fish
28 Roman numeral three
29 A rude, rustic man
31 Thirty-fourth president of U.S. (init.)
34 Corrupted
37 Brand of portable media players
39 WITHOUT THIS MOTHER, THERE WOULD BE NO JUDAH (Genesis 35:23)
40 To finish a cake
41 Meadows
42 "In the beginning God created the heaven and the ____" (Genesis 1:1)
44 Sour
47 European eagle (var.)
48 Elliptical
50 "They plotted to arrest Jesus in some ____ way" (Matthew 26:4 NIV)
51 "The bigger the ____, the harder the fall" (Proverbs 16:18 MSG)
52 Retorts
56 "They. . .went their ways, one to his ____, another to his merchandise" (Matthew 22:5)
59 No longer active
63 Year (Sp.)
64 "Praise the LORD from the earth, you great sea creatures and all ____ depths" (Psalm 148:7 NIV)
66 " 'Do you watch when the doe bears her ____?' " (Job 39:1 NIV)
67 Vietnamese language
68 Gold Rush state (abbr.)
69 "Men and women. . .cursed God for the hail, the ____ disaster of hail" (Revelation 16:17 MSG)
70 Retired persons' group (abbr.)
71 Pastoral scene
72 "By wise counsel you will ____ your own war" (Proverbs 24:6 NKJV)
73 "The people is one, and ____ have all one language" (Genesis 11:6)

DOWN

1 Toothbrush brand
2 Brown pigment
3 Beam
4 " 'I have made you a tester of metals and my people the ____' " (Jeremiah 6:27 NIV)
5 European country

198

6 Middle East country
7 Switzerland's capital
8 Nutritious legume (var.)
9 Scarf of feathers
10 AN ____ CAME TO SAMSON'S MOTHER TO FORETELL OF HIS BIRTH (Judges 13:3)
11 "Thou hast not ____ unto men, but unto God" (Acts 5:4)
12 ZACHARIAS BROKE INTO THIS WHEN ELISABETH GAVE BIRTH TO JOHN THE BAPTIST (Luke 1:67–79)
13 One's share of the cost
21 GOD GAVE ABRAHAM AN ____ THROUGH SARAH (Genesis 17)
22 "Thou shalt not call ____ name Sarai" (Genesis 17:15)
25 "The LORD God. . .had led me in the ____ way" (Genesis 24:48)
27 PRIEST WHO THOUGHT SAMUEL'S MOTHER WAS DRUNK (1 Samuel 1:13)
29 DeMille, director of The Ten Commandments and The King of Kings
30 Port in Yemen
31 "If you judge the law, you are not a ____ of the law but a judge" (James 4:11 NKJV)
32 Battle launching date
33 Female (suffix)

34 "Is Ephraim my ____ son?" (Jeremiah 31:20)
35 Jacob had to ____ his wives with hard labor
36 Female singer
38 "They went in to her, as men go in to a woman who ____ the harlot" (Ezekiel 23:44 NKJV)
39 Sheltered side
43 Pig
45 Deuteronomy 10:12: To fear, love, obey, and walk with God is the ____ of the Law
46 "Therefore my heart is ____" (Psalm 16:9)
49 Amount (abbr.)
51 Electronic correspondence
53 ISAAC'S MOTHER (Genesis 21:3)
54 Harden (var.)
55 Foggy
56 Central points
57 School (abbr.)
58 "Because thou didst ____ on the LORD, he delivered them" (2 Chronicles 16:8)
60 "Abide with us ____ days" (Genesis 24:55) (2 words)
61 Father
62 Draught
65 AFC and NFC (abbr.)
67 "The heron after her kind, and the lapwing, and the ____" (Leviticus 11:19)

Acrostic
by Donna K. Maltese

Trophy Daughter

Long before the term *trophy wife* came into vogue, men offered their daughters as rewards to young men who would fight their battles. Crack this acrostic's code to discover the name of this trophy daughter, the name of her father, and the challenge set before eligible young suitors.

This was the name of the trophy daughter's grandfather
(Joshua 14:13)

___ ___ ___ ___ ___ ___ ___ ___ ___
12 25 39   7 36 43 29 15   3

Her father was given this land as his inheritance (Joshua 14:13)

___ ___ ___ ___ ___ ___
34   8 30 14 42 22

These people inhabited her father's land (Joshua 14:12)

___ ___ ___ ___ ___ ___ ___
 2 11 16 20 33 27   5

The cities in her father's land were "great and _____"
(Joshua 14:12)

___ ___ ___ ___ ___ ___
38   1 32 24 19 10

The name of the suitor who was awarded the daughter's hand
(Joshua 15:17)

___ ___ ___ ___ ___ ___ ___
21   6 28 35 18 41 13

To deliver a bride

___ ___ ___ ___   ___ ___ ___ ___
26   4 37 17   23   9 40 31

23-11-10   24-40-13-25-30   5-2-18-10,   28-15   6-7-2-6

5-27-33-6-41-6-34   20-4-14-12-40-6-3-5-8-39-3-8-14,

23-22-10   6-2-20-17-6-34   33-6,   6-21   28-4-27

9-4-13-13   4   26-4-37-41   16-24-7-5-16-7   27-31

10-16-36-26-7-6-1-14   6-42   9-4-38-19.

Joshua 15:16

Bible Quotation
by Suzanne Stepp

Testing the King
1 KINGS 10:1

Work this Bible quotation puzzle to discover a rich woman who, driven by curiosity, sought a man in whom wisdom reigned.

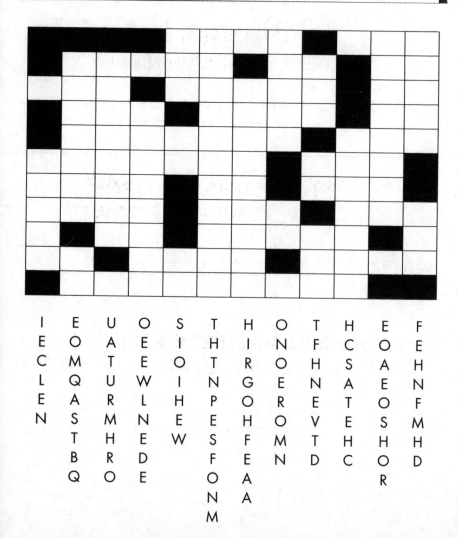

Spotty Headline
by Sara Stoker

Wives of David

The Bible's handsome, popular, and powerful David collected wives like modern guys collect baseball cards. Try to solve these spotty headlines to uncover three of David's women.

**●ROUCHY NABAL D●ES,
LE●VES ●E●UTIFU● W●DOW**

— — — — — — —

**●R●VE ●OLDIER'S ●EAU●Y
●EARS ●ORRIBLE B●TTLE N●WS**

— — — — — — — —

**SAU●'S D●UGHTER ●●ASTISES
●ERRY DAV●D**

— — — — — —

Queen Esther's Appeal
ESTHER 7:3–4

Then Esther the **queen answered** and **said**, If I **have found favour** in thy **sight**, O king, and if it **please** the king, let my **life** be **given** me at my **petition**, and my people at my **request**: For we are sold, I and my **people**, to be **destroyed**, to be **slain**, and to **perish**. But if we had **been sold** for **bondmen** and **bondwomen**, I had **held** my **tongue**, **although** the **enemy could** not **countervail** the **king's damage**.

```
L L E S F C T H E N H N V R V
H X U M X O G J N F A V O U R
T H G I S U U O Y N V W T E C
W Q N A O N I N S M E K F B F
Z Y O H D T E W D B E I R F G
Q L T Q I E E M L U L N N O D
V L J T N R S D O Q H G E A L
A G E V E V I T S W P S M K U
B P I D T A O N R M D A D G O
N P Q V S I S U E O G N N D C
R E S A E L P H Q E Y B O X F
X O S U A N T Y U D U E B B Q
A P Q I E S T H E R L Q D B O
B L N A F Y T H S I R E P B O
B E E N S S U H T L R M H M G
```

Daughters-in-Law

This puzzle highlights some unique Old Testament daughters-in-law—some faithful, some fruitful, and some fickle. Have fun!

[A faithful Ruth said to her mother-in-law Naomi] Whither thou goest, I will go; and where thou lodgest, I will lodge: thy people shall be my people, and thy God my God.
RUTH 1:16

ACROSS
1 City in Japan
6 Seaport in Norway
10 What Peter cut off (Matthew 26:51)
13 "They found him in the temple. . . ____ them questions" (Luke 2:46)
15 "And every man, with ____ was found blue, and purple. . .linen" (Exodus 35:23)
16 Sports group (abbr.)
17 Faithfulness
18 ISAAC'S DAUGHTER-IN-LAW BORE THIS SON (Genesis 35:23)
19 Kindness (abbr.)
20 Capital of Peru
22 TERAH'S DAUGHTER-IN-LAW (Genesis 11:27; 25:1)
24 Before (prefix)
26 ISAAC'S DAUGHTER-IN-LAW ____ BEFORE HE DID (Genesis 35:19)
28 Fill
29 "Using a cattle ____, he killed six hundred Philistines single-handed" (Judges 3:31 MSG)
30 REBEKAH'S DAUGHTER-IN-LAW GAVE BIRTH TO THE ONLY ____ AMONG 12 BROTHERS (Genesis 34:1)
31 Collar
32 " 'This ____ is vanity' " (Ecclesiastes 2:15 NASB)
33 Parks for animals
34 "He scooped Sea into his jug, put Ocean in his ____" (Psalm 33:6 MSG)
35 "He will guide his ____ with discretion" (Psalm 112:5)
37 Low red blood cell count (var.)
41 Compass point (abbr.)
42 A. A. Milne's bear
43 Ear of corn
44 Improvised (2 words)

47 "Hail smote every ____ of the field" (Exodus 9:25)
48 Cold cuts counter
49 "Every vow. . .her husband may make it ____" (Numbers 30:13)
50 One who commands or leads (abbr.)
51 "They. . .brought back sixteen ____ of gold" (1 Kings 9:26 MSG)
52 " 'Because he made his appeal to the ____ I decided to send him to Rome' " (Acts 25:25 NIV)
54 Sixth month of the Jewish calendar
56 Pinch
57 London college (abbr.)
59 "Ye shall destroy their altars, break their ____" (Exodus 34:13)
63 Numero ____
64 HAGAR CHOSE HER OWN DAUGHTER-IN-LAW WHEN SHE "____ [ISHMAEL] A WIFE OUT OF THE LAND OF EGYPT" (Genesis 21:21)
65 Mrs. (Fr.)
66 Cameras in orbit over our planet (abbr.)
67 "Thou shalt not ____ thy brother" (Leviticus 19:17)
68 French sculptor

DOWN
1 Clod
2 Asian stock market (abbr.)
3 Another name for (abbr.)
4 JESSE'S DAUGHTER-IN-LAW'S HUSBAND ____ HER FIRST HUSBAND (2 Samuel 12:9)
5 Against (prefix)
6 "I am like an ____ of the desert" (Psalm 102:6)
7 ABRAHAM'S DAUGHTER-IN-LAW WAS GIVEN EARRINGS THAT WEIGHED HALF OF THIS (Genesis 24:22)

8 THIS DAUGHTER-IN-LAW WAS BEST ____ OUT OF TWO (Genesis 29:30)
9 " 'Tell them everything I command you; do not ____ a word' " (Jeremiah 26:2 NIV)
10 JUDAH'S DAUGHTER-IN-LAW DID ____ HIM TO GIVE HER CHILDREN (Genesis 38)
11 Erode
12 REBEKAH'S DAUGHTER-IN-LAW (Genesis 29:28)
14 Phys. Ed.
21 Good-bye (Sp.)
23 Habit
24 Teacher (abbr.)
25 WHERE DAVID WAS WALKING WHEN HE SAW THIS FUTURE DAUGHTER-IN-LAW OF HIS FATHER (2 Samuel 11:2–3)
27 Treasury Department (abbr.)
29 Give it another try (abbr.)
30 "If an ox ____ a man. . .the ox shall be surely stoned" (Exodus 21:28)
31 NOT SO PRETTY DAUGHTER-IN-LAW OF ISAAC (Genesis 29:16–17)
33 Metallic element
34 "There was a ____ under the first two branches of the same" (Exodus 37:21 NJKV)
36 Positive electrode
37 Main artery

38 Appearance
39 " 'I cannot cure your ____' " (Isaiah 3:7 NJKV)
40 First three vowels in alphabet
42 Bearing or manner
44 Boulevard
45 Game piece
46 Herbivorous mammals (abbr.)
47 WHAT JUDAH'S DAUGHTER-IN-LAW PRETENDED TO BE (Genesis 38:13–15)
48 Dolphin
50 Hot beverage
51 THIS DAUGHTER-IN-LAW WAS WIFE TO TWO SONS (Genesis 38:24–30)
53 ELIMELECH'S DAUGHTER-IN-LAW (Ruth 1:1–4)
55 "His eyes were ____" (Genesis 27:1)
58 Small guitar (abbr.)
60 "Leah said, A troop cometh: and she called his name ____" (Genesis 30:11)
61 Electrical disturbance (abbr.)
62 Japanese money

Acrostic
by Donna K. Maltese

One of Many

Here's an acrostic about a woman who, being married to a polygamist, was one of many. Solve this puzzle to discover her name, as well as those of her husband and son.

Her husband was the second king of Israel, Saul being the ___

___ ___ ___ ___ ___
25 11 29 6   20

She was just one of a king's many ____

___ ___ ___ ___ ___
28 7   19 2   15

Her husband was of this tribe

___ ___ ___ ___ ___
23 12 9   1   17

Her husband had also married Abigail, widow of this man (1 Samuel 27:3)

___ ___ ___ ___ ___
3   22 16 27 10

This man was her brother-in-law (1 Chronicles 2:15)

___ ___ ___ ___
4   21 26 14

Her son violated this woman, his half sister (2 Samuel 13:22)

___ ___ ___ ___ ___
8   13 24 18 5

27-3-9   12-3-20-4   9-18-19-11-9   28-26-5-26

6-4-3-6   16-4-29-3   11-3   17-2-16-5-4-3:   27-3-9

17-11-15   25-7-29-15-8-16-4-29-3   28-22-6

13-14-3-4-3,   4-25   1-17-7-3-4-1-24   20-17-26

23-2-21-5-2-2-10-11-8-2-6-6.

2 SAMUEL 3:2

Old Testament Names

Of the scores of female names and titles in the Old Testament, we've anagrammed three. Can you figure out which three women these are? Hint: The first comes from the book of Genesis, the second from Exodus, and the third from Judges.

Her beak

_ _ _ _ _ _ _

A hug or sharp death

_ _ _ _ _ _ _ ' _

_ _ _ _ _ _ _ _

Ill head

_ _ _ _ _ _

Esther's Predecessor
ESTHER 1:9

Before Esther, someone else ruled the roost in a Persian palace. Can you solve the puzzle to find out the name of King Xerxes' first wife and what she did in the royal house?

Word	Clue	Answer	#	Drop
VOLTAGE	Brag	_____	1.	___ ___
NASCENT	Odor	_____	2.	___ ___
MEASLES	Artist's frame	_____	3.	___ ___
ACALEPH	Table setting	_____	4.	___ ___
TREBLED	Oppose	_____	5.	___ ___
ELLIPSE	Trance	_____	6.	___ ___
ADAPTER	Curtain	_____	7.	___ ___
FLASHED	Distributes cards	_____	8.	___ ___
EROSIVE	Cap front	_____	9.	___ ___
QUARTER	More genuine	_____	10.	___ ___
UNCLOSE	DNA twin	_____	11.	___ ___
TERMITE	Type of joint	_____	12.	___ ___

___ ___ ___ ___ ___ ___ ___ ___ ___ ___ ___ ___

___ ___ ___ ___ ___ ___ ___ ___ ___ ___ ___ ___
1   2   3   4   5   6   7   8   9   10   11   12

Who Loved Him Most?
LUKE 7:37–38, 50

And, **behold**, a woman in the **city**, which was a **sinner**, when she **knew** that **Jesus** sat at **meat** in the **Pharisees house**, **brought** an **alabaster** box of ointment, and **stood** at his feet **behind** him **weeping**, and began to **wash** his feet with **tears**, and did **wipe** them with the **hairs** of her **head**, and **used** his **feet**, and **anointed** them with the **ointment**. . . . And he said to the **woman**, They **faith hath saved thee**; go in **peace**.

Word Search
by John Hudson Tiner
(continued)

```
D H U D S D E S S I K W K M K
B E H O L D A E W C U X E M C
V C H O Y P E M I C D T O M Q
T H A T H S E T V N Z U U G Q
A I Y S I T Y A N S B J N A D
E L M R D A E H C I R O O Z E
M W A S H E F H M E O G T Q S
A H R B H J A S N O U N E J T
P W F T A I U N I U G I A Y J
W G Q N R S I N A T H P R X E
H O U S E S T O D M T E S P S
W K R J P M A E M P O E I T Y
D N I H E B A V R O B W D U F
P E K N Z P P D E M N T A Q D
Y W T E E F F Z C D B K Q M A
```

Mothers-in-Law

The Old Testament is teeming with mothers-in-law, some mentioned by name, some merely referenced as a certain man's wife. Either way, they are still mothers-in-law, women one should never approach empty-handed (see Ruth 3:17 below).

Go not empty unto thy mother in law.
RUTH 3:17

ACROSS

1 More (Sp.)
4 Cravat
9 Beats
14 "Pray over him, anointing him with _____ in the name of the Lord" (James 5:14)
15 Protestant preacher and positive thinker Norman Vincent
16 NAOMI WAS HER MOTHER-IN-LAW (Ruth 1:1–4)
17 Friend (slang)
18 THIS WOMAN BECAME RACHEL'S MOTHER-IN-LAW BECAUSE YEARS BEFORE SHE GAVE WATER TO A SERVANT'S _____ (Genesis 24:15–20)
19 ORPAH'S MOTHER-IN-LAW (Ruth 1:3–4)
20 Edible lily bulb
22 PETER'S MOTHER-IN-LAW WAS _____ OF A FEVER BY JESUS (Matthew 8:15)
24 THE NUMBER OF CAMELS WATERED BY LEAH'S MOTHER-IN-LAW (Genesis 24:10–15)
25 Commotion
27 "She fastened it with the _____" (Judges 16:14)
29 Spread out
32 Declining
35 Broker's organization (abbr.)
36 Japanese city
38 JETHRO'S WIFE WAS THE MOTHER-IN-LAW OF MOSES WHO SAID TO GOD, "SHEW ME THY _____" (Exodus 33:18)
40 "Harness the _____ to the chariot" (Micah 1:13 NIV)
42 Discharges
44 Great Lake
45 Cars
47 Swelling
49 Manuscripts (abbr.)
50 Pictures
52 Prejudiced
54 Arbitrator (abbr.)
55 Theological degree (abbr.)
56 SAUL'S WIFE WAS THE MOTHER-IN-LAW OF DAVID WHOM GOD DELIVERED "OUT OF THE _____ OF THE LION, AND. . .THE BEAR" (1 Samuel 17:37)
59 "To renew them again. . .they crucify to themselves the Son of God _____" (Hebrews 6:6)
63 Insect stage
67 "Woe to _____. . .the city where David dwelt!" (Isaiah 29:1)
69 Garret
71 Young lady (slang)
72 "The voice of the LORD maketh the hinds to _____" (Psalm 29:9)
73 "Refuse to get involved in _____ discussions" (2 Timothy 2:22 MSG)
74 Sweater size (abbr.)
75 Tenth U.S. President
76 Florida Key
77 "_____, he did fly upon the wings of the wind" (Psalm 18:10)

DOWN

1 " 'You treat them like dirt, greeting them with lynch _____' " (Matthew 23:33 MSG)
2 River in Yorkshire, England
3 Plod
4 Military tank (abbr.)
5 Small marine fish whose males become "pregnant"
6 "IN THE LAND OF CANAAN. . . ABRAHAM _____ TO MOURN" FOR THE MOTHER-IN-LAW OF REBEKAH (Genesis 23:2)

7 Olive trees

8 ABRAHAM'S SERVANT SAID TO RACHEL'S FUTURE MOTHER-IN-LAW, "WHOSE DAUGHTER ART THOU? ____ ME, I PRAY" (Genesis 24:23)

9 Fastening

10 Age

11 "That ye may be found. . .without ____" (2 Peter 3:14)

12 "The tongue can no man ____" (James 3:8)

13 "He had bronze ____ armor on his legs and a bronze javelin across his shoulders" (1 Samuel 17:6 AMP)

21 Lout

23 Pollution watchdog (abbr.)

26 Two

28 "Pharaoh's daughter went down to the ____ to bathe" (Exodus 2:5 NIV)

29 Consume completely (2 words)

30 Under (poet.)

31 Plates in armor

32 JACOB HELPED ASENATH'S MOTHER-IN-LAW DRAW ____ (Genesis 29:10)

33 Standards

34 Ground grain

35 Village in Hungary

37 AFTER HER MOTHER-IN-LAW'S DEATH, TAMAR WAS TO RECEIVE THIS, AS PAYMENT FOR SERVICES RENDERED, FROM HER FATHER-IN-LAW (Genesis 38:17)

39 "She answered and said unto him, ____, Lord" (Mark 7:28)

41 Berth

43 "I held the two stone slabs high and threw them down, ____ them to bits" (Deuteronomy 9:15 MSG)

46 Thief

48 "The ____ of violence is in their hands" (Isaiah 59:6)

51 LEAH'S FUTURE MOTHER-IN-LAW "LIGHTED ____ THE CAMEL" WHEN SHE SAW ISAAC (Genesis 24:64)

53 Mischief maker

56 RUTH MADE A ____ WITH HER MOTHER-IN-LAW THAT SHE WOULD NOT LEAVE HER (Ruth 1:16)

57 Pre-Christian Armenians' god of war

58 THE FIRST MOTHER-IN-LAW WAS CREATED WHEN GOD SAID, "I ____ MAKE HIM AN HELP MEET FOR HIM" (Genesis 2:18)

60 "He wrote also letters to ____ on the Lord" (2 Chronicles 32:17)

61 Volcano in Sicily

62 Led the way to Jesus (Matthew 2:9)

64 REBEKAH'S MOTHER-IN-LAW WAS CERTAINLY NOT THIS (Genesis 12:14)

65 "She shall shave her head, and ____ her nails" (Deuteronomy 21:12)

66 Seaweed

68 THE WORLD'S FIRST MOTHER-IN-LAW

70 Top boss (abbr.)

215

Enough's Enough

Depending on the circumstances, extended family can take on a whole new meaning.

1. UEPRSCOI

2. TNFAIONU

3. UNYRLU

4. TSUECRPRI

5. IDUPMET

6. BEIDLR

7. RNDFEI

8. ATWNON

9. MBSMERE

In the Old Testament times, some men had one or more of these.

1. _ _ _ O _ _ _ _

2. _ O _ _ _ _ _ _

3. _ O _ _ _ _

4. _ O _ _ _ _ _ _

5. _ _ _ O _ _ _

6. O _ _ _ _ _

7. _ _ O _ _ _

8. _ _ O _ _ _

9. _ _ _ _ O _ _

Answer: _ _ _ _ _ _ _ _

Telephone Scramble
by Connie Troyer

Regarding Dorcas

God blesses women who are always looking out for others. Can you crack the telephone codes to find out more about Dorcas, a godly do-gooder?

| TUV 8 | ABC 2 | ABC 2 | GHI 4 | TUV 8 | GHI 4 | ABC 2 |

| JKL 5 | MNO 6 | PRS 7 | PRS 7 | ABC 2 |

| DEF 3 | GHI 4 | PRS 7 | ABC 2 | GHI 4 | PRS 7 | JKL 5 | DEF 3 |

| GHI 4 | DEF 3 | MNO 6 | DEF 3 | PRS 7 | MNO 6 | TUV 8 | PRS 7 |

| PRS 7 | DEF 3 | TUV 8 | DEF 3 | PRS 7 |

| MNO 6 | GHI 4 | PRS 7 | ABC 2 | ABC 2 | JKL 5 | DEF 3 |

| ABC 2 | JKL 5 | GHI 4 | TUV 8 | DEF 3 |

Acrostic
by Donna K. Maltese

Setting a Standard

Because of her father's rash vow, scholars believe this maiden was either committed to a life of celibacy or sacrificed to God. Either way, she never married. Solve this puzzle to learn more about this maiden who set a standard for all Israeli women.

Her grandmother was a prostitute or _____

___ ___ ___ ___ ___ ___
3 19 24 9 29 13

Her father was a _____

___ ___ ___ ___ ___
15 20 8 26 31

Vow

___ ___ ___ ___ ___ ___ ___
21 5 11 27 32 16 2

She greeted her father with timbrels and this (Judges 11:34)

___ ___ ___ ___ ___ ___
28 1 12 22 18 7

Number of months she bewailed her virginity (Judges 11:38)

___ ___ ___
6 14 23

Duties she never assumed

___ ___ ___ ___ ___ ___
10 4 25 30 33 17

19-12-28   32-13   10-1-16   19   22-20-7-6-29-27

32-12   4-7-24-1-30-9,   13-3-1-13   13-3-18

28-1-20-26-3-6-2-5-16   11-25   4-7-24-1-30-9   14-2-12-6

17-31-1-5-33-17   6-11   33-1-27-2-12-6   13-3-18

28-1-20-26-3-6-2-5   11-25   15-2-21-3-13-3-1-3   13-3-18

26-4-9-2-1-8-4-6-2   25-23-20-24   8-1-17-16   32-12   19

17-31-1-5.

JUDGES 11:39—40

Sudoku
by Sara Stoker

A Most Amazing Visit

EASY

	A	B	C	D	E	F	G	H	I
1	D	R	U		N			Y	A
2	Y	N	O					R	F
3	A			R	O	Y			
4		U			A		N		
5				F	R		D		
6	M		D			N			R
7	R	O	Y	U		A	F	N	D
8					R				O
9			N				R	M	Y

Hint: Column 4

"And the angel said unto her, Fear not, _____: for thou hast _____ favour with God" (Luke 1:30).

All Things Are Possible
HEBREWS 11:11

God's promises are no laughing matter. Solve this puzzle to discover the woman whose faith prevailed amid the improbable.

```
H   P   A   D   E   G   I   S   C   R   A   T
T   H   R   U   S   L   W   H   E   A   D   E
H   S   R   S   U   S   I   M   R   N   E   V
A   O   S   R   A   O   H   N   F   E   C   T
E   V   T   D   E   L   A   S   A   D   A   T
W   H   E   S   T   D   S   R   E   R   G   D
T   G   U   L   E   C   F   H   E   W   I   W
D   E   A   O   L   S   H   V   O   E   B   S
C   A   E   D   E   M   I   A   E   L   J   A
H   H   P   E   O   H   O   G   N   D   H   E
D       F   O       H   T   E   I   F   A   U
I           N           C   H   E       I   I
        F   S                   H
```

221

Crossword
by Sarah Lagerquist Simmons

Sisters-in-Law

The Old Testament swarms with sisters and sisters-in-law. One example is Abraham who married his sister; so technically Sarah was not only his wife, but his sister *and* sister-in-law. Solve this puzzle to uncover even more intricate webs of family ties—sister-in-law wise!

And yet indeed she is my sister; she is the daughter of my father, but not the daughter of my mother; and she became my wife.

GENESIS 20:12

ACROSS

1 Criminal
7 "Let us build us a _____" (Genesis 11:4)
11 "The strong shall be as _____" (Isaiah 1:31)
14 Relaxed soldiers stance (2 words)
15 "An half _____ of land, which a yoke of oxen might plow" (1 Samuel 14:14)
16 Period of time
17 Lymphoid tissue
18 Freshwater duck
19 ESAU'S SISTER-IN-LAW _____ UPON THE IDOLS SHE HAD TAKEN, TO HIDE THEM (Genesis 31:34)
20 Condiment
22 Eastward flowing river in Nebraska
24 Salutation
27 Tree found in Mexico
29 Person who colors fabric
30 ABRAHAM'S SERVANT GAVE JEWELS OF _____ TO JUDITH'S SISTER-IN-LAW (Genesis 24:53; 26:34)
32 Intimated
35 "When there were no _____, I was given birth" (Proverbs 8:24 NIV)
37 Town in Denmark
38 "They hatch cockatrice' eggs, and weave the spider's _____" (Isaiah 59:5)
41 ESAU'S SISTER-IN-LAW (Genesis 29)
42 City in Oregon
44 Height (abbr.)
45 "All Israel shouted. . .so that the earth _____ again" (1 Samuel 4:5)
48 "Just then someone, without _____, shot an arrow randomly into the crowd" (1 Kings 22:34 MSG)
49 Commander of a fleet
51 BOAZ SAID TO ORPAH'S SISTER-IN-LAW, "IT IS _____ THAT I AM THY NEAR KINSMAN" (Ruth 3:12)
52 "Then did they _____ in his face" (Matthew 26:67)
55 AARON'S SISTER-IN-LAW'S HUSBAND WAS GIVEN "TABLES OF STONE, AND A _____, AND COMMANDMENTS" (Exodus 24:12)
56 Morse code signal
57 Faker
60 Canine's cries
64 Dog group (abbr.)
65 Italian city
67 "You got an _____ of their. . .wood and stone, silver and gold junk-gods" (Deuteronomy 29:14 MSG)
71 "No one will so much as offer a cup of _____" (Jeremiah 16:5 MSG)
72 "People with a big head are headed for a fall, pretentious _____ brought down a peg" (Isaiah 2:11 MSG)
73 "They plotted to _____ Jesus in some sly way and kill him" (Matthew 26:4 NIV)
74 Computer keyboard key
75 ORPAH'S SISTER-IN-LAW (Ruth 1:4)
76 DAVID _____ THE VOICE OF ELIAB'S SOON-TO-BE SISTER-IN-LAW (1 Samuel 25:35)

DOWN

1 Grain
2 City in Japan
3 THE NUMBER OF CAMELS GIVEN WATER BY ISHMAEL'S SISTER-IN-LAW (Genesis 24:10)
4 Maiden
5 "We launched, meaning to sail by the coasts of _____" (Acts 27:2)
6 ESAU'S SISTER-IN-LAW MET HER HUSBAND-TO-BE BY A COVERED _____ (Genesis 29:1–6)

7 Indian bean

8 "He casteth forth his _____ like morsels: who can stand before his cold?" (Psalm 147:17)

9 SAUL USED ABIGAIL'S FUTURE SISTER-IN-LAW TO _____ DAVID (1 Samuel 18:21 NLV)

10 "They shall _____ as lions' whelps" (Jeremiah 51:38)

11 Irritable

12 Speak

13 MALCHIEL'S SISTER-IN-LAW GAVE SISERA MILK WHEN HE ASKED FOR _____, AND THEN KILLED HIM WHILE HE RESTED (Genesis 46:17; Judges 4)

21 "Take the _____ of the sons of Kohath from among the sons of Levi" (Numbers 4:2)

23 WHAT JACOB'S SISTER-IN-LAW SAID UPON THE BIRTH OF HER FIRSTBORN: "THE LORD SHALL _____ TO ME ANOTHER SON" (Genesis 30:24)

24 Israeli monetary unit

25 Uttered

26 "Behold my servant. . .mine _____, in whom my soul delighteth" (Isaiah 42:1)

28 PRIEST WHO PRAYED FOR PENINNAH'S SISTER-IN-LAW (1 Samuel 1:1–17)

31 Longer signal in Morse code

32 Religion of Ishmael's descendants

33 "Not that I have now attained [this _____], or have already been made perfect" (Philippians 3:12 AMP)

34 Toiletry case

36 Dolt

38 "He finds nothing _____ or misguided" (Titus 2:7 MSG)

39 Boredom

40 "Take ye wives, and _____ sons and daughters" (Jeremiah 29:6)

43 Universal time (abbr.)

46 Nix

47 Ashen

49 "I took the little book out of the angel's hand, and _____ it up" (Revelation 10:10)

50 "Stand in _____, and sin not" (Psalm 4:4)

52 Sudden rush

53 "Everyone _____ fun at me" (Psalm 22:6 MSG)

54 UNCLE TO JACOB'S SISTER-IN-LAW (Genesis 28:9)

58 Super (Ger.)

59 Brand of spaghetti sauce

61 ESAU'S OTHER SISTER-IN-LAW (Genesis 33:1)

62 "Its _____ is fire with much wood" (Isaiah 30:33 NJKV)

63 Withered

66 "Chooseth a tree that will not _____" (Isaiah 40:20)

68 "Jacob _____ the rest of Laban's flocks" (Genesis 30:36)

69 "They. . .could _____ both the right hand and the left" (1 Chronicles 12:2)

70 Express (abbr.)

223

The Woman at the Well
JOHN 4

CALL	MOUNTAIN
CITY	MUST
DEEP	PROPHET
DRAW	SAITH
EVERLASTING	SAT
FIVE	SIXTH
GIFT OF GOD	SPRINGING UP
GIVE ME TO DRINK	SYCHAR
HAD	THIRST
HEARD	THOU
HOUR	TOLD
HOW	WATER
HUSBANDS	WEARIED
JACOB'S	WELL
JESUS	WHO
LIFE	WOMAN OF SAMARIA
LIVING	WORSHIPPED
MEAT	

Word Search
by Marijane Troyer
(continued)

```
G  I  F  T  O  F  G  O  D  P  E  E  D  Y  W
I  T  T  T  H  I  R  S  T  U  W  F  Q  A  E
V  E  R  A  H  C  Y  S  D  O  H  A  I  F  A
E  H  L  I  V  I  N  G  H  N  O  R  V  L  R
M  P  M  O  U  N  T  A  I  N  A  P  U  Y  I
E  O  H  U  L  S  N  W  K  M  U  B  T  V  E
T  R  E  L  R  D  U  G  A  T  P  I  S  R  D
O  P  A  R  H  T  C  S  M  R  C  K  E  U  R
D  C  R  A  U  H  F  M  E  H  D  T  A  S  H
R  A  D  T  T  O  H  I  L  J  A  C  O  B  S
I  X  S  S  N  U  H  J  V  W  E  L  L  T  H
N  F  U  A  H  T  I  A  S  E  C  D  L  O  T
K  M  M  S  P  R  I  N  G  I  N  G  U  P  X
L  O  E  V  E  R  L  A  S  T  I  N  G  H  I
W  O  R  S  H  I  P  P  E  D  T  A  E  M  S
```

The Wives of Prophets

The events in a prophet's life—some happy, some sad—often gave the Israelites
an indication of Jerusalem's future. The following cryptoscriptures deal with
two prophets' wives. Can you break their codes?

CPN L RDPH WPHQ HUD BTQBUDHDMM; CPN

MUD JQPJDLFDN, CPN GCTD C MQP. HUDP

MCLN HUD EQTN HQ ID, JCEE ULM PCID

ICUDTMUCECEUCMUGCX.

YBJ BV GEJ, IQOBTK, U LEDQ EFER VHBG LOQQ

LOQ KQYUHQ BV LOUJQ QRQY FULO E YLHBDQ:

RQL JQULOQH YOETL LOBS GBSHJ JBH FQQN,

JQULOQH YOETT LOR LQEHY HSJ KBFJ.

Terrific Troublemakers

Many faithful, gracious women are described in scripture. And then there are those others who go down in history for their wicked acts. Can you figure out these three spotty headlines of the bad girls of the Bible?

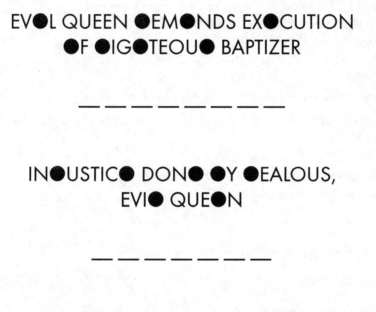

EV●L QUEEN ●EM●NDS EX●CUTION
●F ●IG●TEOU● BAPTIZER

— — — — — — —

IN●USTIC● DON● ●Y ●EALOUS,
EVI● QUE●N

— — — — — — —

WOM●N D●ES IN●T●NTLY FO● KEE●ING
●ROCEEDS IN LYING SC●EME

— — — — — — —

Acrostic
by Donna K. Maltese

An Ambitious Man's Wife

The wrong ambition can sometimes lead to fatal "hang-ups," as proven by the story of this wife who encouraged her husband to build a gallows. Crack this acrostic's code to discover the name of this woman and her ruthless spouse.

This Jew would not bow down to the ambitious man

___ ___ ___ ___ ___ ___ ___ ___
10 20   8   32 27 22   1   15

Lack of the Jew's respect made the ambitious man ____

___ ___ ___ ___ ___
26 14 21 30   6

The name of Ahasuerus's second queen

___ ___ ___ ___ ___ ___
2   18 28   4   12 23

The queen prepared this for the ambitious man

___ ___ ___ ___ ___
3   19 24 11 29

Drink served at the queen's banquet

___ ___ ___ ___
17 25   7   13

Fifty cubits high was the ____ of the gallows

___ ___ ___ ___
9   5   16 31

7-19-21-19-23-28-4-19-26-19-9-9   4-1-10-1-7

8-12-3-8-1-15-7-12-6   4-30-10-18-2-26-3:   24-7-32

17-4-13-7   4-27   22-1-10-27   4-20-10-2,   4-27

18-2-7-29   24-7-32   22-1-26-26-2-6   3-20-8   4-5-11

3-23-14-2-7-6-18,   24-7-32   16-31-8-31-18-4   4-5-11   1

7-25-3-2.

ESTHER 5:10

Crossword

by Sarah Lagerquist Simmons

Women in Jesus' Family Tree

Although the New Testament mostly notes the paternal branches of Jesus' family tree, His male ancestors couldn't have borne fruit without their female counterparts. Here's a puzzle that highlights the many women that played a role in Jesus' descent. If you just take the clues a "line" at a time, you'll "be getting" them all!

The family tree of Jesus Christ, David's son, Abraham's son.
MATTHEW 1:1 MSG

1 Salesmen (abbr.)
5 Store
9 Piling
14 Main stem
15 Water (Sp.)
16 GREAT-GRANDMOTHER OF JUDAH, OF WHOSE TRIBE JESUS CAME FROM (Genesis 17:15; Matthew 1:1–2)
17 "Even the _____ went in after the blade, and the fat closed over the blade" (Judges 3:22 NKJV)
18 Program training college students to be officers (abbr.)
19 "Three things _____ me, no, four things I'll never understand" (Proverbs 30:18 MSG)
20 Southern U.S. state (abbr.)
21 Card game: Crazy _____
23 "In the morning they are like grass which sprouts _____" (Psalm 90:5 NASB)
24 "Lest peradventure mischief _____ him" (Genesis 42:4)
26 "They which lead thee cause thee to _____" (Isaiah 3:12)
28 "A _____ tongue brings angry looks" (Proverbs 25:23 NIV)
29 WOMAN WHO ATE FROM THE _____ IN THE GARDEN WAS ALSO THE FIRST WOMAN IN JESUS' FAMILY TREE (Luke 3:38)
31 Fleet commander (abbr.)
34 Feelers
37 "Samson went and caught three hundred _____" (Judges 15:4)
39 ABRAHAM HAD TWO SONS—ONE BORN OF A SLAVE WOMAN, THE OTHER, OF A _____ WOMAN IN JESUS' FAMILY TREE (Galatians 4:22–31)
40 "Abimelech took an _____ in his hand" (Judges 9:48)
41 "I will requite thee in this _____" (2 Kings 9:26)
42 Unit of length (var.)
44 Seasoning (2 words)
47 Coney

48 Infusions
50 Geological time period
51 Hovercraft (abbr.)
52 Substitute
56 Room-cooling system (abbr.)
58 "He maketh the devices of the people of none _____" (Psalm 33:10)
62 Thousand
63 "God can do anything. . .far more than you could ever imagine or _____" (Ephesians 3:20 MSG)
66 JUDAH'S MOTHER (Matthew 1:3)
67 Utah's state flower: _____ lily
68 ALTHOUGH NOT A BLOOD TIE TO JESUS, BATHSHEBA'S FORMER HUSBAND, _____, IS MENTIONED IN JESUS' FAMILY TREE (Matthew 1:6 NKJV)
69 "Jacob shall return, and be in rest and at _____" (Jeremiah 46:27)
70 Support
71 "Wild animals will like it just fine, filling the vacant houses with _____ night sounds" (Isaiah 13:21 MSG)
72 "Egyptian magicians did the same things by their secret _____" (Exodus 7:22 NIV)
73 JESUS' MOTHER

DOWN
1 HARLOT FROM JERICHO WHO IS MENTIONED IN JESUS' FAMILY TREE (Matthew 1:5 NIV)
2 "The captive _____ hasteneth that he may be loosed" (Isaiah 51:14)
3 Rice dish
4 Aircraft that flies faster than the speed of sound
5 Actress Monroe
6 "The whole earth was _____, gaping at the Beast" (Revelation 13:3 MSG)
7 MOABITE WOMAN IN JESUS' FAMILY TREE (Matthew 1:5)
8 Diplomacy

9 Administers OASDI benefits (abbr.)
10 WOMAN IN JESUS' FAMILY TREE WHO PRETENDED TO BE A HARLOT TO HAVE CHILDREN (Matthew 1:3 NJKV)
11 Formerly Persia
12 "How long are you going to _____ around doing nothing?" (Proverbs 6:9 MSG)
13 Well-developed muscle
21 She (Fr.)
22 "Ye shall _____ my face no more" (Genesis 44:23)
25 Flower
27 Judge (abbr.)
29 Hacks
30 "The earth shall _____ to and fro like a drunkard" (Isaiah 24:20)
31 Spindle
32 WHEN ABIMELECH TOOK THIS ANCESTRESS OF JESUS, GOD CAME TO HIM IN A DREAM AND SAID, "THOU ART BUT A _____ MAN" (Genesis 20:3)
33 Time zone in U.S.
34 "His descendants settled in the _____ from Havilah to Shur" (Genesis 25:18 NIV)
35 "Let the wicked fall into their own _____" (Psalm 141:10)
36 Nothing (Sp.)
38 "The LORD _____ the eyes of the blind" (Psalm 146:8 NJKV)
39 Highly contagious viral disease among cattle and pigs (abbr.)

43 And so on (abbr.)
45 Blood suckers
46 "Two of every _____ shalt thou bring into the ark" (Genesis 6:19)
49 THE NAME OF THE FIRST WOMAN IN JESUS' FAMILY TREE
51 South American palm
53 One-celled protozoa (var.)
54 "You can tame a _____, but you can't tame a tongue" (James 3:7 MSG)
55 Polish money
56 Malady
57 "Yet could he not heal you, nor _____ you of your wound" (Hosea 5:13)
59 "After whom dost thou pursue? after a dead dog, after a _____" (1 Samuel 24:14)
60 IN ANNOUNCING JESUS' BIRTH, THE ANGEL GABRIEL SAID TO JESUS' MOTHER, "_____ NOT" (Luke 1:30)
61 JACOB JOURNEYED "INTO THE LAND OF THE PEOPLE OF THE _____" (Genesis 29:1) TO FIND HIS BRIDE, ANOTHER WOMAN IN JESUS' FAMILY TREE (Matthew 1:2)
64 Norse goddess
65 THE WOMAN OF 49 DOWN WAS SO NAMED "BECAUSE _____ WAS THE MOTHER OF ALL LIVING" (Genesis 3:20)
67 Book following Ruth (abbr.)

Highly Favored
Luke 1:29–31, 38

And **when** she saw him, she was **troubled** at his **saying**, and **cast** in her **mind what manner** of **salutation** this **should** be. And the angel said unto her, **Fear** not, Mary: for thou hast **found favour** with God. And, behold, **thou** shalt **conceive** in thy **womb**, and **bring forth** a son, and **shalt call** his **name Jesus**. . . . And **Mary said, Behold** the **handmaid** of the **Lord**; be it unto me **according** to thy **word**. And the **angel departed** from her.

```
N  M  L  B  E  H  O  L  D  Q  T  K  B  M  X
E  O  I  W  G  J  M  E  F  C  A  L  L  X  D
D  V  I  N  O  M  T  W  B  I  T  N  A  Z  I
D  R  I  T  D  R  U  O  V  A  F  S  E  H  T
M  R  A  E  A  I  D  U  G  X  D  D  A  H  S
B  H  T  P  C  T  P  F  N  D  N  N  O  C  N
W  A  E  R  C  N  U  F  I  N  D  U  K  E  F
F  D  B  M  O  W  O  L  Y  M  F  O  D  O  J
D  I  A  S  R  U  O  C  A  J  D  F  R  D  Y
V  R  R  U  D  W  B  I  S  S  E  T  O  E  W
Y  B  B  A  I  H  D  L  U  O  H  S  L  Z  S
M  M  A  N  N  E  R  M  E  K  T  N  U  X  S
A  O  O  G  G  N  A  M  E  D  P  B  D  S  P
J  V  K  E  D  D  E  E  I  Q  Q  K  U  P  Z
U  U  Z  L  Z  U  F  C  K  A  I  V  L  T  E
```

An Adorning Wife

This woman, whose name means "adornment," is the second female named in the Bible. Solve to discover her nomenclature and that of her firstborn, along with the latter's occupation.

Lamech was her _____

$\overline{3} \quad \overline{16} \quad \overline{30} \quad \overline{22} \quad \overline{12} \quad \overline{25} \quad \overline{6}$

Methusael was her husband's _____

$\overline{26} \quad \overline{1} \quad \overline{15} \quad \overline{21} \quad \overline{2} \quad \overline{11}$

Her husband was a descendent of this man, Eve's firstborn

$\overline{19} \quad \overline{28} \quad \overline{9} \quad \overline{14}$

The name of her son, the musician

$\overline{17} \quad \overline{27} \quad \overline{8} \quad \overline{20} \quad \overline{7}$

The number of sons she bore

$\overline{5} \quad \overline{13} \quad \overline{24}$

She was one of two _____

$\overline{10} \quad \overline{18} \quad \overline{29} \quad \overline{23} \quad \overline{4}$

28-14-6   12-6-12-21   22-1-11-23   17-12-8-12-7:

3-2   10-20-30   15-3-2   26-1-5-3-2-11   24-26

4-16-19-21   20-30   6-13-23-7-7   9-25   15-2-25-15-4,

28-14-6   24-26   4-27-19-21   20-30   3-1-29-2

19-1-5-5-7-2.

GENESIS 4:20

Anagram
by Paul Kent

Widows

In Bible times, widows lived especially hard lives—but God was always faithful to His own. Can you solve these three anagrams relating to Bible widows? Hint: You may be looking for names, hometowns, or other details.

Zap her hat

_ _ _ _ _ _ _ _ _

Swim tote

_ _ _   _ _ _ _ _

Hard mountain

_ _ _ _   _ _ _   _ _ _ _ _

A Bitter Woman
RUTH 1:20

In the midst of tribulation, God is still working to fill our lives. Work this puzzle to find the woman who was once bitter and later blessed.

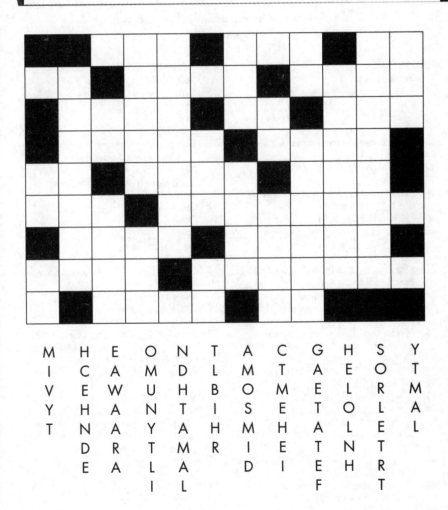

Crossword
by Sarah Lagerquist Simmons

Crowning Qualities of Womanhood

A woman with a good head on her shoulders is a blessing to her husband. As you solve this puzzle, you'll discover what qualities she must have in order to make her man feel like a king.

A virtuous woman is a crown to her husband.
PROVERBS 12:4

ACROSS
1 Semitic people
6 Cough for attention
10 Talk
14 "He called for his _____. 'Get rid of this woman' " (2 Samuel 13:17 MSG)
15 Stage between larvae and adult
16 Stupid (var.)
17 Musical composition
18 Chieftain
19 "When you get on each other's nerves. . . don't _____ at each other" (1 Thessalonians 5:14 MSG)
20 "Peter remembered how Jesus had made the _____ to him" (Mark 14:72 NASB)
22 Organization that defends individual liberties (abbr.)
24 " 'He searches the farthest recesses for _____ in the blackest darkness' " (Job 28:3 NIV)
25 "He had no _____ with her until she gave birth to a son" (Matthew 1:25 NIV)
27 Lifeless
29 A WISE WIFE HONORS HER _____
32 Fall month (abbr.)
33 Insect discussed in Proverbs
34 Eating regimens
37 "Skin or sack, whatever _____ it is. . . must be put in water" (Leviticus 11:32 NKJV)
41 "If my _____ hath turned out of the way" (Job 31:7)
43 "_____ not liberty for an occasion to the flesh" (Galatians 5:13)
44 OLDER WOMEN MUST TEACH YOUNGER WOMEN TO _____ THEIR HUSBANDS (Titus 2:4)

45 WIVES ARE COMMANDED TO BE "KEEPERS AT _____" (Titus 2:5)
46 " 'You, however, _____ me with lies' " (Job 13:4 NIV)
48 To a _____
49 Copy (abbr.)
51 Openwork embroidery
54 "The LORD smelled a soothing _____" (Genesis 8:21 NKJV)
56 "_____ there is no vision, the people perish" (Proverbs 29:18)
57 Grunt
58 Constellation
60 Caller
64 He _____ the line
66 Make over
68 Genus of plant in the Verbena family
69 Affected
70 "Now the men took this as an _____" (1 Kings 20:33 NASB)
71 Catcher of snakelike fish
72 "But what I _____, that do I" (Romans 7:15)
73 THIS KIND OF WOMAN BUILDS HER HOUSE (Proverbs 14:1)
74 Monotone

DOWN
1 Attest
2 "The price for his release is to be based on the _____ paid to a hired man" (Leviticus 25:50 NIV)
3 Potash _____
4 Plaster
5 Breast bones
6 Parrot
7 "There were certain men who were defiled by a _____ corpse" (Numbers 9:6 NKJV)

8 Long story
9 Saltwater game fishes
10 Today's albums (abbr.)
11 "A GRACIOUS WOMAN RETAINS ____" (Proverbs 11:16 NKJV)
12 "The LORD hath set ____ him that is godly" (Psalms 4:3)
13 "Adam. . .is a ____ of Him who was to come" (Romans 5:14 NKJV)
21 CHARACTERISTIC OF A GODLY WOMAN
23 Card game
26 Hatred
28 A VIRTUOUS WOMAN DOES HER HUSBAND NO ____ (Proverbs 31:12)
29 "God will make ____ of these squatters, send them packing for good" (Psalm 53:5 MSG)
30 THE PROVERBS 31 WOMAN MAKES CLOTHING AND DELIVERS THEM ____ A MERCHANT (Proverbs 31:24)
31 "There shall come forth. . .out of the ____ of Jesse" (Isaiah 11:1)
35 Compass point (abbr.)
36 OLDER WOMEN NEED TO ____ YOUNGER WOMEN TO BE GODLY (Titus 2:4)
38 Dorothy's dog

39 "So shall we ____ be with the LORD" (1 Thessalonians 4:17)
40 WOMEN ARE TO ADORN THEMSELVES WITH THIS KIND OF SPIRIT (1 Peter 3:4)
42 But (Sp.)
46 "Yea, the ____ hath found a house" (Psalm 84:3)
47 Regretted
50 System for measuring electricity and magnetism (abbr.)
52 Three-legged
53 THE VIRTUOUS WOMAN WAS A ____ OF SILK AND PURPLE (Proverbs 31:22)
54 Greek marketplace
55 Scarlett's husband
56 Walks through water
57 New Mexico's neighbor
59 Partially
61 Inventory accounting term
62 "____ a child is known by his doings" (Proverbs 20:11)
63 A VIRTUOUS WOMAN IS ____
65 Color
67 "Hear, O Israel: The LORD our God is ____" (Deuteronomy 6:4)

Moses' Mother
Exodus 1–2, 6; Hebrews 11:23; Numbers 26:59

AARON	LEVI
AMRAM	MAID
ARK	MIRIAM
BRINK	MONTHS
BULRUSHES	MOSES
CHILD	MOTHER
COMMANDMENT	NURSE
CONCEIVED	PARENTS
DAUBED	PITCH
DAUGHTER	PROPER
EGYPT	SISTER
FAITH	SLIME
FLAGS	SON
HID	THREE
GOODLY	WATER
JOCHEBED	WOMAN

```
M  O  S  E  S  M  R  M  A  R  K  Q  U  T  H
O  P  E  D  R  O  D  I  N  S  Z  U  P  C  E
N  O  R  A  A  N  L  J  A  H  L  U  T  H  D
E  S  R  U  N  T  C  O  N  C  E  I  V  E  D
G  O  G  G  N  H  X  C  C  M  P  K  M  R  J
O  C  T  H  P  S  U  H  M  I  S  B  Z  E  O
O  H  V  T  R  B  I  E  A  X  E  G  Y  P  T
D  I  Y  E  O  D  R  B  R  Y  H  T  I  A  F
L  L  S  R  P  M  E  E  M  L  S  T  T  R  O
Y  D  O  W  E  O  T  D  A  I  U  H  B  E  K
Q  U  N  S  R  T  A  N  S  V  R  P  T  N  W
R  X  D  C  V  H  W  T  M  E  L  I  I  T  O
A  W  I  S  D  E  E  L  E  L  U  R  A  S  M
S  G  A  L  F  R  R  D  A  U  B  E  D  M  A
C  O  M  M  A  N  D  M  E  N  T  Z  E  I  N
```

Drop Two
by Dorothy Pryse

Mary Is Chosen
LUKE 1:27

When the angel Gabriel came to town, he headed straight for Joseph's fiancé. Solve this drop two to figure out the phrase describing the woman to whom Gabriel made a startling proclamation.

SCALING	Hold fast	_____	1. ___ ___
NEUTRON	Highway	_____	2. ___ ___
DECADAL	Sticker	_____	3. ___ ___
TRAMPED	Removed skin	_____	4. ___ ___
HEARTED	Business	_____	5. ___ ___
ENDWAYS	Light brown	_____	6. ___ ___
AVAILED	Felt ill	_____	7. ___ ___
ISLAMIC	Demand	_____	8. ___ ___
ROSTRUM	Pull out of bed	_____	9. ___ ___
GREAVES	Work for	_____	10. ___ ___
IGNORAL	Over the length	_____	11. ___ ___
NASTILY	Not heads	_____	12. ___ ___

___ ___ ___ ___ ___ ___ ___ ___ ___ ___ ___ ___

1   2   3   4   5   6   7   8   9   10   11   12

Cryptoscripture
by Sharon Y. Brown

Womanly Advice

They say beauty is only skin deep. Crack these cryptoscripture codes to find proverbs that support this "admirable" adage.

VTRZBW QP GOSOQUVBD, TEG IOTBUM QP

RTQE: IBU T FZNTE UATU VOTWOUA UAO

DZWG, PAO PATDD IO CWTQPOG.

L DGBKTFTN YFHLU GN L PBFYU KF ZOB

ZTNCLUJ: CTK NZO KZLK HLAOKZ LNZLHOJ GN

LN BFKKOUUONN GU ZGN CFUON.

Acrostic
by Donna K. Maltese

A Woman of Vision

Pilate's wife was definitely a woman of vision. Solve this puzzle to learn what message she sent to her husband during an extremely crucial period in history.

Her husband's title

—— —— —— —— —— —— —— ——
11 19 27 31 35 8 16 23

Pilate sat on this seat

—— —— —— —— —— —— —— ——
18 21 32 28 3 6 15 1

Jesus _____ before Pilate

—— —— —— —— ——
34 29 14 9 25

The crowd quickly turned into this

—— —— ——
13 22 26

Pilate did _____ his hands

—— —— —— ——
24 7 2 5

Her husband ordered his men to _____ Christ

—— —— —— —— —— —— ——
10 30 17 33 4 12 20

5-4-2   24-4-12-6   34-31-15-29   21-15-29-14

5-4-13,   34-7-20-4-8-28,   5-7-27-31   1-5-16-17

8-22-1-5-4-8-11   29-9   32-9   24-4-1-5   1-5-7-1

18-21-34-29   3-7-15:   12-19-23   4   5-7-27-31

34-17-12-12-6-35-6-25   3-7-15-20   1-5-4-8-11-34

1-5-4-2   25-7-20   4-8   7   32-30-6-7-13

26-6-10-7-21-2-6   9-12   5-4-3.

MATTHEW 27:19

Crossword
by Sarah Lagerquist Simmons

A Good Woman Is Hard to Find

They say a good woman is hard to find, but there are plenty in the Bible and a few featured in this crossword. Have fun solving this puzzle and tracking down those first-class females—who may never have had a "cross word"!

Now there was at Joppa a certain disciple named Tabitha,
which by interpretation is called Dorcas: this woman was
full of good works and almsdeeds which she did.

ACTS 9:36

ACROSS

1 "My _____ are many" (Lamentations 1:22)
6 Type of carpet
10 Winglike
14 Pentateuch
15 "Back to that old rule-keeping, _____-pleasing religion would be an abandonment" (Galatians 2:21 MSG)
16 "The land was _____, and quiet" (1 Chronicles 4:40)
17 Jesus' death did _____ for our sins
18 Italian coin
19 TIMOTHY'S GRANDMOTHER, SPOKEN HIGHLY OF BY PAUL (2 Timothy 1:5)
20 Gape
21 Collisions followed by rebounds
23 "He shall pluck my feet out of the _____" (Psalm 25:15)
24 BECAUSE OF ABIGAIL'S WISDOM, DAVID WENT _____ AND DID NOT HARM HER OR HER HUSBAND (1 Samuel 25)
26 Married woman
28 Waiter at a drive-in restaurant
31 Hack
32 Rhea
33 SHE RISKED HER OWN LIFE TO SAVE HER PEOPLE
36 Upon
40 "He makes my feet like the feet of _____" (2 Samuel 22:34 NKJV)
42 A wife is supposed to be as a pleasant _____ (Proverbs 5:19)
43 " 'So, how long are you going to _____ over Saul?' " (1 Samuel 16:1 MSG)
44 "All the _____ of the world" (Psalm 22:27)
45 Lassoer
48 " 'Get up, take your _____ and go home' " (Matthew 9:6 NIV)

49 "They _____, but the [Holy] Spirit remains the same" (1 Corinthians 12:4 AMP)
51 "You will speak from the ground; your speech will _____ out of the dust" (Isaiah 29:4 NIV)
53 LYDIA, A SELLER OF _____ CLOTH, GAVE HOSPITALITY TO PAUL AND SILAS (Acts 16)
56 Life
57 One (Sp.)
58 Thrashed
61 Movie: *Saving Private* _____
65 "His violent dealing shall come down upon his own _____" (Psalm 7:16)
67 River that runs through France and Germany
68 Pack or stow cargo
69 "I will make your heaven as _____, and your earth as brass" (Leviticus 26:19)
70 "He who hurries his footsteps _____" (Proverbs 19:2 NASB)
71 Siamese natives
72 "Let them sing praises to Him with timbrel and _____" (Psalm 149:3 NASB).
73 Eye infection
74 " 'Keep a distance of about a thousand _____ between you and the ark' " (Joshua 3:4 NIV)

DOWN

1 THE SHUNAMMITE WOMAN MADE A PLACE FOR ELISHA TO _____ (2 Kings 4)
2 Jot
3 THE VIRTUOUS WOMAN BOUGHT A FIELD TO _____ A VINEYARD IN (Proverbs 31:16)
4 THIS WOMAN GAVE HER FIRSTBORN SON TO THE LORD (1 Samuel 1:11, 20)
5 "_____ shall be called Woman" (Genesis 2:23)

6 Bevel

7 Isaac was Abraham's ____

8 Relating to aircraft (abbr.)

9 " 'The ____ is clear: God says, "I am—not was—the God of Abraham" ' " (Matthew 22:29 MSG)

10 " 'His master shall pierce his ear with an ____' " (Exodus 21:6 NKJV)

11 "They were stronger than ____" (2 Samuel 1:23)

12 Good-bye

13 "He made narrowed ____ round about" (1 Kings 6:6)

21 " 'You shall make ____ for them, for glory and for beauty' " (Exodus 28:40 NASB)

22 "Noah was ____ hundred years old when the flood of waters was upon the earth" (Genesis 7:6)

25 "____ to thee, Moab!" (Numbers 21:29)

27 Former name of Thailand

28 Surrender

29 "And all the people shall say, ____" (Deuteronomy 27:16)

30 Lamented

31 "God said, 'Let the water ____ with living creatures' " (Genesis 1:20 NIV)

34 Ilium

35 "____ dreadful is this place!" (Genesis 28:17)

37 Sarah's ____ is a cave in the field of Machpelah (Genesis 23:19)

38 Gem

39 Nickname for the disciple who denied Jesus three times

41 Reply

45 Wrinkles

46 "God has ascended ____ shouts of joy" (Psalm 47:5 NIV)

47 "I went down to the orchard of ____ trees" (Song of Solomon 6:11 NASB)

50 "Rejoice with ____ the heart" (Zephaniah 3:14)

52 SISTER WHO FED JESUS

53 MARY WAS A ____ OF JESUS; SHE SAT AT HIS FEET

54 Single element

55 Stator

56 "Jesus wept" (John 11:35) is the Bible's shortest ____

59 Store

60 WOMAN WHO BORE THE MESSIAH

62 "His parents went to Jerusalem every ____ at the feast of the Passover" (Luke 2:41)

63 Enthusiastic

64 Headland

66 Chemical suffix

68 Pigpen

247

Regarding Lydia

The first Christian convert in Europe was a woman named Lydia. Decipher the telephone codes below to find out more about this "first lady" of faith.

| PRS 7 | TUV 8 | PRS 7 | PRS 7 | JKL 5 | DEF 3 |

| TUV 8 | GHI 4 | WXY 9 | ABC 2 | TUV 8 | GHI 4 | PRS 7 | ABC 2 |

| MNO 6 | DEF 3 | PRS 7 | ABC 2 | GHI 4 | ABC 2 | MNO 6 | TUV 8 |

| ABC 2 | DEF 3 | JKL 5 | GHI 4 | DEF 3 | TUV 8 | DEF 3 | PRS 7 |

| PRS 7 | ABC 2 | TUV 8 | JKL 5 |

| ABC 2 | ABC 2 | PRS 7 | TUV 8 | GHI 4 | QZ 0 | DEF 3 | DEF 3 |

| ABC 2 | JKL 5 | MNO 6 | TUV 8 | GHI 4 |

All She Wanted

EASY

	A	B	C	D	E	F	G	H	I
1			K	E	G		A		
2	I			N		S	B		K
3	E				A	K			G
4	B			S		G	H	A	
5		K	A	H	B	E		S	N
6	H				I				
7			N	G			E	B	
8	A	H			E	I			
9		G		B	N	A	K		

Hint: Row 7

"And _____ Solomon gave unto the queen of _____ all her desire, whatsoever she asked, beside that which Solomon gave her of his royal bounty" (1 Kings 10:13).

Virtuous Woman
Proverbs 31:10–31

BLESSED
BRINGETH
BUYETH
CLOTHING
CONSIDERETH
EXCELLEST
FOOD
GOOD
HEART
HER
HONOUR
HOUSEHOLD
KINDNESS
LINEN
MAKETH
MERCHANDISE

PERCEIVETH
PLANTETH
PURPLE
REJOICE
RUBIES
SCARLET
SELLETH
SILK
SPINDLE
STRENGTH
VINEYARD
VIRTUOUS
WILLINGLY
WISDOM
WORKETH

```
S W I S D O M R M O E A L H E
P S V C H A E S E B U Y E T H
I T I C K H M X R R U B I E S
N E R E O P E R C E I V E T H
D S T R E N G T H E D K W N W
L H U L F W S K A K L I E A O
E S O D E O G I N H L L D L R
C E U O E V O N D L O L E P K
I L S O H S I D I E O N O S E
O L O G J P S N S H R U O Q T
J E J T U F G E E I L E B U H
E T Z R H L F S L Y L I T Q R
R H P A Y I U S A B A K N H V
Z L J E F O N K S C A R L E T
E D T H H T E G N I R B D B N
```

by Donna K. Maltese

A Promise-Breaker's Daughter

This princess could have been a queen, except for her father's reneging on a promise. Crack the code to discover her name and those of her immediate family.

Name of Israel's first king's wife and this princess's mother
(1 Samuel 14:50)

__ __ __ __ __ __ __
20 32 27 12 24 2 16

This princess was to marry David, Israel's ____ king

__ __ __ __ __ __
31 11 25 22 3 15

Her brother gave David this (1 Samuel 18:4)

__ __ __
19 5 34

What her father felt toward David

__ __ __ __ __ __ __ __
30 10 36 33 28 23 6 17

David ____ Philistines for her hand

__ __ __ __ __ __
9 14 35 18 4 8

She was given to this man instead of David (1 Samuel 18:19)

__ __ __ __ __ __
13 29 7 26 1 21

12-24-34   8-4-1   6-28-12-6   5-9   6-20-35-21

34-11-7-11   30-22-12-20-8-32-20-12,   2-3-15

26-6-32-23-26,   2-3-15   16-1-33-25-4-26-6-4-35-36:

2-3-15   8-4-1   12-13-16-10-6   5-9   4-27-6   8-34-5

29-36-23-18-4-8-1-7-6   34-11-7-11   8-4-1-6-1;   8-4-1

12-13-16-10   5-9   8-4-1   9-27-7-6-8-19-14-7-3

16-1-7-20-19,   2-3-15   8-4-1   12-13-16-10   5-9   8-4-1

17-14-23-3-18-1-7   16-27-25-32-20-21.

1 SAMUEL 14:49

Women Who Suffered

"Trials and tribulations" the Bible calls them—those hard experiences we all go through from time to time. Can you solve these spotty headlines to uncover three biblical women who really suffered?

M●THER RETURNS HO●E AFTER
YE●RS OF A●GU●SH

— — — — —

●OM HE●RS C●OWD SHOUT "CRUCIF●"!

— — — —

SURRO●ATE MOTHE● CH●SED
AW●Y FROM ●OME

— — — — —

Favorable Hospitality

Under stress, sibling rivalry can occasionally rear its ugly head.

1. SEEKEMNS

2. RPEACILU

3. ROSIAV

4. RAINSGAYE

5. SAMETSITARG

6. CREGA

7. ROVEL

8. ROETHX

9. NADH

10. READPEAP

They were always ready to have Jesus as their guest.

1. ◯ _ _ _ _ _ _ _

2. _ _ _ _ _ _ ◯ _

3. _ _ _ _ _ ◯

4. _ _ _ _ _ _ ◯ _ _

5. ◯ _ _ _ _ _ _ _ _ _

6. _ _ ◯ _ _

7. _ _ _ _ ◯

8. _ _ _ _ _ ◯

9. ◯ _ _ _

10. _ _ _ _ ◯ _ _ _

Answer: _ _ _ _ _ and _ _ _ _ _ _ _

Crossword
by Sarah Lagerquist Simmons

Behind Every Man. . .

It is said that behind every man is a good woman. Whether this is true or not depends, of course, on the individual makeup of each man and woman and their relationship to God. Have fun solving this puzzle, which includes the good and the bad of both the sexes.

For as the woman is of the man, even so is the man also by the woman; but all things of God.
1 Corinthians 11:12

ACROSS

1 A GOOD WOMAN _____ GOODNESS TO HER HUSBAND'S LIFE
5 "The stones of the wall will cry out, and the beams of the woodwork will _____ it" (Habakkuk 2:11 NIV)
9 "He had bronze _____ armor on his legs and a bronze javelin across his shoulders" (1 Samuel 17:6 AMP)
13 "So she wove it tightly with the batten of the _____" (Judges 16:14 NKJV)
14 BEHIND THIS MAN WAS A VERY WICKED WOMAN (1 Kings 16:30–31)
15 Egyptian city
16 Mentor
17 Place to store grain
18 BEFORE MARRYING BOAZ'S DAD, RAHAB HID JOSHUA'S SPIES "WITH THE STALKS OF FLAX, WHICH SHE HAD LAID IN _____ UPON THE ROOF" (Joshua 2:6)
19 THIS WOMAN WAS MARRIED FIRST TO ONE WICKED MAN AND THEN ONE GODLY MAN (1 Samuel 25:39)
21 Volcano
23 And so on (abbr.)
24 Drafter and publisher of U.S. law restatements (abbr.)
25 Prickly (prefix)
29 "I will melt them, and _____ them" (Jeremiah 9:7)
30 WOMAN BEHIND ISRAEL (Genesis 30:17)
32 River in Portugal
33 Remove cover
36 "Weep for my people's gardens and _____" (Isaiah 32:13 MSG)
37 ISAAC LOVED _____ WIFE AT FIRST SIGHT
38 _____ Basin, a coal-producing region in W. Germany
39 States of unconsciousness
40 Weighted average of rates of interest on deposit accounts (abbr.)

41 Certifier of radiologists (abbr.)
42 Supports
43 " 'Who _____ open the doors of his mouth. . . with his fearsome teeth?' " (Job 41:14 NIV)
44 " _____ those loudmouthed liars who heckle me" (Psalm 31:14 MSG)
45 Warren Beatty film based on the life of communist John Reed
46 "Their _____ calveth, and casteth not her calf" (Job 21:10)
47 Married in secret
49 Cry for help (abbr.)
50 Measurement (abbr.)
53 "God caused a deep sleep to fall _____ Adam" (Genesis 2:21)
55 SECOND WIFE BEHIND MAN WHO WAS ALSO A FRIEND OF GOD (Genesis 25:1)
57 Capital of Ghana
60 Nisan
62 Worth of virtuous woman far above one of these jewels (Proverbs 31:10)
63 Tall and thin
64 Capital of Vanuatu
65 "FOR THE LORD SHALL _____ SISERA INTO THE HAND OF A WOMAN" (Judges 4:9)
66 "Give me children, or _____ I die" (Genesis 30:1)
67 "They shall _____ as lions' whelps" (Jeremiah 51:38)
68 "The whole _____ surrounding the mountaintop is most holy" (Ezekiel 43:12 NKJV)

DOWN

1 Seaweed
2 "Wherefore didst thou _____?" (Matthew 14:31)
3 Dialect of Ancient Greek
4 "I'm no longer _____ in my sin" (Psalm 38:18 MSG)
5 "Lay aside every weight. . .which doth so _____ beset us" (Hebrews 12:1)

6 Bean dish

7 Salt (prefix)

8 Woodwind

9 WOMAN BEHIND A MAN OF GREAT FAITH (Genesis 17:15)

10 RACHEL ____ HER IDOLS TO KEEP THEM FROM BEING FOUND (Genesis 31:34)

11 Rage

12 "There shall neither be earing ____ harvest" (Genesis 45:6)

15 Shells used as horns

20 Seniors' association (abbr.)

22 "He sees chariots with ____ of horses" (Isaiah 21:7 NIV)

26 Watery, acrid discharge from a wound

27 ATHALIAH, THE WICKED WIFE OF JORAM, WAS KILLED SOON AFTER SHE HEARD THE ____ OF THE PEOPLE IN THE TEMPLE OF THE LORD (2 Kings 11:13)

28 "Hot sands will become a cool ____" (Isaiah 35:7 MSG)

29 "She got him a wicker basket and covered it over with ____ and pitch" (Exodus 2:3 NASB)

30 "Ten virgins. . .took their ____" (Matthew 25:1)

31 Ages

33 Customs

34 THIS MAN'S WIFE SAVED HIS LIFE, BY PUTTING HERS ON THE LINE (1 Samuel 25)

35 "There the ship was to unload her ____" (Acts 21:3 NKJV)

36 ABIGAIL BROUGHT ____ TO APPEASE HER FUTURE HUSBAND FOR HER THEN HUSBAND'S STUPIDITY (1 Samuel 25:18)

39 Belief

40 Crow's cry

42 Remunerate before receipt of goods

43 WHAT JOB'S NOT-SO-ENCOURAGING WIFE SAID TO HIM: "____ THOU STILL RETAIN THINE INTEGRITY? CURSE GOD, AND DIE" (Job 2:9)

46 Contemporary

48 "____ me with hyssop" (Psalm 51:7)

49 "God gave them knowledge and ____ in all learning" (Daniel 1:17)

50 "It is much ____ that the members of the body which seem to be weaker are necessary" (1 Corinthians 12:22 NASB)

51 Weasel-like mammal

52 Divisions of the animal kingdom

54 "Solomon made a ____ of ships" (1 Kings 9:26)

56 ____ Minor

57 "Ye ____ my witnesses" (Isaiah 43:10)

58 State (abbr.)

59 System of the body (abbr.)

61 Strive

Word Search
by Janet W. Adkins

Unwanted Wife
Exodus 2–4, 18

BREAD	LAND
CAST	MAN
CONTENT	MIDIAN
DAUGHTERS	MOSES
DELIVERED	PHARAOH
DROVE	PRIEST
DWELL	REUEL
EAT	SENT HER BACK
EGYPTIAN	SEVEN
ELIEZER	SHARP
FATHER-IN-LAW	SHEPHERDS
FEET	SON
FILLED	STOOD
FLOCK	TROUGHS
GERSHOM	WATERED
HELPED	WIFE
HUSBAND	ZIPPORAH
JETHRO	

```
R E Z E I L E D W I F E C A P
Z E G Y P T I A N E A T A N H
I B N O N A M L J E T H R O A
P R U P R I E S T M H G S S R
P E D K D M T E A G E Z H R A
O A N I C O V D D R R Z A E O
R D A X O O I E S O I K R T H
A N B D R E L H S O N F P H E
H C S D N I O F G T L L N G L
Y O U F V M O S E S A L E U P
L N H E D E R E T A W E V A E
A T R E U E L D A C H W E D D
N E B T S H E P H E R D S S R
D N X R S E N T H E R B A C K
O T F I L L E D T R O U G H S
```

Acrostic
by Donna K. Maltese

A Peg above the Rest

This resourceful woman used the tools at hand to kill a Canaanite chieftain. Crack the code to solve this puzzle of an "intense" heroine who was a peg above the rest.

Her husband's tribe

‾‾16‾ ‾‾24‾ ‾‾1‾ ‾‾21‾ ‾‾7‾ ‾‾12‾

The chieftain she slew

‾‾31‾ ‾‾17‾ ‾‾6‾ ‾‾11‾ ‾‾22‾ ‾‾4‾

He ____ down from his chariot

‾‾29‾ ‾‾33‾ ‾‾19‾ ‾‾10‾ ‾‾2‾ ‾‾26‾

He ____ away on his feet, to her door

‾‾14‾ ‾‾9‾ ‾‾20‾ ‾‾27‾

She was sly or ____

‾‾30‾ ‾‾8‾ ‾‾15‾ ‾‾23‾

The name of the prophetess who sung of this woman's deeds

‾‾32‾ ‾‾18‾ ‾‾28‾ ‾‾5‾ ‾‾13‾ ‾‾25‾ ‾‾3‾

7-3-2-1   29-4-18-9   3-11-28-11-22-'6   30-17-14-18

7-5-5-16   4   1-25-21-15   5-14   7-3-2   7-20-1-7,   4-1-26

7-5-5-16   4-1   3-4-19-19-11-13   8-1   3-18-13   3-4-1-26,

4-1-27   30-24-1-7   31-5-14-7-9-23   33-1-7-5   3-8-19,

4-1-27   6-19-5-7-12   7-3-2   1-25-21-15   8-1-7-5   3-8-6

7-20-19-10-9-20-6. . .14-5-13   3-2   30-4-6   14-4-6-7

4-6-9-12-12-10   4-1-32   30-24-4-13-23.

JUDGES 4:21

Anagram
by Paul Kent

New Testament Names

Of the dozens of female names in the New Testament, we've anagrammed three. Can you figure out which three women these are? Hint: You'll find all three of these in the Gospel accounts.

Ham art

— — — — — —

Lithe base

— — — — — — — — —

Arm may end a leg

— — — — — — — — — — — —

Cryptoscripture
by Donna K. Maltese

Wise Women

Some women demonstrate their wisdom through their creativeness and others through their courage to speak out. Can you break the alphabet codes to discover these nameless wise women who showed their dedication and daring, all to God's glory?

GHH UAY JIBYD UAGU JYLY JSQY AYGLUYW

WSW QVSD JSUA UAYSL AGDWQ, GDW

MLICZAU UAGU JASTA UAYO AGW QVCD, MIUA

IX MHCY, GDW IX VCLVHY, GDW IX QTGLHYU,

GDW IX XSDY HSDYD.

CZFH MYDFO I EDXF ETSIH TPC TQ CZF MDCJ,

ZFIY, ZFIY; XIJ, D AYIJ JTP, PHCT WTIK, MTSF HFIY

ZDCZFY, CZIC D SIJ XAFIR EDCZ CZFF.

Crossword

by Dorothy Pryse

Family Ties

Athaliah, daughter of Jezebel, was a rotten apple that fell not far from a wickedly wanton family tree. As you solve this puzzle, check out the deeds of devilry done by Athaliah and other nefarious ne'er-do-wells in her family.

When Athaliah the mother of Ahaziah saw that her son was dead, she arose and destroyed all the seed royal.

2 KINGS 11:1

ACROSS

1 Am not (contraction)
5 JEHOIADA ARMED MEN WITH "SPEARS AND SHIELDS" OF KING ____ TO GUARD JOASH, THE ONLY ROYAL ATHALIAH DID NOT KILL (2 Kings 11:10)
10 "One ____ or one tittle shall in no wise pass from the law" (Matthew 5:18)
13 SOON AFTER ATHALIAH "CAME TO THE ____ GATHERED AT THE TEMPLE," SHE WAS SLAIN (2 Kings 11:13 MSG)
15 Aflame
16 Republic of fifty states (abbr.)
17 "Let not my ____ be united to their assembly" (Genesis 49:6 NKJV)
18 "Out of the abundance of my complaint and ____ have I spoken" (1 Samuel 1:16)
19 "Thou shalt not take the ____ with the young" (Deuteronomy 22:6)
20 Compass point (abbr.)
21 "Go in to her. . .that through her ____ may have children " (Genesis 30:3 NASB) (2 words)
23 JEHU, RESPONSIBLE FOR JEZEBEL'S AND AHAZIAH'S DEATHS, TOLD HIS MEN TO "BRAKE DOWN THE ____ OF BAAL" 2 Kings 10:27)
25 "Heareth the word, and ____ with joy receiveth it" (Matthew 13:20)
26 "God shall ____" (Psalm 46:5) (2 words)
28 Adhesive
31 "He took. . .a cake of ____ bread" (Leviticus 8:26)
32 "Thine enemies shall be found ____ unto thee" (Deuteronomy 33:29)
33 WHEN ATHALIAH'S SON AHAZIAH SAW JEHU KILL JEHORAM, "HE ____ BY THE WAY OF THE GARDEN HOUSE" (2 Kings 9:27)
34 "Leah. . .called his name ____" (Genesis 30:11)
37 "The Pharisees began to ____ him" (Luke 11:53)
38 "He maketh the storm ____, so that the waves. . .are still" (Psalm 107:29) (2 words)
40 Tree trunk
41 Earth (prefix)

42 WHEN THEY WENT TO BURY JEZEBEL, "THEY FOUND NO MORE OF HER ____ THE SKULL, AND THE FEET, AND THE PALMS OF HER HANDS" (2 Kings 9:35)
43 JEZEBEL WAS A PRINCESS HERE (1 Kings 16:31) (modern spelling)
44 Meat juice
45 "Provide neither gold, nor silver, nor brass in your ____" (Matthew 10:9)
46 "They. . .found Mary, and Joseph, and ____" (Luke 2:16) (2 words)
49 Pirate captain
50 Moved hurriedly
51 WHEN JEZEBEL CUT OFF GOD'S PROPHETS, THE LAND SUFFERED A DROUGHT FORCING AHAB TO "____ GRASS TO SAVE THE. . .BEASTS" (1 Kings 18:5)
52 Brief sleep
55 Historic time
56 Kenneth Lay's fraudulent corporation
59 "They shall see ____ eye" (Isaiah 52:8) (2 words)
61 Small child
62 Covered in a long garment
63 JEHORAM, ATHALIAH'S BROTHER, "CLEAVED UNTO THE SINS OF JEROBOAM THE SON OF ____" (2 Kings 3:1–3)
64 "Why make ye this ____, and weep?" (Mark 5:39)
65 Type of cheese
66 JEHOSHEBA TOOK JOASH, "STOLE HIM FROM AMONG THE KING'S ____. . .," AND HID HIM (2 Kings 11:2)

DOWN

1 Hurt
2 "And ____, and Migdalel, Horem" (Joshua 19:38)
3 "JEHU SLEW ALL THAT REMAINED OF THE HOUSE OF AHAB. . .UNTIL HE LEFT HIM ____ REMAINING" (2 Kings 10:11)
4 "____ AND TWENTY YEARS OLD WAS AHAZIAH WHEN HE BEGAN TO REIGN. . . . AND HIS MOTHER'S NAME WAS ATHALIAH" (2 Kings 8:26)

5   "The Philistines took the ark. . .and set it by _____" (1 Samuel 5:2)
6   Hairstyle
7   Roman numeral seven
8   Anger
9   "He had _____ Dinah their sister" (Genesis 34:13)
10 ATHALIAH WAS QUEEN HERE (2 Kings 8:25; 11:3)
11 Native American tribe
12 Animal trainer
14 "Which stood only in meats and _____" (Hebrews 9:10)
22 Child's object
24 Psychological malady (abbr.)
25 "As it were an half _____ of land, which a yoke of oxen might plow" (1 Samuel 14:14)
26 "They set them up images and groves in every high _____" (2 Kings 17:10)
27 Grade school (abbr.)
28 Round bullet
29 "Bind the _____ of thine head" (Ezekiel 24:17)
30 Villain in Hamlet
31 "There failed not ought _____ good thing" (Joshua 21:45) (2 words)
34 JEZEBEL TOLD ELIJAH, "SO LET THE _____ DO TO ME. . .IF I MAKE NOT THY LIFE AS THE LIFE OF ONE OF THEM" (1 Kings 19:2)
35 Medicinal plant
36 "Look. . .from the lions' _____" (Song of Solomon 4:8)
38 ATHALIAH'S FATHER (2 Kings 8:18–26)
39 WHEN JEZEBEL CUT OFF THE LORD'S PROPHETS, OBADIAH "HID THEM BY FIFTY IN A _____" (1 Kings 18:4)

40 AFTER ANNOUNCING A DROUGHT TO AHAB, ELIJAH WENT INTO HIDING AND WAS FED BY WHAT? (1 Kings 17:4)
42 Dealers
43 "Be not afraid of _____ fear" (Proverbs 3:25)
44 Group of Kwa languages
45 "She fastened it with the _____" (Judges 16:14)
46 Greek letter
47 "Jerubbaal. . .pitched beside the well of _____" (Judges 7:1)
48 Poetry muse
49 "The people heard. . .all _____ of musick" (Daniel 3:7)
51 "I will beat down his _____ before his face" (Psalm 89:23)
52 "Get thee up. . .unto Mount _____, which is in the land of Moab" (Deuteronomy 32:49)
53 "Every one could sling stones _____ hair breadth" (Judges 20:16) (2 words)
54 "Hold the tradition of men, as the washing of _____ and cups" (Mark 7:8)
57 AFTER ORDERING THE KILLING OF JEZEBEL, JEHU SAID, "GO, SEE _____ THIS CURSED WOMAN, AND BURY HER: FOR SHE IS A KING'S DAUGHTER" (2 Kings 9:34)
58 Baseball statistic (abbr.)
60 "She answered and said unto him, _____, Lord" (Mark 7:28)

265

A Bride for Isaac
GENESIS 24:2–67

ABRAHAM
ANGEL
APPOINTED
BLESSED
CAMELS
COMFORTED
DAMSEL
DRINK
EARRING
GOLD
HAND
HEART
ISAAC
JEWELS
LABAN
LAHAIROI

LORD
LOVED
MESOPOTAMIA
OATH
PITCHER
PRAY
PRECIOUS
RAIMENT
REBEKAH
SERVANT
SILVER
VIRGIN
WELL
WIFE
WORSHIPPED

```
M  A  E  F  I  W  E  L  L  I  V  I  C  T  S
A  P  S  H  T  A  O  M  O  U  A  P  R  O  L
H  P  I  T  C  H  E  R  Y  V  N  A  P  S  E
A  O  N  I  G  R  I  V  S  I  E  Y  U  E  M
R  I  L  A  B  A  N  B  I  H  X  O  Z  D  A
B  N  M  A  H  E  N  C  L  D  I  S  A  A  C
A  T  E  A  D  L  O  G  V  C  B  P  K  M  L
F  E  L  S  T  G  H  I  E  J  L  M  P  S  O
G  D  O  T  L  O  S  R  R  L  E  D  R  E  Q
N  D  R  U  V  E  P  W  E  X  S  R  T  L  D
I  E  D  E  D  R  W  O  C  B  S  I  B  A  Z
R  V  T  N  A  V  R  E  S  F  E  N  G  H  A
R  O  R  Y  Q  M  P  L  J  E  D  K  J  K  I
A  L  S  I  T  N  O  T  N  E  M  I  A  R  N
E  C  O  M  F  O  R  T  E  D  D  N  A  H  N
```

Bible Quotation
by Suzanne Stepp

Given to Moses
EXODUS 2:21–22

When Moses fled to Midian, he was given the gift of a priest's daughter. Work this puzzle to discover the name of Moses' wife and the son she delivered.

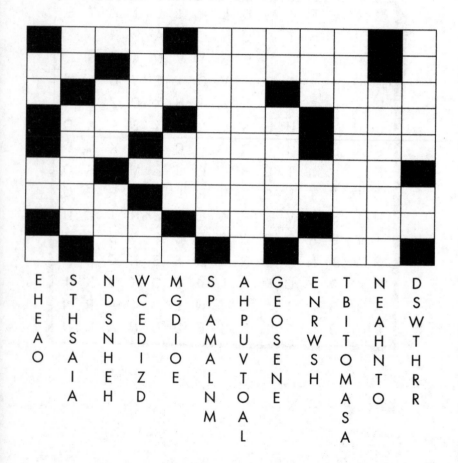

Mothers

Moms are great. In fact, they are so great that the very word *mom*, when turned upside down, reads *wow!* Unscramble these telephone codes to discover the names of some biblical moms who were absolutely wow-some.

| DEF 3 | TUV 8 | MNO 6 | GHI 4 | ABC 2 | DEF 3 |

| QZ 0 | GHI 4 | JKL 5 | JKL 5 | ABC 2 | GHI 4 |

| PRS 7 | ABC 2 | ABC 2 | GHI 4 | DEF 3 | JKL 5 |

| DEF 3 | JKL 5 | GHI 4 | PRS 7 | ABC 2 | ABC 2 | DEF 3 | TUV 8 | GHI 4 |

| TUV 8 | ABC 2 | MNO 6 | ABC 2 | PRS 7 |

| ABC 2 | ABC 2 | TUV 8 | GHI 4 | PRS 7 | GHI 4 | DEF 3 | ABC 2 | ABC 2 |

| JKL 5 | MNO 6 | ABC 2 | GHI 4 | DEF 3 | ABC 2 | DEF 3 | DEF 3 |

Acrostic
by Donna K. Maltese

Mother of a Priestly Line

This woman, whose name means "God is an oath," is the ancestress of the entire Levitical priesthood. Crack the code to uncover the names of this amazing matriarch and her immediate family members.

Her husband's uncle's name (Leviticus 10:4)

—— —— —— —— —— ——
37   30   18   15   2   25

Another word for priest

—— —— —— —— —— —— —— ——
31   8   36   24   16   3   12   20

Offerings were made _____ the Lord

—— —— —— —— —— ——
9   34   22   6   17   29

Two sons offered this kind of fire to the Lord (Leviticus 10:1)

—— —— —— —— —— —— ——
35   26   13   11   7   21   32

Two sons suffered God's _____

—— —— —— —— ——
28   14   1   23   4

They were not to _____ wine (Leviticus 10:9)

—— —— —— —— ——
5   33   27   10   19

11-10-5   1-1-14-6-36   3-6-6-19   4-15-31

12-25-24-16-4-12-9-1,   5-1-37-21-4-26-32-33   6-22

1-31-31-27-7-1-5-1-9,   16-8-16-23-29-13   6-22

7-1-1-35-4-6-7,   3-6   28-8-22-34;   11-10-5   35-4-2

9-1-20-2   4-15-31   7-1-5-1-9,   11-10-5   1-9-8-4-37,

2-25-2-1-18-1-17,   11-10-5   8-26-4-1-31-1-14.

Exodus 6:23

Crossword
by Dorothy Pryse

The Enticing Tale of Adam's Rib

God formed woman by taking a rib out of Adam's *side*—not to have the man lord over her, but to be equal with him, under his arm to be sheltered by him, and near his heart to be loved by him. As you solve this puzzle, remember the alluring story of this first couple and their loving Creator.

And the rib, which the LORD God had taken from man,
made he a woman, and brought her unto the man.
GENESIS 2:22

ACROSS

1 Resort
4 Coffeehouse
8 Cite
14 Thousand
15 Musical composition
16 Creep (slang)
17 "When your children shall _____. . . What mean these stones?" (Joshua 4:21)
18 Part of a church
19 "For the turn of _____ was from the LORD" (1 Kings 12:15 NKJV)
20 "Terrors _____ him on every side and dog his every step" (Job 18:11 NIV)
22 "A man shall _____ a pit, and not cover it" (Exodus 21:33)
23 "Jehoiada the priest took a chest, and bored a _____ in the lid of it" (2 Kings 12:9)
24 THE FIRST GARDEN (Genesis 2:8)
27 Relating to a rounded projection
31 Green citrus fruit
33 Ballet step
35 ADAM'S WAS 130 WHEN HIS WIFE GAVE BIRTH TO SETH (Genesis 5:3)
36 _____ Maria
38 Baboon
39 Veer
40 "By the _____ of the countenance the heart is made better" (Ecclesiastes 7:3)
44 Intellectual
46 BECAUSE THE FIRST WOMAN DID NOT _____ THE LORD'S INSTRUCTIONS, SIN ENTERED THE WORLD (Genesis 3)
47 Office of the U.S. Surgeon General (abbr.)
49 "God said, Let us make man in _____ image" (Genesis 1:26)
50 "They are lively, and are delivered _____ the midwives come" (Exodus 1:19)

51 AFTER THE FALL, GOD TOLD THE FIRST WOMAN, "IN PAIN _____ SHALL BRING FORTH CHILDREN" (Genesis 3:16 NKJV)
52 "As cold waters to a thirsty soul, so is good _____ from a far country" (Proverbs 25:25)
55 "ADAM SAID. . .SHE SHALL BE CALLED _____, BECAUSE SHE WAS TAKEN OUT OF MAN" (Genesis 2:23)
58 GOD TOLD ADAM AND HIS WIFE THAT IF THEY ATE THE FRUIT THEY WOULD "BE AS GODS, KNOWING GOOD AND _____" (Genesis 3:5)
61 Rider's command
63 Brief report (abbr.)
65 "And Rachel _____ was buried" (Genesis 35:19) (2 words)
67 Large desert
70 "God sent me. . .to _____ your lives by a great deliverance" (Genesis 45:7)
71 Card game
72 Tennis player Andre
73 AFTER THE BIRTH OF HER GRANDSON ENOS, "_____ BEGAN MEN TO CALL UPON THE NAME OF THE LORD" (Genesis 4:26)
74 "He that hath an _____, let him hear" (Revelation 3:6)
75 THE FIRST WOMEN "WAS THE _____ OF ALL LIVING" (Genesis 3:20)
76 Curious
77 "ADAM KNEW. . .HIS WIFE; AND _____ CONCEIVED, AND BARE CAIN" (Genesis 4:1)

DOWN

1 "Break down their altars, _____ their sacred stones" (Exodus 34:13 NIV)
2 Small firearm

3 Strong chemical base

4 TO COVER THE NAKEDNESS OF ADAM AND HIS WIFE, GOD MADE EACH ONE A _____ OF SKINS (Genesis 3:21)

5 FRUIT OFTEN ASSOCIATED WITH THE GARDEN

6 Joined together

7 Native of (suffix)

8 "The people. . .fell on their faces in _____ worship" (1 Kings 18:39 MSG)

9 Jesus was later "tempted of the _____" in the wilderness (Matthew 4:1)

10 San _____ (CA city)

11 Vase

12 U.S. time zone

13 Goddess of the dawn

21 Return to custody

25 Pollution watchdog (abbr.)

26 "She took the goatskins and covered. . . the smooth _____ of his neck" (Genesis 27:15 MSG)

28 Hay bundle

29 Water (Sp.)

30 "The LORD shall smite Israel, as a _____ is shaken in the water" (1 Kings 14:15)

32 "ADAM CALLED HIS WIFE'S NAME _____" (Genesis 3:20)

34 Type of lily

37 "Stand by the way, and _____" (Jeremiah 48:19)

39 THE SERPENT WAS THIS, OR CANNY (Genesis 3:1)

40 "_____ kindness unto my master Abraham" (Genesis 24:12)

41 Relating to aircraft

42 "Members of the body which we _____ less honorable. . .we bestow more abundant honor (1 Corinthians 12:23 NASB)

43 "Loose thy _____ from off thy foot" (Joshua 5:15)

45 Rifle

48 Type of vehicle (abbr.)

53 "And God created great _____" (Genesis 1:21)

54 "_____ knew that the waters were abated" (Genesis 8:11) (2 words)

56 Embarass

57 "Deborah, Rebekah's _____ died" (Genesis 35:8)

59 Northwestern state

60 "And deliver our _____ from death" (Joshua 2:13)

62 "We _____ you as the one who is over all things" (1 Chronicles 29:11 NLT)

64 "He has left His _____ like the lion" (Jeremiah 25:38 NKJV)

66 _____ meany, miney, moe

67 Books 1 and 2 following Ruth (abbr.)

68 "Thine asses that were lost three days _____" (1 Samuel 9:20)

69 "You walk away from your God at the drop of a _____" (Hosea 9:1 MSG)

70 Depot (abbr.)

Word Search
by Marijane Troyer

Sisters of Bethany
LUKE 10; JOHN 11

A CERTAIN WOMAN	LAZARUS
ALONE	LIFE
ART	LORD
BETHANY	MANY THINGS
BID	MARTHA
BROTHER	MARY
CAREFUL	NEEDFUL
CHOSEN	RECEIVED
CUMBERED	RISE
DEAD	SAT AT
ENTERED	SHE
FEET	SERVING
GLORY	SICKNESS
GOOD PART	SISTERS
HEARD	TAKEN
HELP ME	TROUBLED
HOUSE	VILLAGE
JESUS	WORD
JEWS	

```
J  N  E  E  D  F  U  L  R  E  H  T  O  R  B
E  N  T  E  R  E  D  E  V  I  E  C  E  R  E
S  H  N  E  K  A  T  G  O  O  D  P  A  R  T
U  V  E  A  S  E  R  V  I  N  G  S  Y  C  H
S  I  A  A  M  I  E  F  I  L  H  H  A  D  A
U  L  L  T  R  O  U  B  L  E  D  T  R  E  N
A  L  O  B  I  D  W  O  L  D  E  E  U  R  Y
M  A  N  Y  T  H  I  N  G  S  T  B  S  E  S
E  G  E  D  A  E  D  L  I  E  I  W  M  B  U
N  E  A  D  F  U  L  R  E  A  E  Q  A  M  R
E  E  M  P  L  E  H  F  O  J  T  P  R  U  A
S  I  S  T  E  R  S  A  G  L  O  R  Y  C  Z
O  E  S  U  O  H  M  A  R  T  H  A  E  E  A
H  S  I  C  K  N  E  S  S  D  R  O  W  C  L
C  A  R  E  F  U  L  S  A  T  A  T  T  R  A
```

by Sara Stoker

No Secrets

MEDIUM

	A	B	C	D	E	F	G	H	I
1	H	A		I		S			T
2		G					H	I	N
3	I		Y		N				
4	A			Y	H			G	S
5		N				I		H	
6	G		H	A	E	N	Y		
7	S						T	E	
8						H		A	Y
9	T	H		S	A		I		

Hint: Row 9

"And many of the Samaritans of that city believed on him for
_____ _____ of the woman, which testified, He told me
all that ever I did" (John 4:39).

Sarah Births Isaac
SEE GENESIS 21:7

Sarah laughed when she overheard God tell Abraham she would soon be pregnant. Solve this puzzle to find out why she thought God's prediction amazingly ridiculous.

Word	Clue	Answer	#
INSTEAD	Depressions	_____	1. ___ ___
HIGHEST	Black pool ball	_____	2. ___ ___
ACINOSE	Long gone	_____	3. ___ ___
NERVING	Rule	_____	4. ___ ___
INGRATE	Consent to	_____	5. ___ ___
NOBLEST	Took another's	_____	6. ___ ___
ORATORY	Delay	_____	7. ___ ___
RECLINE	Brother's daughter	_____	8. ___ ___
DROWNED	Used oars	_____	9. ___ ___
ABROACH	Snake	_____	10. ___ ___
GRACILE	Settle debt	_____	11. ___ ___
MADNESS	Harbor fill	_____	12. ___ ___

___ ___ ___ ___ ___ ___ ___ ___ ___ ___ ___ ___

1　2　3　4　5　6　7　8　9　10　11　12

by Donna K. Maltese

The Frustrated Temptress

Here's a woman who had no scruples when it came to lusting after handsome men. Crack the code to discover this wily, wicked woman's passion-filled proposition to a valiant, virtuous servant.

Her husband's name

‾‾ ‾‾ ‾‾ ‾‾ ‾‾ ‾‾ ‾‾ ‾‾
38 33 19 10 28   3 35 22

His position in Pharaoh's guard

‾‾ ‾‾ ‾‾ ‾‾ ‾‾ ‾‾ ‾‾
14   9 23 34 29   4 26

Pharaoh's country

‾‾ ‾‾ ‾‾ ‾‾ ‾‾
 1 15 27 20   6

Her servant was this

‾‾ ‾‾ ‾‾ ‾‾ ‾‾ ‾‾
37 32 16 11   5 21

He fueled her _____ of desire

‾‾ ‾‾ ‾‾ ‾‾ ‾‾
30 12   8 25 18

Where her servant wound up

‾‾ ‾‾ ‾‾ ‾‾ ‾‾ ‾‾ ‾‾
17 36   7 24   2 13 31

35-7-17   10-34   14-8-25-2   19-33   20-9-5-5

8-30-19-1-22   6-3-2-5-2   6-3-11-31-15-5,   6-3-8-6

3-4-5   25-9-5-6-1-22-'5   16-4-30-2   14-8-5-19   3-32-22

1-27-1-5   36-23-13-26   37-33-5-18-28-21;   35-7-17

5-3-32   5-29-4-17,   12-4-1   16-4-6-21   25-32.

GENESIS 39:7

Crossword
by Dorothy Pryse

Rachel, the Shepherdess

The Lord God used a flock of sheep to bring together the shepherdess Rachel, whose name means "ewe," and her one true love, a man who was also a keeper of sheep. As you solve this puzzle, wonder anew at the Good Shepherd's hand in Rachel's life story as well as your own. "Ewe" will be amazed!

Rachel came with her father's sheep; for she kept them.
Genesis 29:9

ACROSS

1 "Where is the _____ for a burnt offering?" (Genesis 22:7)
5 "For the LORD shall rise up. . .and bring to pass his _____" (Isaiah 28:21)
8 "_____ him in thine hand" (Genesis 21:18)
12 "Cain talked with _____ his brother" (Genesis 4:8)
13 Greek marketplace
15 Fencing sword
16 Sample (abbr.)
17 Small young chicken
18 "What was being done by the angel was _____" (Acts 12:9 NASB)
19 Common finch
21 Cheap art
23 "They _____ fig leaves together" (Genesis 3:7)
25 "I will give you rain in _____ season" (Leviticus 26:4)
26 "As a _____ which melteth, let every one of them pass away" (Psalm 58:8)
29 "MAY GOD GIVE YOU OF THE _____ OF HEAVEN," WAS PART OF THE BLESSING ISAAC GAVE TO RACHEL'S HUSBAND-TO-BE (Genesis 27:28 NKJV)
31 RACHEL'S HUSBAND'S CHALLENGE TO GOD: "I WILL NOT LET THEE GO, EXCEPT THOU _____ ME" (Genesis 32:26)
35 "They shall be as though they _____ been" (Obadiah 1:16) (2 words)
37 Bad (prefix)
39 "Then she shall be _____" (Numbers 5:28)
40 One (Ger.)
41 Capital of Cyprus
44 Road or street (abbr.)
45 Explosive sound
47 "_____ his son, Jehoshuah his son" (1 Chronicles 7:27)

48 Puckered
50 "And _____ with her suburbs" (1 Chronicles 6:59)
52 Pen brand
54 Small
55 "AND _____ REMEMBERED RACHEL. . . AND OPENED HER WOMB" (Genesis 30:22)
57 Chocolate substitute
59 Paul Reubens's character _____ Herman
62 RACHEL'S FIRST CHILD (Genesis 30:25)
65 "_____ again unto the LORD God" (2 Chronicles 30:6)
66 HE LOVED RACHEL (Genesis 29:28)
68 Capital of Ukraine
70 Narrow opening
71 GOD HAD _____ IN JACOB'S MARRIAGE (2 words)
72 "As it were an half _____ of land, which a yoke of oxen might plow" (1 Samuel 14:14)
73 BECAUSE THE LORD GRANTED HER FATHER-IN-LAW'S _____, RACHEL'S HUSBAND-TO-BE WAS CONCEIVED (Genesis 25:21 NKJV)
74 Saint (Fem.)
75 "The cock shall not crow, till thou _____ denied me thrice" (John 13:38)

DOWN

1 "God was with the _____; and he grew" (Genesis 21:20)
2 Encourage
3 Note
4 "As surely as rain _____ from the north, anger is caused by cruel words" (Proverbs 25:23 CEV) (2 words)
5 "Can two walk together, except they be _____?" (Amos 3:3)
6 Reserved

7 Long journey

8 "She maketh _____ coverings of tapestry; her clothing is silk" (Proverbs 31:22)

9 Petroleum organization (abbr.)

10 RACHEL'S SISTER (Genesis 29:16)

11 Eastern state (abbr.)

13 THE YEARS JACOB WAITED FOR RACHEL SEEMED BUT _____ DAYS (Genesis 29:20) (2 words)

14 "It roams through dry [_____] places in search of rest" (Matthew 12:43 AMP)

20 "Eliab the son of _____ shall be captain" (Numbers 2:7)

22 "You got fat, became obese, a _____ of lard" (Deuteronomy 32:15 MSG)

24 Satanic

26 "The queen of _____ heard of the fame of Solomon" (1 Kings 10:1)

27 "His _____ [were grown] like birds' claws" (Daniel 4:33)

28 "_____ the chief, and with him mighty men of valour" (2 Chronicles 17:14)

30 "LABAN HAD TWO DAUGHTERS. . .THE YOUNGER _____ RACHEL" (Genesis 29:16)

32 Rub out

33 JACOB'S YEARS OF LABOR FOR RACHEL (Genesis 29:18)

34 Run down

36 "They are brass, and _____, and iron" (Ezekiel 22:18)

38 "They shoot out the _____, they shake the head" (Psalm 22:7)

42 Male swan

43 Cars

46 Reddish-purple color

49 JACOB'S MOTHER (Genesis 27:11)

51 "_____ RACHEL HAD TAKEN THE IMAGES . . .AND SAT UPON THEM" (Genesis 31:34)

53 Wheedle

56 _____ vu

58 RACHEL'S FIRSTBORN WAS SO FAVORED BY HIS FATHER THAT HE MADE HIM THIS GARMENT (Genesis 37:3 NIV)

59 "Then will I build you, and not _____ you down" (Jeremiah 42:10)

60 Pennsylvania canal

61 "Seven _____ of corn came up upon one stalk" (Genesis 41:5)

63 Type size

64 "Restore all that was _____. . .since the day that she left" (2 Kings 8:6)

65 Measurement (abbr.)

67 Narrow bed

69 Animal doctor (abbr.)

281

Scrambled Circle
by Suzanne Stepp

No Way to Treat a Guest

Sometimes we lose our heads when confronted with unexpected joy.

1. NOSRIP

2. SEOUH

3. CIVOE

4. LEDSAM

5. TGEA

She left an important guest at the door.

1. _ O _ _ _ _

2. O _ _ _ _

3. _ O _ _ _

4. O _ _ _ _ _

5. _ O _ _

Answer: _ _ _ _ _

Old Testament Mothers

Ancient cultures expected women to be mothers, and the Bible contains the stories of many. Can you solve these spotty headlines to discover three Old Testament women known for their mothering?

WOMAN H●S FI●ST CHILD W●EN ●HE'S NINETY YE●RS OLD

_ _ _ _ _

SNEA●Y MOTHE● ●ELPS YOUNG●R SON CHE●T OLD●R ●ROTHER

_ _ _ _ _ _

WOMAN'S ●NGUIS●ED PRAYERS ●●SWERED T●ROUGH BIRTH OF SO●

_ _ _ _ _ _

Hagar
GENESIS 16:8, 10–11

And he **said**, **Hagar**, Sarai's **maid**, **whence camest thou**? and **whither wilt** thou go? And she said, I **flee** from the **face** of my **mistress Sarai**. . . . And the **angel** of the LORD said **unto** her, I will **multiply** thy **seed exceedingly**, that it shall **not** be **numbered** for **multitude**. And the angel of the LORD said unto **her**, **Behold**, thou **art** with **child** and **shalt bear** a **son**, and shalt **call his name Ishmael; because** the LORD hath **heard** thy **affliction**.

```
E D U T I T L U M M B L O R D
C X E H T N U M B U E F L E E
N P C A M E S T F R H E R L Y
E L H E A R D M A W N E U S R
H H I S E S U A C E B E A R M
W I L T M D V B E M E V W Q U
P O R H V E I T U V H C A L L
E C E O E M A N N A O L A R T
L H T U L Z A N G E L U B E I
D I H A E I Z G H L D C C H P
Y L S C A U A C M D Y E I T L
R D I A M N N R T U N T O I Y
R A G A H O T P A V T L A H S
S H M I S T R E S S E E D W P
A F F L I C T I O N O S A I D
```

Acrostic
by Donna K. Maltese

A Well-Thought-Of Woman

This verse is about a woman who, at a moment's notice, implemented a plan that brooked no objection from the men who needed to hide from their enemies. Solve to discover what she did to help save the kingdom of Israel.

The king Absalom tried to usurp

$\overline{\hspace{0.5em}}_{37}$ $\overline{\hspace{0.5em}}_{7}$ $\overline{\hspace{0.5em}}_{22}$ $\overline{\hspace{0.5em}}_{31}$ $\overline{\hspace{0.5em}}_{15}$

The man who counseled against the king (2 Samuel 17:21)

$\overline{\hspace{0.5em}}_{25}$ $\overline{\hspace{0.5em}}_{36}$ $\overline{\hspace{0.5em}}_{12}$ $\overline{\hspace{0.5em}}_{38}$ $\overline{\hspace{0.5em}}_{17}$ $\overline{\hspace{0.5em}}_{2}$ $\overline{\hspace{0.5em}}_{29}$ $\overline{\hspace{0.5em}}_{21}$ $\overline{\hspace{0.5em}}_{5}$ $\overline{\hspace{0.5em}}_{14}$

The men she hid were _____ of the king

$\overline{\hspace{0.5em}}_{23}$ $\overline{\hspace{0.5em}}_{11}$ $\overline{\hspace{0.5em}}_{40}$ $\overline{\hspace{0.5em}}_{34}$ $\overline{\hspace{0.5em}}_{30}$ $\overline{\hspace{0.5em}}_{1}$ $\overline{\hspace{0.5em}}_{16}$ $\overline{\hspace{0.5em}}_{10}$

What the two men carried to the king

$\overline{\hspace{0.5em}}_{19}$ $\overline{\hspace{0.5em}}_{35}$ $\overline{\hspace{0.5em}}_{39}$ $\overline{\hspace{0.5em}}_{32}$ $\overline{\hspace{0.5em}}_{3}$ $\overline{\hspace{0.5em}}_{9}$ $\overline{\hspace{0.5em}}_{26}$

What cisterns hold

$\overline{\hspace{0.5em}}_{8}$ $\overline{\hspace{0.5em}}_{27}$ $\overline{\hspace{0.5em}}_{4}$ $\overline{\hspace{0.5em}}_{20}$ $\overline{\hspace{0.5em}}_{13}$

Corn shell

$\overline{\hspace{0.5em}}_{28}$ $\overline{\hspace{0.5em}}_{6}$ $\overline{\hspace{0.5em}}_{18}$ $\overline{\hspace{0.5em}}_{33}$ $\overline{\hspace{0.5em}}_{24}$

3-1-15   4-6-11   8-2-19-30-1   16-2-2-24   3-1-15

32-29-13-35-3-37   27   33-2-22-26-40-12-1-9

2-34-20-13   4-6-11   8-5-14-14-10   19-2-18-4-36,

3-1-15   23-29-13-35-7-37   9-40-2-18-1-15   33-2-40-1

4-17-5-40-5-2-1;   3-1-15   4-6-11   4-21-31-1-9   8-25-28

1-2-38   24-1-2-8-1.

2 SAMUEL 17:19

Anagram
by Paul Kent

Esther's Story

Beautiful, courageous Esther saved her fellow Jews from a terrible slaughter. Can you reassemble the letters of the three phrases below to create names and words from her story?

Road mice

— — — — — — —

Charm sale bin

— — — — — — — — — —

Yard saver

— — — — — — — —

Heroines

Extraordinary strength of character can give birth to heroic deeds. Work the telephone scramble puzzle below to identify the nomenclatures of some awesome biblical heroines.

| MNO 6 | GHI 4 | PRS 7 | GHI 4 | ABC 2 | MNO 6 |

| PRS 7 | ABC 2 | GHI 4 | ABC 2 | ABC 2 |

| MNO 6 | GHI 4 | ABC 2 | GHI 4 | ABC 2 | JKL 5 |

| JKL 5 | ABC 2 | DEF 3 | JKL 5 |

| JKL 5 | DEF 3 | GHI 4 | MNO 6 | PRS 7 | GHI 4 | DEF 3 | ABC 2 | ABC 2 |

| DEF 3 | PRS 7 | TUV 8 | GHI 4 | DEF 3 | PRS 7 |

Crossword

by Dorothy Pryse

The Vindication of Jacob's Daughter

Here's a puzzle about Jacob's daughter Dinah, a girl who, after leaving the security of her family's tent, attracted a prince's attention and brought trouble upon herself and her entire family. Check out the full flap in Genesis 34, wherein her brothers managed to take a whole community down a peg.

Dinah. . .went out to visit the daughters of the land.
When Shechem the son of Hamor the Hivite, the prince of the land,
saw her, he took her and lay with her by force.
GENESIS 34:1–2

ACROSS

1 "They look and ____ upon me" (Psalm 22:17)
6 "____ no man any thing" (Romans 13:8)
9 "AND LEAH ____ WITH HER CHILDREN CAME NEAR" (Genesis 33:7)
13 "I would not write with ____ and ink" (2 John 12)
14 "ON THE THIRD ____, WHEN THEY WERE SORE. . .DINAH'S BRETHREN, TOOK EACH MAN HIS SWORD" (Genesis 34:25)
15 "And ____, whom the men of Gath. . . slew" (1 Chronicles 7:21)
16 "The sons of Shobal; ____, and Manahath" (1 Chronicles 1:40)
17 DINAH'S BROTHERS SAID TO SHECHEM, "WE CANNOT. . .GIVE OUR SISTER TO ____ THAT IS UNCIRCUMCISED" (Genesis 34:14)
18 "Get thee. . .unto ____ that I will shew thee" (Genesis 12:1) (2 words)
19 DINAH'S AUNT RACHEL DID ____ HER FATHER'S SHEEP (Genesis 29:9)
20 Initial stage of something
22 REGARDING HER FATHER, DINAH'S UNCLE SAID, "____ TAKEN MY BLESSING!" (Genesis 27:36 NIV)
23 Insert (abbr.)
24 "All that handle the ____, the mariners" (Ezekiel 27:29)
25 James ____, American author
27 "Ye shall not ____ the LORD your God" (Deuteronomy 6:16)
29 DINAH'S FATHER, JACOB, DREAMT OF A LADDER AND THE ____ STANDING ABOVE IT (Genesis 28:13) (2 words)
33 Affirmative
34 Campers (abbr.)
35 DINAH, HER BROTHERS, AND HER MOTHER BOWED TO THIS UNCLE (Genesis 30:19–21; 33:1–7)

36 "He may ____ to fear the LORD" (Deuteronomy 17:19)
39 RACHEL ENVIED DINAH'S FERTILE MOTHER AND SAID TO JACOB, "GIVE ME CHILDREN, OR ELSE I ____" (Genesis 30:1)
40 Satan took the form of a ____ (Genesis 3:1)
41 Leave out
42 Drink in small quantities
43 Jacob said to his father, "____ and eat of my venison" (Genesis 27:19)
44 "And others save with fear, ____ them out of the fire" (Jude 1:23)
46 "I came to ____ to preach" (2 Corinthians 2:12)
49 Send out
50 Change color
51 SHECHEM'S OFFER TO JACOB FOR DINAH'S HAND: "____ GIVE ME THE DAMSEL TO WIFE" (Genesis 34:12)
53 "But be gentle unto all men, ____ to teach" (2 Timothy 2:24)
56 Farthest point
58 Champion
59 "Taking out a stone, he ____ it and struck the Philistine" (1 Samuel 17:49 NIV)
61 Sheep's cry
62 DINAH'S BROTHERS' COUNTEROFFER TO SHECHEM: "WE WILL GIVE OUR CONSENT. . .[IF YOU CIRCUMCISE] ALL YOUR ____" (Genesis 34:15 NIV)
63 Weird
64 Building wing
65 "Not a belt is loosened at the waist, or ____ string broken" (Isaiah 5:27 NLV) (2 words)
66 "Godless nations ____ and rave" (Psalm 46:4 MSG)
67 Petrol
68 "If the ____ be certainly found in his hand. . .he shall restore double" (Exodus 22:4)

DOWN

1 SHECHEM LOVED DINAH "AND _____ KINDLY UNTO THE DAMSEL" (Genesis 34:3)

2 "I. . .hid thy _____ in the earth" (Matthew 25:25)

3 "Take nothing. . .neither have two coats _____" (Luke 9:3)

4 "Ye _____ the harvest of your land" (Leviticus 19:9)

5 Sea eagle

6 "The house was filled with the _____ of the ointment" (John 12:3)

7 "Embrace the rock for _____ of a shelter" (Job 24:8)

8 "Anoint thine eyes with _____" (Revelation 3:18)

9 DINAH'S BROTHERS "SLEW _____ THE MALES" (Genesis 34:25)

10 MOTHER OF DINAH (Genesis 34:1)

11 " 'I'm not crazy. I'm both accurate and _____ in what I'm saying' " (Acts 26:25 MSG)

12 "No one against us, nothing at _____ with us" (1 Kings 5:1 MSG)

15 "Maketh it. . .bud, that it may give. . .bread to the _____" (Isaiah 55:10)

20 Grain (plural)

21 "People with a big head are headed for a fall, pretentious _____ brought down" (Isaiah 2:11 MSG)

24 DINAH'S UNCLE WAS "A MAN OF THE _____ COUNTRY" (Genesis 25:27 NIV)

26 "A river went out of _____ water the garden" (Genesis 2:10) (2 words)

28 "The brier shall come up the _____ tree" (Isaiah 55:13)

30 Youth organization for girls (abbr.)

31 DINAH'S FATHER HID "STRANGE GODS. . .UNDER THE _____ WHICH WAS BY SHECHEM" (Genesis 35:4)

32 "I will give you rain in _____ season" (Leviticus 26:4)

34 "Thou wilt. . . _____ up their women with child" (2 Kings 8:12)

36 "The LORD. . .shall _____ the bough with terror" (Isaiah 10:33)

37 Australian bird

38 Hurt

39 "I cannot _____ I am ashamed" (Luke 16:3) (3 words)

40 JACOB WAS DINAH'S _____ (Genesis 34:1)

42 Clip

43 Eye inflammation

45 "In the _____ of God created he him" (Genesis 1:27)

47 "And _____ also brought of the firstlings of his flock" (Genesis 4:4) (2 words)

48 "No man is _____ life" (Job 24:22) (2 words)

50 "The meat offering. . .shall be two tenth _____ of fine flour" (Leviticus 23:13)

52 "And in cutting of stones, _____ them" (Exodus 31:5) (2 words)

53 "Anna. . .of the tribe of _____" (Luke 2:36)

54 DINAH'S HALF BROTHER DAN WAS BORN TO BILHAH AFTER GOD LISTENED TO RACHEL'S _____ (Genesis 30:6 NIV)

55 DINAH'S DAD USED TREE BRANCHES TO _____ SOLID-COLORED SHEEP INTO SPECKLED ONES (Genesis 30:37–39)

57 Festive occasion

58 "Maher-Shalal-_____-Baz" (Isaiah 8:3)

60 Louse egg

62 "Uriah went out to sleep on his _____" (2 Samuel 11:13 NIV)

291

Word Search
by David Austin

Hannah's Hope
1 Samuel 1:9–2:21

ASKED	PRAYED
BARREN	PRIEST
BLESSED	REMEMBER
CALLED	SAMUEL
CHILD	SON
FAVOUR	SOUL
HANDMAID	VISITED
HANNAH	VOWED
HUSBAND	WEPT
MOTHER	WIFE
PETITION	YEARLY
POURED	

```
H  A  M  F  E  D  C  A  C  E  F  I  W  S  T
M  I  F  R  M  W  Y  E  B  A  R  R  E  N  E
E  G  P  R  I  E  S  T  V  L  L  P  P  H  O
J  U  Q  O  A  O  J  O  F  O  E  L  T  B  Z
F  Q  A  R  U  V  U  Z  V  T  W  S  E  J  F
K  D  L  L  T  R  B  T  I  U  A  E  S  D  O
D  Y  I  Q  Q  V  E  T  S  F  S  X  D  E  A
W  S  H  M  O  H  I  D  I  M  K  J  L  Y  D
M  L  A  A  V  O  M  O  T  H  E  R  D  A  V
J  P  N  M  N  B  U  Y  E  T  D  N  X  R  M
Q  K  N  Q  U  D  P  P  D  R  A  S  O  P  Q
W  M  A  P  R  E  M  E  M  B  E  R  S  N  S  V
B  T  H  N  G  Z  L  A  S  T  E  F  P  S  I
B  X  V  V  C  J  E  U  I  L  L  V  W  O  B
M  H  F  S  U  P  H  N  J  D  L  I  H  C  K
```

Cryptoscripture
by Sharon Y. Brown

The Story That Began It All

In the beginning was man, but he was soon followed by woman. Ah, paradise! Solve the puzzles below to find verses dealing with the fruitful mother of us all.

JSZ PBI FNYZ TNZ HJLZ, LP LH SNP TNNZ PBJP

PBI RJS HBNCFZ OI JFNSI; L ULFF RJQI BLR JS

BIFA RIIP WNY BLR.

CAL XWP IGTL YGL VCRL ZAXG XWP QGDCA,

QWCX RV XWRV XWCX XWGZ WCVX LGAP? CAL

WXP QGDCA VCRL, WXP VPTJPAX EPYZRIPL DP,

CAL R LRL PCX.

Truth or Consequences

EASY

	A	B	C	D	E	F	G	H	I
1			B	Y	D	T			R
2		T		E	R	B		Y	I
3	D	Y	R			U			
4		U	I		B		Y	E	
5	Y			H			B		
6	B			T	Y				U
7		D		B	E	H		R	Y
8				R				D	B
9	R		Y	U	I	D	E		

Hint: Column 3

"Then Peter said unto her, How is it that ye have agreed together to tempt the Spirit of the Lord? behold, the feet of them which have _____ _____ husband are at the door, and shall carry thee out" (Acts 5:9).

The Prophetess

Amid evil days, the prophetess Huldah kept the divine light of God's law and truth burning in her heart. Crack the code to uncover her insight regarding the foreseeable future of Israel.

The wife of Shallum, whom Josiah sought for advice
(2 Kings 22:14)

—— —— —— —— —— ——
4   49   34   23   51   8

Priest of King Josiah (2 Kings 22:4)

—— —— —— —— —— —— ——
21   43   12   50   31   18   3

King Josiah's evil grandfather (2 Kings 21)

—— —— —— —— —— —— —— ——
9   33   2   37   25   42   7   27

National enemies of Judah (2 Kings 23:29)

—— —— —— —— —— —— —— and —— —— —— —— ——
14   36   45   16   28   46   10   and   22   30   48   11   38

This was found when Josiah had the temple renovated
(2 Chronicles 34:14)

—— —— —— —— —— —— —— —— —— —— —— ——
6   47   29   15   39   19   5   44   26   17   40   35

These types of images were among what Josiah destroyed after the prophetess spoke (2 Chronicles 34:3)

—— —— —— —— —— ——
20   41   1   32   24   13

10-2-13   45-3-22   36-18-31-23   49-2-38-47

38-21-26-9,   5-4-49-45   25-41-46-5-4   38-27-26

17-47-28-13   30-29-13   39-19   43-25-1-10-7-12. . .

6-22-21-29-17-23,   31   35-46-34-12   6-28-46-2-30

24-32-31-34   49-11-29-2   5-8-43-25

11-12-33-20-7,   14-2-23   49-11-39-2   5-3-26

31-2-3-14-6-46-38-51-2-5-36   5-27-22-28-7-29-19. . .

6-22-20-18-49-42-26   38-44-22-16   27-40-32-26

19-39-1-45-37-50-7-2   9-22.

2 Kings 22:15–17

Crossword
by Dorothy Pryse

A Steward's Wife

Among the many women who followed Jesus was the wife of Herod's steward. How amazing it must have been to not only follow Jesus, but to *nurture* the Great Nurturer Himself! As you solve this puzzle, you'll be learning more about this female follower of the Greatest Man to ever walk the earth!

Many women were there beholding afar off, which followed Jesus from Galilee, ministering unto him.
MATTHEW 27:55

ACROSS

1 Acadian
6 "So I ____ a girdle according to the word of the LORD" (Jeremiah 13:2)
9 "The throne had six steps leading up to it, its back shaped like an ____" (1 Kings 10:18 MSG)
13 Nut
14 Street (abbr.)
15 JOANNA'S HUSBAND (Luke 8:3)
16 "Get past the elementary ____ in the teachings and doctrine of Christ" (Hebrews 6:1 AMP)
17 WHEN THIS FEMALE FOLLOWER WENT BACK TO CHRIST'S TOMB, "BEHOLD, TWO ____ STOOD. . .IN SHINING GARMENTS" (Luke 24:4)
18 Doppler
19 "Seven other ____ came up after them out of the river" (Genesis 41:3)
20 THIS STEWARD'S WIFE WAS PART OF CHRIST'S INNER ____ (Luke 8:1–3)
22 "While the flesh was yet between their teeth, ____ it was chewed" (Numbers 11:33)
23 THE STEWARD'S WIFE WAS THERE WHEN CHRIST SAW JOHN AND SAID TO HIS MOTHER, "WOMAN, BEHOLD THY ____!" (John 19:26)
24 AFTER THE FEMALE FOLLOWERS REPORTED CHRIST'S MISSING BODY AND THE ANGELS' APPEARANCE, PETER "____ UNTO THE SEPULCHRE" (Luke 24:12)
25 "An adulterous woman: She ____ and wipes her mouth" (Proverbs 30:20 NKJV)
26 AFTER THE CRUCIFIXION OF CHRIST, THE FEMALE FOLLOWERS AND THE DISCIPLES WERE AT THIS LOWEST POINT
29 TV rating
33 Lung disease group (abbr.)
34 Restricted (abbr.)
35 "We departed in a ship of Alexandria, which had wintered in the" (Acts 28:11)

36 "Save your lives, and be like the ____ in the wilderness" (Jeremiah 48:6)
39 Romaine
40 THIS FEMALE FOLLOWER WITNESSED THE SOLDIERS WHO CROWNED JESUS AND "____ DOWN BEFORE HIM AND MOCKED HIM" (Matthew 27:29 NASB)
41 Dark liquids ejected by octopus
42 AT CHRIST'S EMPTY TOMB, THE ANGELS TOLD THE STEWARD'S WIFE AND OTHER FEMALE FOLLOWERS, "HE IS ____ HERE, BUT IS RISEN" (Luke 24:6)
43 Spree (slang)
44 Procurer
46 Malicious burning
49 Geek
50 "Why make ye this ____, and weep?" (Mark 5:39)
51 "Put it. . .upon the great ____ of his right foot" (Leviticus 14:25)
53 Collection
56 THE BOOK OF LUKE IS OUR ____ OF INFORMATION ABOUT THE STEWARD'S WIFE (see Luke 8:3; 24:10)
58 Small licorice treats
59 "Thou shalt ____ sons and daughters" (Deuteronomy 28:41)
61 Card game (var.)
62 "The rain also filleth the ____" (Psalm 84:6)
63 THE STEWARD'S WIFE WAS PRESENT HERE (Luke 23:49)
64 SHE WAS ALSO THERE WHEN "____ OF THE MALEFACTORS WHICH WERE HANGED RAILED ON [JESUS]" (Luke 23:39)
65 "After these things Jesus shewed himself again to the disciples ____ the ____ of Tiberias (John 21:1) (2 words)
66 Trigonometric function
67 "She answered and said unto him, ____, Lord" (Mark 7:28)
68 Distrustful

DOWN

1. "Silos full of grain, _____ of wine and barrels of olive oil" (Joel 2:24 MSG)
2. THE STEWARD'S WIFE FOLLOWED JOSEPH, A COUNCIL MEMBER "WHO HAD NOT CONSENTED TO THEIR DECISION AND _____," TO THE SEPULCHRE (Luke 23:50–55 NIV)
3. THE NAME OF THE STEWARD'S WIFE, WHO WAS ALSO HEALED BY JESUS (Luke 8:3)
4. "The scribes and the Pharisees began to _____ him vehemently" (Luke 11:53)
5. Compass point (abbr.)
6. Street urchin
7. THE STEWARD'S WIFE SAW THE SIGN "WRITTEN _____ HIM, [SAYING], THIS IS THE KING OF THE JEWS" (Luke 23:38)
8. Dime (2 words)
9. "He warmeth himself, and saith, _____, I am warm" (Isaiah 44:16)
10. "Though I be _____ in speech, yet not in knowledge" (2 Corinthians 11:6)
11. Russian monarch
12. "The _____. . .cheweth the cud" (Leviticus 11:6)
15. "We sailed under _____, over against Salmone" (Acts 27:7)
20. Autos
21. THE STEWARD'S WIFE "BEHELD THE SEPULCHRE, AND HOW HIS BODY WAS _____" (Luke 23:55)
24. THE STEWARD'S WIFE'S FAMILY WAS _____ (Luke 8:3)
26. "Uzziah prepared for them. . .bows, and _____ to cast stones" (2 Chronicles 26:14)
28. Pre-Nissan

30. Compass point (abbr.)
31. Wing
32. "Peter went up, and drew the _____ to land full of great fishes" (John 21:11)
34. THE STEWARD'S WIFE WAS THERE WHEN EACH SOLDIER CAST A _____ FOR JESUS' GARMENTS (Mark 15:24)
36. WHEN SHE AND THE OTHER WOMEN REALIZED CHRIST HAD RISEN, "THEY REMEMBERED _____ WORDS" (Luke 24:8)
37. Chemical compound (suffix)
38. Pedigree registry (abbr.)
39. Ribbed fabric
40. Corn syrup brand
42. Roman emperor
43. Precious stone
45. "In the wall of the house he made narrowed _____ round about" (1 Kings 6:6)
47. Useless
48. "It. . .rests upon more important (sublimer, higher, and _____) promises" (Hebrews 8:6 AMP)
50. Peaks
52. Literary composition
53. Elementary stages
54. "The son of Salathiel, which was the son of _____" (Luke 3:27)
55. Conflict between protagonist and antagonist
57. Character from an ancient German alphabet
58. "Write it before them in a table, and _____ it in a book" (Isaiah 30:8)
60. Native of (suffix)
62. "I don't hang out with tricksters, I don't _____ around with thugs" (Psalm 26:4 MSG)

Drop Two
by Dorothy Pryse

Eunice's Mother
SEE 2 TIMOTHY 1:5

Women of faith are wonderful examples to their children. Work out this puzzle to determine which of Timothy's female relatives was instrumental in nurturing his burgeoning devotion to God.

FLEDGED	Rock shelf	_____ 1. ___ ___
ALMONER	Avoids company	_____ 2. ___ ___
INBOARD	Trademark	_____ 3. ___ ___
TRIDENT	Small restaurant	_____ 4. ___ ___
CHERISH	Weeps	_____ 5. ___ ___
IMAGINE	Urchin	_____ 6. ___ ___
NOCTURN	Nobleman	_____ 7. ___ ___
GHASTLY	Speedy	_____ 8. ___ ___
OVERSAW	Hand signals	_____ 9. ___ ___
AVARICE	Slice	_____ 10. ___ ___
SNIPPED	Conveyed liquid	_____ 11. ___ ___

__ __ __ __ __ __ __ __ __ __ __

1   2   3   4   5   6   7   8   9   10   11

The First Lady
GENESIS 3:20

Work this Bible quotation puzzle to discover the name of the lady who, being the first to bear fruit and multiply, super-seeded all.

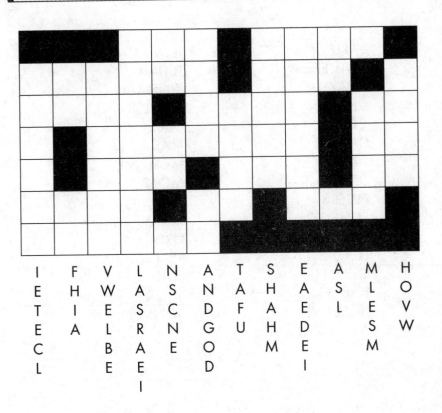

Ruth

BARLEY	JESSE
BETHLEHEM	JUDAH
BOAZ	KINSMAN
CHILION	MAHLON
CORN	MAIDENS
DAMSEL	MARA
DAUGHTER	MEALTIME
DAVID	MOAB
ELDERS	NAOMI
ELIMELECH	OBED
FEET	ORPAH
FLOOR	REAPERS
GLEAN	RUTH
HARVEST	SHOE
HUSBAND	SONS

```
S H A M O B D J S S D V D M H
R E T H G U A D N A M S N I K
U D E L D E R S O N A U R G S
T H R B A R L E Y O H O T E N
H S A O E N S M C I O B E D E
A H A P L T E E F L E S M A D
E O N R R C H H F I I H H H I
M S L L A O N L M H A D U J A
I R E L I M E L E C H O S E M
T E A O N A E L G H M I B S D
L P O A S H O E M I E I A S A
A A G H M L S T B A O M N E V
E E B U X O X S O N S O D S I
M R Z Q Z N X H A M O A R T D
H A R V E S T M Z O A N R O C
```

Acrostic

by Tenley Osberg

Deborah's Song

Deborah hit the nail on the head in this final verse of her song celebrating Jael's courageous yet deadly deed. Crack this acrostic's code to learn more about the prophetess's tuneful tale of victory and the peace that followed.

The Israelites' enemy (Judges 4:24)

$\overline{55}$ $\overline{45}$ $\overline{17}$ $\overline{42}$ $\overline{10}$ $\overline{36}$ $\overline{30}$ $\overline{61}$ $\overline{23}$ $\overline{5}$

The current Canaanite king (Judges 4:23)

$\overline{58}$ $\overline{18}$ $\overline{6}$ $\overline{46}$ $\overline{39}$

Where Sisera and his army were lured (Judges 4:7)

$\overline{59}$ $\overline{40}$ $\overline{31}$ $\overline{22}$ $\overline{43}$ $\overline{2}$ $\overline{24}$ $\overline{50}$ $\overline{32}$ $\overline{7}$ $\overline{16}$

Barak _____ Sisera's chariots (Judges 4:16)

$\overline{60}$ $\overline{44}$ $\overline{27}$ $\overline{12}$ $\overline{19}$ $\overline{37}$ $\overline{8}$

The children of Israel _____ and _____ the king of Canaan (Judges 4:24)

$\overline{25}$ $\overline{66}$ $\overline{56}$ $\overline{1}$ $\overline{47}$ $\overline{62}$ $\overline{51}$ $\overline{64}$ $\overline{38}$ and

$\overline{3}$ $\overline{13}$ $\overline{26}$ $\overline{65}$ $\overline{41}$ $\overline{57}$ $\overline{33}$ $\overline{11}$ $\overline{63}$

Place of battle of the kings (Judges 5:19)

$\overline{9}$ $\overline{28}$ $\overline{48}$ $\overline{15}$ $\overline{53}$ $\overline{20}$ $\overline{54}$ $\overline{34}$

$\overline{4}$ $\overline{52}$ $\overline{29}$ $\overline{14}$ $\overline{49}$ $\overline{21}$ $\overline{35}$

31-35   51-23-48   18-51-51   48-22-40-36-37

64-2-11-4-62-23-20   60-23-16-40-12-22,   43

51-54-27-8:   6-44-65   51-7-61   65-22-37-4

48-22-42-61   51-35-32-15   22-30-4   6-11

10-26   61-22-52   5-19-17   9-22-56-2   22-15

29-35-7-48-22   34-43-24-61-22   46-2   22-14-26

4-50-29-22-61.   28-39-21   48-22-37   51-10-36-3

22-45-49   53-56-26-65   34-57-41-48-33

33-13-47-66-5.

JUDGES 5:31

Crossword
by Dorothy Pryse

The Harlot with a Lot of Heart

Because of her faith, the prostitute Rahab not only saved the lives of Joshua's men but also those of herself and her household, and *then* she went on to become part of Jesus' family tree! What a woman! Have fun learning more about this harlot with a lot of heart as you work your way through this puzzle.

By faith the harlot Rahab perished not with them that believed not, when she had received the spies with peace.
HEBREWS 11:31

ACROSS

1 Biblical fisherman (Matthew 4:18)
6 Individual rights defender (abbr.)
10 Clutch
13 Pineapple
15 Blacken
16 Language used by the deaf (abbr.)
17 "An anxious heart ____ a man down" (Proverbs 12:25 NIV)
18 "The people. . .baked it in ____" (Numbers 11:8)
19 Pressure unit (abbr.)
20 "The people shall go out and gather a certain ____ every day" (Exodus 16:4)
22 JOSHUA'S MEN TOLD RAHAB TO HANG THIS COLOR CORD FROM HER WINDOW (Joshua 2:18)
24 RAHAB'S SON MARRIED A WOMAN FROM THIS COUNTRY (Ruth 4:10)
26 Memorization process
28 "The cave. . .was from the children of ____" (Genesis 49:32)
29 Seed
30 RAHAB LET THE SPIES "DOWN BY A ____ THROUGH THE WINDOW" (Joshua 2:15 NKJV)
31 RAHAB'S GREAT-GRANDSON (Matthew 1:5 NIV)
32 Native of (suffix)
33 JOSHUA, WHO SENT OUT THE SPIES INTO RAHAB'S TOWN, HAD BEEN THE ____ OF MOSES (Joshua 1:1 NIV)
34 "Fiery serpents. . .____ the people" (Numbers 21:6)
35 Layered Italian dish (var.)
37 Seaplane float

41 "Ye shall not eat of them that chew the ____" (Deuteronomy 14:7)
42 RAHAB HID THE SPIES "WITH THE STALKS OF ____" (Joshua 2:6)
43 By way of
44 Travesty
47 Test
48 "I was pricked in my heart [as with the sharp ____ of an adder]" (Psalm 73:21 AMP)
49 Gelatinous seaweed substance
50 "Be ____ your sin will find you out" (Numbers 32:23)
51 Abruptly refuse
52 Indian bean
54 "A front behind which I worked an elaborate ____" (2 Corinthians 12:16 MSG)
56 Relating to (suffix)
57 "You were putting on ____, acting so high and mighty" (Ezekiel 16:55 MSG)
59 Straitlaced
63 "____ did that which was right in the eyes of the LORD" (1 Kings 15:11)
64 Disallow
65 "____ their fathers, they quickly turned from the way" (Judges 2:17 NIV)
66 American sculptor and architect Maya Ying
67 Organization (abbr.)
68 "David put garrisons in ____ of Damascus" (2 Samuel 8:6)

DOWN

1 THE LORD DELIVERED RAHAB'S GREAT-GREAT-GRANDSON "OUT OF THE ____ OF THE LION" (1 Samuel 17:37; Matthew 1:5–6)
2 Chemical compound suffix

3 Siamese
4 Memory trace
5 THIS WOMAN GAVE JOSHUA'S SPIES LODGING (Joshua 2:3)
6 Internists' organization (abbr.)
7 WHAT RAHAB THE HARLOT WAS NOT (Joshua 2:1)
8 "They shall hold the bow and the ____" (Jeremiah 50:42)
9 ____ Minor (Little Dipper)
10 City in Italy
11 Things of value
12 Untroubled
14 Concord, e.g.
21 Eat away
23 Gone with the Wind's Mr. Butler
24 Plateau
25 Mined metals
27 Unlock (poet.)
29 Mousse
30 Peel
31 Hex
33 Flu
34 RAHAB'S SON (Matthew 1:5 NIV)
36 Capital of Ghana
37 Thicknesses
38 President's office

39 Squeal
40 "He doesn't endlessly ____ and scold" (Psalm 103:9 MSG)
42 Animal pelt
44 Beauty treatment
45 Tennis player Andre
46 Wickerwork material
47 "'Three ____ of barley for a denarius'" (Revelation 6:6 NKJV)
48 "JOSHUA SPARED RAHAB THE PROSTITUTE, WITH HER ____" (Joshua 6:25 NIV)
50 "THE YOUNG MEN THAT WERE ____ WENT IN, AND BROUGHT OUT RAHAB" (Joshua 6:23)
51 "Thy ____ be filled with plenty" (Proverbs 3:10)
53 "'The pressure has built up, like ____ beneath the earth'" (Job 32:19 MSG)
55 Computer component (abbr.)
58 BOAZ TO RAHAB (Matthew 1:5 NIV)
60 "The woman saith unto him, ____, give me this water" (John 4:15)
61 Slalom
62 "____, though I walk through the valley of the shadow of death" (Psalm 23:4)

307

Close to Jesus

Though Jesus' twelve disciples were all men, a number of women contributed to His ministry from the very earliest days of His life. These spotty headlines describe three women who were close to Jesus—can you solve each one?

BABY JESUS ME●TIO●ED BY ELDERLY
JERUS●LEM TEMPLE L●DY

— — — —

F●IT●FUL ELD●R●Y PRIE●T'S W●FE
EXP●C●ING BA●Y

— — — — — — — —

AGGR●VATED SISTER ●ORE CONCERNED
●BOUT CHO●ES ●HAN T●E GUEST

— — — — — —

Sharing the News

God's great works can stun even the most avid believers into silence.

1. THIOSUGRE

2. LRTAA

3. ESNICEN

4. MOTUSC

5. NALGE

6. MESLBSAEL

7. TSIPER

8. OTL

9. DLIHC

Her husband returned home excited but speechless.

1. _ _ _ _ _ O _ _ _

2. _ O _ _ _

3. O _ _ _ _ _ _

4. _ _ O _ _ _

5. O _ _ _ _

6. O _ _ _ _ _ _ _

7. _ _ _ O _ _

8. _ _ O

9. _ O _ _ _

Answer: _ _ _ _ _ _ _ _ _

Word Search
by Angela Fletcher

Song of Deborah
JUDGES 5:2–31

ARCHERS	LIVES
AWAKE	LORD
BENJAMIN	MEROZ
BREACHES	MIGHTY
DEBORAH	MOUNTAINS
DISH	PRAISE
FLOCKS	REUBEN
GATES	SHAMGAR
HAMMER	SHIELD
HEART	SINAI
HEBER	SISERA
HORSEHOOFS	SPEAK
JAEL	SPEAR
KINGS	SUN
KISHON	

```
B F N R B C M O U N T A I N S
L G I U A S K L V F L O C K S
E H M S S F J K I N G S F L Q
S I A K P O S M S N Z E E P L
Q J J A E O R S H I E L D O O
E D N V A H E E A K N B G N R
K I E M R E H H M I A D U M D
A S B X Z S C C G S R T H E R
E H Q G I R R A A H E R I R R
P K P A R O A E R O M A J O S
S L N T E H I R W N M E L Z J
D I O E B D E B O R A H I M A
S S I S E R A T X Y H C V L E
B M N Y H M I G H T Y B E K L
A A W A K E H U P R A I S E U
```

Acrostic
by Tenley Osberg

Ruth's Commitment

Because of Ruth's promise, her mother-in-law, although embittered, did not become "ruth-less." Solve to uncover a vow of commitment that reaped prophetic benefits.

A determined promise

‾‾ ‾‾ ‾‾ ‾‾ ‾‾ ‾‾ ‾‾ ‾‾ ‾‾ ‾‾
22 42 10 46 15 19 27 31 52 3

Ruth's mother-in-law (Ruth 1:3–4)

‾‾ ‾‾ ‾‾ ‾‾ ‾‾
2   34 38 51 6

Two of Boaz's crops (Ruth 2:23)

‾‾ ‾‾ ‾‾ ‾‾ ‾‾ and ‾‾ ‾‾ ‾‾ ‾‾ ‾‾ ‾‾
13 17 26 29 1   21 41 9   45 49 33

To follow behind the harvesters (Ruth 2:3)

‾‾ ‾‾ ‾‾ ‾‾ ‾‾
14 18 25 30 50

The place Boaz winnowed barley (Ruth 3:2)

‾‾ ‾‾ ‾‾ ‾‾ ‾‾ ‾‾ ‾‾ ‾‾ ‾‾
35 39 53 7   43 54 23 47 11

‾‾ ‾‾ ‾‾ ‾‾ ‾‾
5   37 16 20 28

To disavow or reject

‾‾ ‾‾ ‾‾ ‾‾ ‾‾ ‾‾ ‾‾ ‾‾ ‾‾
4   32 36 40 44 8   48 24 12

10-34-33   19-17-31   18-42-9-44   44-25-29-45

13-15-1-39   46-49. . .6-5   41-50-33-19-17-15-2-14

21-40-24   44-25-34-19-39   43-7-36-34-28-34-19-31-43

33-42-40   48-50-44   10-25.

RUTH 1:17 NIV

Drop Two
by Dorothy Pryse

An Example of Loyalty
RUTH 1:16

Some people you just can't get rid of. Solve this puzzle to find out what Ruth said to Naomi as she was heading out of town.

SCARLET	Loves	_____	1. ___ ___
NIGHTLY	Knotting	_____	2. ___ ___
BLARNEY	Discover	_____	3. ___ ___
PLEASES	Gross receipts	_____	4. ___ ___
INFLAME	Last	_____	5. ___ ___
ALIMONY	Italian city	_____	6. ___ ___
PROPHET	Spasm	_____	7. ___ ___
MISDEAL	Female servants	_____	8. ___ ___
COASTER	Vehicles	_____	9. ___ ___
SPARING	Corn	_____	10. ___ ___
SHINGLE	Burn	_____	11. ___ ___
EATABLE	Sheep sound	_____	12. ___ ___

___ ___ ___ ___ ___ ___ ___ ___ ___ ___ ___ ___

___ ___ ___ ___ ___ ___ ___ ___ ___ ___ ___ ___
1   2   3   4   5   6   7   8   9   10   11   12

Answers

Drop Twos

One of a Kind
LEARN, STOLE, WINDS, TREES, AMBLE, RATED, GLUED, CANED,
NOBLE, BLASÉ, CHINA, VINES, VERGE
"The king made Daniel a great man." Daniel 2:48

Paul in Prison
TANGO, FLARE, LOSER, RATED, SIRES, CELLS, RANDY, AMPLE, EERIE,
SLATE, DALLY, HAIRY, SLITS
"But Paul cried with a loud voice." Acts 16:28

Check Your Hearing
BALED, DENSE, MEATY, SEAMS, ASIDE, SAGES, BLAST, GOING,
THERE, STAKE, IMAGE
"So Samuel went and lay down." 1 Samuel 3:9

Israel's First King
BREAD, CHAIN, CHIME, DAMES, SCARF, APING, ACUTE, FIRST,
MOIRE, RISEN, CRIBS, SOBER, CAUSE
"Is Saul also among the prophets?" 1 Samuel 10:12

Over the Rainbow
DOING, PANIC, VERSE, LIKED, ABATE, CARRY, TRIAD, MINED, WALLS,
MANNA, CASTE, BREED
"God blessed Noah and his sons." Genesis 9:1

A Patient Man
VICAR, ELATE, CHAIN, ROSIN, QUIET, ABIDE, BRACE, PLUME, IDEAL,
LEGGY, GLADE, REACH, TARDY
"After this opened Job his mouth." Job 3:1

Jacob Picks a Wife
SLIME, STRUM, STEED, INERT, TAXED, DEEDS, VERBS, EYING,
ROAST, DRIVE, CLIME, ACHED
"And he loved also Rachel more." Genesis 29:30

Esther's Predecessor
GLOAT, SCENT, EASEL, PLACE, REBEL, SPELL, DRAPE, DEALS,
VISOR, TRUER, CLONE, MITER
"Vashti the queen made a feast." Esther 1:9

Mary Is Chosen
CLING, ROUTE, DECAL, PARED, TRADE, SANDY, AILED, CLAIM,
ROUST, SERVE, ALONG, TAILS
"And the virgin's name was Mary." Luke 1:27

Sarah Births Isaac
DENTS, EIGHT, SINCE, REIGN, GRANT, STOLE, TARRY, NIECE,
ROWED, COBRA, CLEAR, SANDS
"I have born him a son in old age." Genesis 21:7

Eunice's Mother
LEDGE, LONER, BRAND, DINER, CRIES, GAMIN, COUNT,
HASTY, WAVES, CARVE, PIPED
"Faith in grandmother Lois." See 2 Timothy 1:5

An Example of Loyalty
CARES, TYING, LEARN, SALES, FINAL, MILAN, THROE, MAIDS,
CARTS, GRAIN, SINGE, BLEAT
"Thy people shall be my people." Ruth 1:16

Acrostics

A Brotherly Brother
JUDAH, BRETHREN, FLOCKS, WANDERING, PIECES, MANY
"Reuben said unto them, Shed no blood, but cast him into this pit that is in the wilderness, and lay no hand upon him." Genesis 37:22

A Burning Sentence
IMAGE, FURY, KING, DECREE, BROUGHT, WORSHIP
"He commanded the most mighty men that were in his army to bind Shadrach, Meshach, and Abednego, and to cast them into the burning fiery furnace." Daniel 3:20

A Criminal or a King
BLOOD, JUDGMENT, PERSUADED, WASHED, SAYING, CRUCIFIED
"They had then a notable prisoner, called Barabbas. Therefore when they were gathered together, Pilate said unto them, Whom will ye that I release unto you? Barabbas or Jesus?" Matthew 27:16–17

A Right-Hand Man
BURDENS, WILDERNESS, AFFLICTION, GATHERED, WORSHIP, TASKMASTERS
"Aaron spake all the words which the LORD had spoken unto Moses, and did the signs in the sight of the people." Exodus 4:30

A Serious Misstep
HOUSE, FATHER, RECKONED, MIDST, POWER, BEHOLD
"His nurse took him up, and fled: and it came to pass, as she made haste to flee, that he fell, and became lame. And his name was Mephibosheth." 2 Samuel 4:4

A Special Friend
COVENANT, BOW, JAVELIN, SACRIFICE, HEARKENED, COMMUNE
"The soul of Jonathan was knit with the soul of David, and Jonathan loved him as his own soul." 1 Samuel 18:1

A True Blessing
GATHERED, BLESSED, VESSELS, SYMPATHIZED, SUFFICED, RECOMPENSE
"Boaz commanded his young men, saying, Let her glean even among the sheaves, and reproach her not: And let fall also some of the handfuls of purpose for her." Ruth 2:15–16

Beloved Brother
BETHEL, BENONI, CULPABLE, FAVORED, SMALLEST, JUDGE
"To all of them he gave each man changes of raiment; but to Benjamin he gave three hundred pieces of silver, and five changes of raiment." Genesis 45:22

Christ's Purpose
BETHLEHEM, DISCIPLES, SON OF GOD, ANDREW, GARDEN, CALVARY
"For to this end Christ both died, and rose, and revived, that he might be Lord both of the dead and living." Romans 14:9

Craving Jesus
SPEAKING, SABBATH, WOMEN, JEWS, CRUCIFY, REVILED
"Joseph of Arimathaea, an honourable counsellor, which also waited for the kingdom of God, came, and went in boldly unto Pilate, and craved the body of Jesus." Mark 15:43

Father of a Great King
OBED, JESSE, KING DAVID; SAMUEL; EIGHT; BRANCH; PAW; SACRIFICE
"And the LORD said unto Samuel. . .Fill thine horn with oil, and go, I will send thee to Jesse the Bethlehemite: for I have provided me a king among his sons." 1 Samuel 16:1

Goodness Rewarded
WORKED, ADVANCE, CHRONICLES, MIGHTY, PURIM, FOE
"Mordecai was great in the king's house, and his fame went out throughout all the provinces." Esther 9:4

He Always Loved Him Best
PEACEABLY, UPRIGHT, DREAMING, WIVES, JACOB, FLOCK
"Now Israel loved Joseph more than all his children, because he was the son of his old age: and he made him a coat of many colours." Genesis 37:3

High Priest of the Jews
FATHER-IN-LAW, LAZARUS, EXCEEDING, SERVANT, BLASPHEMY, PETER AND JOHN
"Now Caiaphas was he, which gave counsel to the Jews, that it was expedient that one man should die for the people." John 18:14

Master of the World
ESPOUSED, SWADDLING, BETHLEHEM, PRAYERFUL, COUNTRY, WAX
"And it came to pass in those days, that there went out a decree from Caesar Augustus, that all the world should be taxed." Luke 2:1

Saul's Servant
HADADEZER, WHITHERSOEVER, MAGNIFIED, BEHOLD, KINDNESS, CONTINUALLY
"When they had called him unto David, the king said unto him, Art thou Ziba? And he said, Thy servant is he." 2 Samuel 9:2

Second-Best but Blessed
WALK, LAUGHED, COVENANT, ESTABLISH, FLESH, MOTHER
"And as for Ishmael, I have heard thee: Behold, I have blessed him, and will make him fruitful." Genesis 17:20

Strangers on the Road
CONDEMNED, SEPULCHRE, ASTONISHED, FRIGHTENED, KNEW, JOY
"One of them, whose name was Cleopas, answering said unto him, Art thou only a stranger in Jerusalem, and hast not known the things which are come to pass there in these days?" Luke 24:18

An Issue of Faith
STANCHED, STRAIGHTWAY, VIRTUE, TREMBLING, DAUGHTER, COMFORT
"A woman, which was diseased with an issue of blood twelve

years, came behind him, and touched the hem of his garment: For she said within herself, If I may but touch his garment, I shall be whole." Matthew 9:20–21

The Girl Who Betrayed the Betrayer
JERUSALEM, PETER, ZEAL, OATH, FORETOLD, CROWING
"And when he was gone out into the porch, another maid saw him, and said unto them that were there, This fellow was also with Jesus of Nazareth." Matthew 26:71

The Woman Who Rocked
ENCAMPED, FLED, SHECHEM, WICKED, TOWER, ARMOURBEARER
"And a certain woman cast a piece of a millstone upon Abimelech's head, and all to brake his skull." Judges 9:53

A Showy yet Shallow Woman
AGRIPPA, CAESAREA, MEN, BROUGHT, TESTIMONY, OVERWORKED
"And when he had thus spoken, the king rose up, and the governor, and Bernice, and they that sat with them." Acts 26:30

Trophy Daughter
JEPHUNNEH, HEBRON, ANAKIMS, FENCED, OTHNIEL, GIVE AWAY
"And Caleb said, He that smiteth Kirjathsepher, and taketh it, to him will I give Achsah my daughter to wife." Joshua 15:16

One of Many
FIRST, WIVES, JUDAH, NABAL, OZEM, TAMAR
"And unto David were sons born in Hebron: and his firstborn was Amnon, of Ahinoam the Jezreelitess." 2 Samuel 3:2

Setting a Standard
HARLOT, JUDGE, PROMISE, DANCES, TWO, WIFELY
"And it was a custom in Israel, that the daughters of Israel went yearly to lament the daughter of Jephthah the Gileadite four days in a year." Judges 11:39–40

An Ambitious Man's Wife
MORDECAI, LIVID, ESTHER, FEAST, WINE, SIZE
"Nevertheless Haman refrained himself: and when he came home, he sent and called for his friends, and Zeresh his wife." Esther 5:10

An Adorning Wife
HUSBAND, FATHER, CAIN, JUBAL, TWO, WIVES
"And Adah bare Jabal: he was the father of such as dwell in tents, and of such as have cattle." Genesis 4:20

A Woman of Vision
GOVERNOR, JUDGMENT, STOOD, MOB, WASH, CRUCIFY
"His wife sent unto him, saying, Have thou nothing to do with that just man: for I have suffered many things this day in a dream because of him." Matthew 27:19

A Promise-Breaker's Daughter
AHINOAM, SECOND, BOW, JEALOUSY, FOUGHT, ADRIEL
"Now the sons of Saul were Jonathan, and Ishui, and Melchishua: and the names of his two daughters were these; the name of the firstborn Merab, and the name of the younger Michal."
1 Samuel 14:49

A Peg above the Rest
KENITE, SISERA, JUMPED, FLED, WILY, DEBORAH
"Then Jael Heber's wife took a nail of the tent, and took an hammer in her hand, and went softly unto him, and smote the nail into his temples. . .for he was fast asleep and weary." Judges 4:21

Mother of a Priestly Line
UZZIEL, MINISTER, BEFORE, STRANGE, WRATH, DRINK
"And Aaron took him Elisheba, daughter of Amminadab, sister of Naashon, to wife; and she bare him Nadab, and Abihu, Eleazar, and Ithamar." Exodus 6:23

The Frustrated Temptress
POTIPHAR, CAPTAIN, EGYPT, JEWISH, FLAME, DUNGEON

"And it came to pass after these things, that his master's wife cast her eyes upon Joseph; and she said, Lie with me." Genesis 39:7

A Well-Thought-of Woman
DAVID, AHITHOPHEL, SERVANTS, MESSAGE, WATER, SHUCK

"And the woman took and spread a covering over the well's mouth, and spread ground corn thereon; and the thing was not known." 2 Samuel 17:19

The Prophetess
HULDAH, HILKIAH, MANASSEH, ASSYRIA and EGYPT, BOOK OF THE LAW, CARVED

"And she said unto them, thus saith the LORD God of Israel. . . Behold, I will bring evil upon this place, and upon the inhabitants thereof. . .because they have forsaken me." 2 Kings 22:15–17

Deborah's Song
CANAANITES, JABIN, KISHON RIVER, PURSUED, PREVAILED and DESTROYED, WATERS OF MEGIDDO

"So let all thine enemies perish, O Lord: but let them that love him be as the sun when he goeth forth in his might. And the land had rest forty years." Judges 5:31

Ruth's Commitment
COMMITMENT, NAOMI, WHEAT and BARLEY, GLEAN, THRESHING FLOOR, REPUDIATE

"May the Lord deal with me. . .if anything but death separates you and me." Ruth 1:17

Word Searches

The Prodigal Son

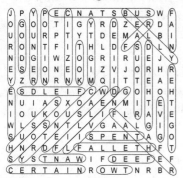

Zacchaeus

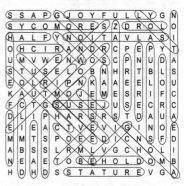

Jewish Mother, Greek Father

Paul's Fellow Helper

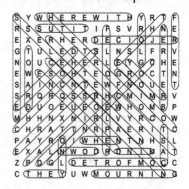

Evangelists

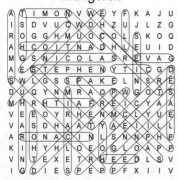

Faithful Father of Nations

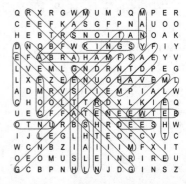

324

Job

Fifteen Years Added to His Life

A Prepared Heart

Prepare the Way

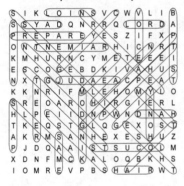

Faithful Centurion

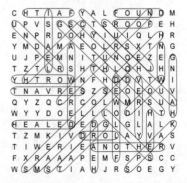

Tax Collector

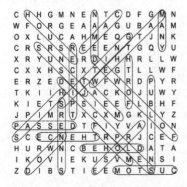

King David

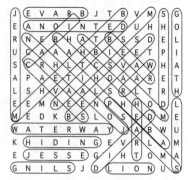

Wise Men

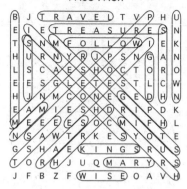

Noah

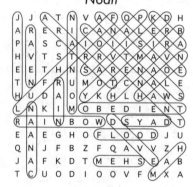

Followers of Christ

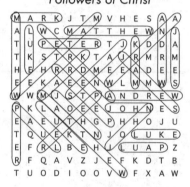

Daniel

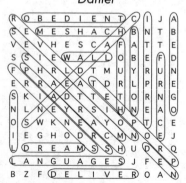

Only One

J	S	E	S	S	J	S	S	J	S	J	S	U
J	J	U	J	S	S	S	S	J	J	E	J	J
S	E	S	S	J	J	E	S	J	S	J	U	S
E	S	E	J	U	J	J	J	E	S	U	J	U
J	S	J	J	J	J	J	J	E	E	J	S	E
E	J	S	U	J	J	J	J	S	S	S	J	J
U	J	J	S	S	E	E	S	S	S	S	S	S
S	S	J	E	J	E	U	E	E	S	J	S	J
J	E	U	J	S	E	J	S	S	J	E	S	S
J	J	J	J	J	U	J	J	J	E	U	J	S
J	U	J	J	J	E	S	J	J	E	J	E	U
U	J	U	J	S	J	S	S	J	E	J	S	J
E	S	J	S	J	S	S	S	J	S	S	E	S

A Surprised Servant-Girl

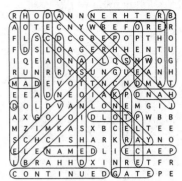

Lady Merchant

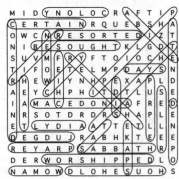

Lady Departed

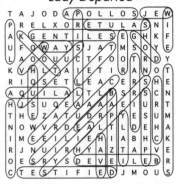

King Saul's Daughter

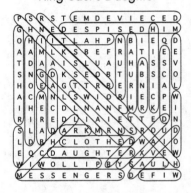

David's Warmth

Queen Esther's Appeal

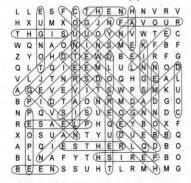

Who Loved Him Most?

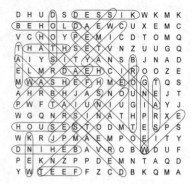

The Woman at the Well

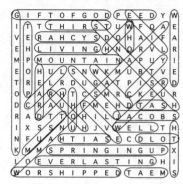

Highly Favored

Moses' Mother

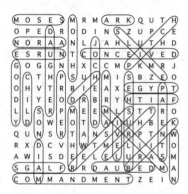

Virtuous Woman

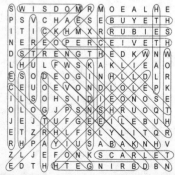

Unwanted Wife

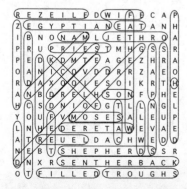

A Bride for Isaac

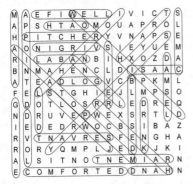

Sisters of Bethany

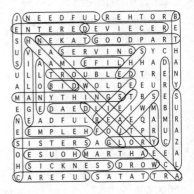

Hagar

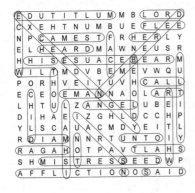

Hannah's Hope

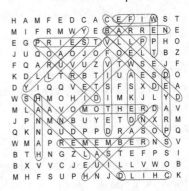

Ruth

Song of Deborah

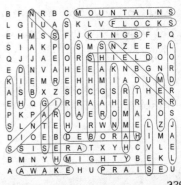

Cryptoscriptures

Biblical Battlers

"And the woman bare a son, and called his name Samson: and the child grew, and the Lord blessed him." Judges 13:24

"And there went out a champion out of the camp of the Philistines, named Goliath, of Gath, whose height was six cubits and a span." 1 Samuel 17:4

Taking a Stand

"He took water, and washed his hands before the multitude, saying, I am innocent of the blood of this just person." Matthew 27:24

"Put up again thy sword into his place: for all they that take the sword shall perish with the sword." Matthew 26:52

Great Love

"Then Paul answered, What mean ye to weep and to break mine heart? for I am ready not to be bound only, but also to die at Jerusalem for the name of the Lord Jesus." Acts 21:13

"Among them that are born of women there hath not risen a greater than John the Baptist." Matthew 11:11

The Wisdom of Kings

"And God gave Solomon wisdom and understanding exceeding much, and largeness of heart, even as the sand that is on the sea shore." 1 Kings 4:29

"Josiah was eight years old when he began to reign, and he reigned in Jerusalem one and thirty years." 2 Chronicles 34:1

Following the Lord

"For Ezra had prepared his heart to seek the law of the LORD, and to do it, and to teach in Israel statutes and judgments." Ezra 7:10

"Be strong and of a good courage; be not afraid, neither be thou dismayed: for the LORD thy God is with thee whithersoever thou goest." Joshua 1:9

The Patriarchs

"And Noah was five hundred years old: and Noah begat Shem, Ham, and Japheth." Genesis 5:32

"And the boys grew: and Esau was a cunning hunter, a man of the field; and Jacob was a plain man, dwelling in tents." Genesis 25:27

Two Important Women

"Now when Jesus was risen early the first day of the week, he appeared first to Mary Magdalene, out of whom he had cast seven devils." Mark 16:9

"Behold, thou art fair, my love; behold, thou art fair; thou hast doves' eyes within thy locks: thy hair is as a flock of goats, that appear from mount Gilead." Song of Solomon 4:1

The Little Maid

"And the Syrians had gone out by companies, and had brought away captive out of the land of Israel a little maid; and she waited on Naaman's wife." 2 Kings 5:2

"And she said unto her mistress, Would God my lord were with the prophet that is in Samaria! for he would recover him of his leprosy." 2 Kings 5:3

The Wives of Prophets
"And I went unto the prophetess; and she conceived, and bare a son. Then said the LORD to me, Call his name Mahershalalhashbaz." Isaiah 8:3

"Son of man, behold, I take away from thee the desire of thine eyes with a stroke: yet neither shalt thou mourn nor weep, neither shall thy tears run down." Ezekiel 24:16

Womanly Advice
"Favour is deceitful, and beauty is vain: but a woman that feareth the LORD, she shall be praised." Proverbs 31:30

"A virtuous woman is a crown to her husband: but she that maketh ashamed is as rottenness in his bones." Proverbs 12:4

Wise Women
"All the women that were wise hearted did spin with their hands, and brought that which they had spun, both of blue, and of purple, and of scarlet, and of fine linen." Exodus 35:25

"Then cried a wise woman out of the city, Hear, hear; say, I pray you, unto Joab, Come near hither, that I may speak with thee." 2 Samuel 20:16

The Story That Began It All
"And the LORD God said, It is not good that the man should be alone; I will make him an help meet for him." Genesis 2:18

"And the LORD God said unto the woman, What is this that thou hast done? And the woman said, The serpent beguiled me, and I did eat." Genesis 3:13

Sudoku

God's Favored

	A	B	C	D	E	F	G	H	I
1	G	S	I	O	T	U	H	E	R
2	R	H	U	G	E	S	O	T	I
3	T	O	E	R	I	H	S	U	G
4	I	T	S	E	R	G	U	O	H
5	H	E	R	U	S	O	I	G	T
6	U	G	O	T	H	I	R	S	E
7	E	U	H	S	G	R	T	I	O
8	S	R	G	I	O	T	E	H	U
9	O	I	T	H	U	E	G	R	S

RIGHTEOUS

The Perfect One

	A	B	C	D	E	F	G	H	I
1	D	E	F	U	R	W	O	L	N
2	O	W	U	L	D	N	E	F	R
3	R	N	L	F	O	E	W	D	U
4	N	F	R	E	L	U	D	O	W
5	L	D	W	R	F	O	U	N	E
6	E	U	O	N	W	D	L	R	F
7	W	O	N	D	E	R	F	U	L
8	F	R	E	O	U	L	N	W	D
9	U	L	D	W	N	F	R	E	O

WONDERFUL

The Brothers Boanerges

	A	B	C	D	E	F	G	H	I
1	T	U	R	F	H	N	D	E	O
2	D	N	O	E	T	R	U	H	F
3	F	E	H	U	O	D	N	R	T
4	E	F	D	N	U	O	R	T	H
5	N	H	T	R	D	F	E	O	U
6	R	O	U	T	E	H	F	D	N
7	H	R	E	O	F	U	T	N	D
8	U	D	N	H	R	T	O	F	E
9	O	T	F	D	N	E	H	U	R

OF THUNDER

A Whale of a Story

	A	B	C	D	E	F	G	H	I
1	H	A	F	E	I	R	T	G	S
2	E	T	R	G	F	S	A	H	I
3	S	G	I	T	H	A	F	R	E
4	R	E	T	F	S	I	H	A	G
5	F	H	G	R	A	E	S	I	T
6	A	I	S	H	G	T	R	E	F
7	I	F	H	S	R	G	E	T	A
8	G	R	E	A	T	F	I	S	H
9	T	S	A	I	E	H	G	F	R

GREAT FISH

Gospel Bad Guy

	A	B	C	D	E	F	G	H	I
1	B	H	A	T	I	M	Y	R	E
2	E	R	M	Y	B	H	T	I	A
3	T	I	Y	R	E	A	M	B	H
4	R	M	H	E	A	T	B	Y	I
5	A	T	I	H	Y	B	R	E	M
6	Y	E	B	I	M	R	H	A	T
7	H	A	E	B	T	Y	I	M	R
8	I	Y	R	M	H	E	A	T	B
9	M	B	T	A	R	I	E	H	Y

BETRAY HIM

Winning God's Approval

	A	B	C	D	E	F	G	H	I
1	N	A	V	Y	T	M	R	E	S
2	M	Y	S	E	R	V	A	N	T
3	R	E	T	S	A	N	M	Y	V
4	A	V	R	M	S	E	Y	T	N
5	S	T	N	R	V	Y	E	A	M
6	Y	M	E	A	N	T	V	S	R
7	V	S	A	T	Y	R	N	M	E
8	E	N	Y	V	M	S	T	R	A
9	T	R	M	N	E	A	S	V	Y

MY SERVANT

Sarah

	A	B	C	D	E	F	G	H	I
1	A	P	S	H	R	C	U	D	E
2	R	D	H	A	E	U	P	C	S
3	E	C	U	S	D	P	R	H	A
4	C	S	E	R	U	D	A	P	H
5	P	U	R	C	H	A	S	E	D
6	H	A	D	E	P	S	C	U	R
7	S	R	P	D	C	H	E	A	U
8	D	E	C	U	A	R	H	S	P
9	U	H	A	P	S	E	D	R	C

PURCHASED

The Family of Zelophehad

	A	B	C	D	E	F	G	H	I
1	U	T	A	D	S	G	H	R	E
2	D	R	E	A	H	T	S	G	U
3	S	H	G	U	R	E	A	D	T
4	A	D	R	G	E	U	T	S	H
5	G	U	T	H	A	S	D	E	R
6	H	E	S	T	D	R	U	A	G
7	R	A	H	E	U	D	G	T	S
8	T	S	D	R	G	H	E	U	A
9	E	G	U	S	T	A	R	H	D

DAUGHTERS

A Most Amazing Visit

	A	B	C	D	E	F	G	H	I
1	D	R	U	M	N	F	O	Y	A
2	Y	N	O	A	D	U	M	R	F
3	A	M	F	R	O	Y	U	D	N
4	O	U	R	Y	A	D	N	F	M
5	N	Y	A	F	R	M	D	O	U
6	M	F	D	O	U	N	Y	A	R
7	R	O	Y	U	M	A	F	N	D
8	F	D	M	N	Y	R	A	U	O
9	U	A	N	D	F	O	R	M	Y

MARY FOUND

All She Wanted

	A	B	C	D	E	F	G	H	I
1	N	S	K	E	G	B	A	I	H
2	I	A	G	N	H	S	B	E	K
3	E	B	H	I	A	K	S	N	G
4	B	N	I	S	K	G	H	A	E
5	G	K	A	H	B	E	I	S	N
6	H	E	S	A	I	N	G	K	B
7	K	I	N	G	S	H	E	B	A
8	A	H	B	K	E	I	N	G	S
9	S	G	E	B	N	A	K	H	I

KING SHEBA

No Secrets

	A	B	C	D	E	F	G	H	I
1	H	A	N	I	G	S	E	Y	T
2	E	G	S	T	Y	A	H	I	N
3	I	T	Y	H	N	E	G	S	A
4	A	E	I	Y	H	T	N	G	S
5	Y	N	T	G	S	I	A	H	E
6	G	S	H	A	E	N	Y	T	I
7	S	Y	A	N	I	G	T	E	H
8	N	I	G	E	T	H	S	A	Y
9	T	H	E	S	A	Y	I	N	G

THE SAYING

Truth or Consequences

	A	B	C	D	E	F	G	H	I
1	I	E	B	Y	D	T	H	U	R
2	H	T	U	E	R	B	D	Y	I
3	D	Y	R	I	H	U	T	B	E
4	T	U	I	D	B	R	Y	E	H
5	Y	R	E	H	U	I	B	T	D
6	B	H	D	T	Y	E	R	I	U
7	U	D	T	B	E	H	I	R	Y
8	E	I	H	R	T	Y	U	D	B
9	R	B	Y	U	I	D	E	H	T

BURIED THY

Crosswords

"Simon, Simon"

A Pinwheel of Prophets

Biblical Warriors

Fathers-in-Law

Fathers and Sons

What's His Line?

King After King

```
L E G A L . A F A C E . E R E
A T O N E . S O D A S . V A T
I N A N D . T R E S S . I N C
N A D A B B A A S H A E L A H
. . . Y O N . . . B Y E . . .
H I D A . A D D T O . L A D A
A R O M A . O H O H . S E S .
M E N A H E M P E K A H I A H
A N N . L E E . S I D L E . .
N E E D . E N D O R . T E S S
. . . A S P . . . N A Y . . .
O M R I A H A B A H A Z I A H
P E A . R A Z O R . G E T S O
E R G . A N O N O . I R A T E
L E E . S T R E W . S O N A S
```

Brothers-in-Law

```
A C S . J A C O B . A T S E A
P O T . A L U L A . J U R O R
A R E . C A R E T . A L I S T
C R E A K S . . T A X I . . .
H A L L . B U L B . P T S D .
E L S E . T A P E R . A H A .
. . R A I N S . . A A R O N .
. J E T T E D . H I S S E D .
F O S S E . . P E C K S . . .
C W A . I T A L Y . A P S E .
A L U M . N E R D . I O T A .
. . O N C E . . W A L T E R .
C H A S E . I S A A C . E R N
D U N E S . N E R V E . N N E
T R Y S T . G A M E S . T A D
```

Biblical Brothers

```
M O D E L . L A M B . B A R
O P E R A . A S I A . I R A
S I M O N A N D A N D R E W
E N O S . D O O . D I D . .
S E N . L A S . R A E . R C A
. . J A M E S A N D J O H N
B A R O N S . T I A . A T A N
A R E Y E . M A N . A D O R E
N E A T . C A N . A L A R M S
J A C O B A N D E S A U . .
O S H . E T E . L I D . D I E
. . M A C . A I N . C O S T
S H E M A N D J A P H E T H
R O T . L E D A . L A T H E
A T E . L A S H . O T H E R
```

Jesus, My Rock

```
O R A L . S A S . L O R D . R
S A . A N T I C S . D E E . E
. M E R C Y . A . H E A L E D
G . S D . E R I E . L I V E .
L E A . R R . T A T . V I E .
O . U T T E R S . V A . E L M
R S . O O . S T . E V E R . E
Y E A R L Y . A I N . R E A R
. R E E D . A L A . C A R D .
R E O . T I E G S . S . A S .
E . N E W . R . O . T O R A .
F D . L A D E N . S A U L . V
U . E . N E . A K A . S E T I
G A L . D A M P . T O . H O .
E L S H A D D A I . T O W E R
```

Joshua's Proclamation

```
P A P A . P E R U . P L E A D
I B I S . A R A B . L U N G E
C A N T . L I M A . U N D E R
A S F O R M E A N D M Y . . .
S H E R E . . G A B . . C O R
S E A M A N S H I P . G O N E
O R T . D O S O . S A L E M .
. . H O U S E W E W I L L . .
W H E L P . V A I N . A I M .
H A R D . G R E T A G A R B O
O D S . T A I . . L I B E L .
. . S E R V E T H E L O R D .
R O M A N . E L S E . E N I E
A B O V E . R O A R . R E A R
T I B E T . S I R S . S S N S
```

The "Ahs" Have It

```
I W O . E N N U I . J O N A H
M E N . M O O R S . U V U L A
P S T . M A N N A . D E N I M
E L I J A H . . I C O N . . .
D E M O . S C A R . . S P O T
E Y E S . G U S H Y . A D E .
. . I N E R T . . R I L E D .
. L I A B L E . S C O T E R .
M O C H A . F A N T A . . . .
O R E . E V E N S . L U S T .
O D D S . K I N G . I N C A .
. . H E E L . . M A C R O N .
S A M O A . I N N E R . E O N
A V O W S . F R O N T . A T E
P E N N Y . Y A R E . L S D .
```

338

Men Who Led the Charge

Head Honchos

Men of Valor

Leaders Who Feared God

Faithful Ministers

Delivering the Message

Esther's People

E	S	A	U		O	F	Y	A		S	H	A	M	E
R	A	S	P		N	O	O	P		E	A	T	U	P
A	H	A	S	U	E	R	U	S		A	D	A	L	E
		A	T	E	L	I	E	R		A	L	E	E	
T	H	E	L	I	P	O	F		A	S	S	E	S	S
H	A	T	A	C	H			A	G	E	S			
A	S	H		A	A	R	O	N		C	A	N	I	T
I	T	E	M		H	A	M	A	N		H	I	R	E
S	O	L	O	T		M	Y	H	A	T		G	A	P
		R	E	A	P		V	A	S	H	T	I		
G	R	A	D	E	S		E	L	I	C	I	T	E	D
R	A	T	E		U	N	T	O	G	O	G			
O	N	I	C	E		S	H	A	A	S	H	G	A	Z
S	A	M	A	R		W	E	N	T		T	O	R	E
S	T	E	I	N		E	R	S	E		S	T	A	R

Women of the Bible

A	S	K	E	D		E	L	L	A		R	U	G	
P	H	E	B	E		N	E	O	N		A	P	R	S
R	E	P	E	L		A	M	I	D		I	S	U	P
	M	I	R	I	A	M		S	E	A	S	I	D	E
				R	E	A		S	L	E	D	G	E	
P	R	I	S	C	I	L	L	A		G	R	E	E	D
A	U	D	I	O	S		L	I	C	E				
L	E	A	R	N	E	D		R	E	B	E	C	C	A
			T	A	O	S		A	R	B	O	R	S	
C	I	R	C	E		E	L	I	S	A	B	E	T	H
A	N	I	O	N	S		O	D	E					
P	I	V	O	T	A	L		E	S	T	H	E	R	
O	R	E	L		L	E	N	A		H	O	V	E	L
S	O	R	I		V	A	A	L		I	R	E	N	E
N	A	T		O	H	M	S		S	A	R	A	I	

Happy Mother's Day

W	H	O		A	L	L	I	S		S	T	R	E	E	T
A	I	R		T	O	O	T	H		T	O	A	C	T	O
A	T	A		H	O	R	S	E		A	U	G	H	T	S
C	A	N	F	I	N	D	A	V	I	R	T	U	O	U	S
			A	S	S			A	R	T	S				
S	A	L	T		G	O	T	A		L	A	U	D		
A	R	A		D	A	L	E		P	U	E	B	L	O	
W	O	M	A	N	F	O	R	H	E	R	P	R	I	C	E
E	S	A	U	A	T		O	R	E	O		D	E	R	
D	E	S	K		C	A	R	E			H	E	R	S	
		T	H	A	T			T	C	U					
I	S	F	A	R	A	B	O	V	E	R	U	B	I	E	S
C	O	O	L	E	D		N	A	D	E	R		H	A	H
A	L	A	S	K	A		E	L	I	A	B		A	T	E
N	O	L	O	S	S		D	E	E	D	S		D	I	M

The "Ah's Have It!"

P	A	S	H	A		T	R	I	P		P	A	T	H
U	N	C	A	P		R	U	T	H		O	B	I	E
A	T	O	N	E		I	N	C	A		T	U	B	A
H	E	W	N		L	A	T	H	E	R		Z	I	T
			A	M	I	D		T	I	R	Z	A	H	
E	U	C	H	R	E		N	O	A	H				
D	R	Y		S	U	L	T	A	N		B	I	D	
A	S	S	N		I	O	U		N	O	S	E		
M	A	T	E		H	O	G	L	A	H		O	L	E
			C	Y	A	N		H	U	N	T	E	R	
P	O	L	K	A	S		D	A	N	E				
U	S	A		K	H	A	M	I	S		A	C	T	S
R	A	C	E		M	U	A	N		F	R	U	I	T
S	K	E	W		A	L	M	A		F	E	R	M	I
E	A	S	E		P	E	A	H		A	D	D	E	R

Mothers of Great Men

O	S	L	O		R	I	B	S		B	A	L	S	A
R	E	A	R		O	R	E	O		O	N	I	O	N
A	P	S	E		M	A	R	Y		A	G	E	N	T
L	I	E		H	A	N	N	A	H		E	D	G	E
B	A	R	R	E	N			E	E	L				
			I	I	I		C	A	R	L		D	D	E
D	E	G	R	A	D	E	D		I	P	O	D	S	
L	E	A	H			I	C	E			L	E	A	S
E	A	R	T	H		V	I	N	E	G	A	R	Y	
E	R	N		O	V	A	L		S	L	Y			
			E	G	O			S	A	S	S	E	S	
F	A	R	M		L	A	P	S	E	D		A	N	O
O	C	E	A	N		F	A	W	N		B	R	U	U
C	A	L	I	F		E	P	I	C		A	A	R	P
I	D	Y	L	L		W	A	G	E		T	H	E	Y

Daughters-in-Law

O	S	A	K	A		O	S	L	O		E	A	R	
A	S	K	I	N	G		W	H	O	M		N	B	A
F	E	A	L	T	Y		L	E	V	I		T	L	C
			L	I	M	A		K	E	T	U	R	A	H
P	R	E		D	I	E	D		S	A	T	E		
P	R	O	D		G	I	R	L		L	A	P	E	L
T	O	O		Z	O	O	S		K	E	G			
A	F	F	A	I	R	S		A	N	A	E	M	I	A
N	N	E		P	O	O	H		I	L	E			
A	D	H	O	C		H	E	R	B		D	E	L	I
V	O	I	D		C	A	P	T		T	O	N	S	
E	M	P	E	R	O	R		A	D	A	R			
N	I	P		U	C	L	U		I	M	A	G	E	S
U	N	O		T	O	O	K		M	A	D	A	M	E
E	O	S		H	A	T	E		R	O	D	I	N	

Mothers-in-Law

```
M A S   A S C O T   B E S T S
O I L   P E A L E   O R P A H
B R O   C A M E L   N A O M I
S E G O   H E A L E D   T E N
    A D O         P I N
  U N F U R L   W A N I N G
A S E   O S A K A   G L O R Y
T E A M   E M I T S   E R I E
A U T O S   E D E M A   M S S
  P H O T O S   R A C I S T
      R E F     S T M
P A W   A F R E S H   P U P A
A R I E L   A T T I C   G A L
C A L V E   I N A N E   L R G
T Y L E R   L A R G O   Y E A
```

Sisters-in-Law

```
O U T L A W   C I T Y   T O W
A T E A S E   A C R E   E R A
T O N S I L   T E A L   S A T
    S A L S A   P L A T T E
A V E     U L E     D Y E R
G O L D   I M P L I E D
O C E A N S   A I D T   W E B
R A C H E L     E U G E N E
A L T   R A N G   A I M I N G
    A D M I R A L   T R U E
S P I T     L A W     D I T
P O S E U R   Y E L P S
A K A   B A R I   E Y E F U L
T E A   E G O S   A R R E S T
E S C   R U T H   H E E D E D
```

Women in Jesus' Family Tree

```
R E P S   M A R T   S T I L T
A X I S   A G U A   S A R A H
H I L T   R O T C   A M A Z E
A L A   E I G H T S   A N E W
B E F A L L       E R R
    S L Y   T R E E   A D M
A N T E N N A E   F O X E S
F R E E   A X E   P L A T
M E T R E   D I L L S E E D
D A S   T E A S   E O N
    A C V     E R S A T Z
A C S   E F F E C T   M I L
G U E S S   L E A H   S E G O
U R I A H   E A S E   A B E T
E E R I E   A R T S   M A R Y
```

Crowning Qualities of Womanhood

```
A R A B S   A H E M   C H A T
V A L E T   P U P A   D O P Y
E T U D E   E M I R   S N A P
R E M A R K   A C L U   O R E
      U N I O N   I N E R T
H U S B A N D     N O V
A N T   D I E T S   I T E M
S T E P   U S E   L O V E
H O M E   S M E A R   T E E
    R E P   C U T W O R K
A R O M A   W H E R E
U G H   U R S A   D I A L E R
T O E D   R E D O   P R I V A
A R T Y   O M E N   E E L E R
H A T E   W I S E   D R O N E
```

A Good Woman Is Hard to Find

```
S I G H S   S H A G   A L A R
T O R A H   P E E R   W I D E
A T O N E   L I R A   L O I S
Y A W N   C A R O M S   N E T
    A W A Y   M I S S U S
C A R H O P   T A X I
E M U   E S T H E R   A T O P
D E E R   R O E   M O P E
E N D S   C O W M A N   M A T
    V A R Y   M U M B L E
P U R P L E   V I T A
U N O   L A M M E D   R Y A N
P A T E   S A A R   S T E V E
I R O N   E R R S   T H A I S
L Y R E   S T Y E   Y A R D S
```

Behind Every Man...

```
A D D S   E C H O   S H I N
L O O M   A H A B   C A I R O
G U R U   S I L O   O R D E R
A B I G A I L   E T N A
E T C   A L I   E C H I N O
    T R Y   L E A H   C O A
U N C A P   F A R M S   H I S
S A A R   C O M A S   C O S I
A B R   P R O P S   D A R E S
G A G   R E D S   C O W
E L O P E D   S O S   T S P
  U P O N   K E T U R A H
A C C R A   A V I V   R U B Y
R A N G Y   V I L A   S E L L
E L S E   Y E L L   A R E A
```

341

Family Ties

AINT · DAVID · JOT
CROWD · AFIRE · USA
HONOR · GRIEF · DAM
ENE · ITOO · IMAGE
ANON · HELPHER
STICKY · OILED
LIARS · FLED · GAD
URGE · ACALM · BOLE
GEO · THAN · SIDON
GRAVY · PURSES
THEBABE · KIDD
HARED · FIND · NAP
ERA · ENRON · EYETO
TOT · ROBED · NEBAT
ADO · SWISS · SONS

The Enticing Tale of Adam's Rib

SPA · CAFE · ADDUCE
MIL · OPUS · WEIRDO
ASK · APSE · EVENTS
STARTLE · DIG
HOLE · EDEN · LOBAR
LIME · PAS · AGE
AVE · APE · SLUE
SADNESS · EGGHEAD
HEED · PHS · OUR
ERE · YOU · NEWS
WOMAN · EVIL · WHOA
BUL · DIEDAND
SAHARA · SAVE · LOO
AGASSI · THEN · EAR
MOTHER · NOSY · SHE

Rachel, the Shepherdess

LAMB · ACT · HOLD
ABEL · AGORA · EPEE
DEMO · FRYER · REAL
TOWHEE · KITSCH
SEWED · DUE
SNAIL · DEW · BLESS
HADNOT · MAL · FREE
EIN · NICOSIA · AVE
BLAM · NON · PURSED
ASHAN · BIC · TEENY
GOD · CAROB
PEEWEE · JOSEPH
TURN · JACOB · KIEV
SLIT · AROLE · ACRE
PLEA · STE · HAST

The Vindication of Jacob's Daughter

STARE · OWE · ALSO
PAPER · DAY · ELEAD
ALIAN · ONE · ALAND
KEEP · OUTSET · HES
ENC · OAR · AGEE
TEMPT · LORDGOD
YES · RVS · ESAU
LEARN · DIE · SNAKE
OMIT · SIP · SIT
PULLING · TROAS
EMIT · DYE · BUT
APT · APOGEE · HERO
SLUNG · BAA · MALES
EERIE · ELL · ASHOE
RANT · GAS · THEFT

A Steward's Wife

CAJUN · GOT · ARCH
ACORN · AVE · CHUZA
STAGE · MEN · RADAR
KINE · CIRCLE · ERE
SON · RAN · EATS
NADIR · NIELSEN
ACS · LTD · ISLE
HEATH · COS · KNELT
INKS · NOT · JAG
SECURER · ARSON
NERD · ADO · TOE
ANA · SOURCE · NIBS
BEGET · RUM · POOLS
CROSS · ONE · ATSEA
SINE · YES · LEERY

The Harlot with a Lot of Heart

PETER · ACLU · NAB
ANANAS · CHAR · ASL
WEIGHS · PANS · PSI
RATE · SCARLET
MOAB · ROTE · HETH
GERM · ROPE · JESSE
ESE · AIDE · BIT
LASAGNE · PONTOON
CUD · FLAX · VIA
FARCE · QUIZ · FANG
AGAR · SURE · BALK
CATALPA · SCAM
IST · AIRS · PRISSY
ASA · VETO · UNLIKE
LIN · ASSN · SYRIA

Scrambled Circle Puzzles

Questioning the Master
He had some serious questions for Jesus.
NICODEMUS
1. HEAVENLY 2. LIGHT 3. RECEIVE 4. LOVED 5. EARTHLY
6. MASTER 7. RULER 8. PERISH

Surprise!
He threw a party for Jesus but was not prepared for the woman with the perfume.
SIMON
1. BLESSED 2. SPIRIT 3. MOURN 4. FORBADE 5. PINNACLE

Rome Rules
Paul was kept under arrest for two years by these two Roman governors.
FELIX and FESTUS
1. FLESH 2. MANNER 3. DEALT 4. PERISH 5. EXECUTE
6. FALLEN 7. STRETCH 8. DESIRE 9. DESPITE 10. MOURN
11. WASHED

The Substitute
He was chosen to replace Judas as one of the twelve apostles.
MATTHIAS
1. MEDITATE 2. WAVES 3. RIGHT 4 TREMBLE 5. HANDMAID
6. MINE 7. STATUTES 8. CURSED

Who Am I?
He was a physician and historian.
LUKE
1. DELIVERED 2. INSTRUCTED 3. MARKETPLACE 4. EXCELLENT

Family History
This prophet was the son of Berechiah.
ZECHARIAH
1. BAPTIZE 2. WONDER 3. SORCERY 4. YOUTH 5. DECLARE
6. STRICKEN 7. MULTIPLY 8. EARTH 9. HANDS

Personal Professions
GOMER
She was a prostitute married to a prophet.
1. AVENGE 2. HOUSE 3. MERCY 4. CEASE 5. SWORD

That's Some Bath!
PHARAOH'S DAUGHTER
She found more than she expected in the river.
1. PITCH 2. HERSELF 3. WATER 4. INCREASED 5. BORN
6. CHILD 7. SLIME 8. MIDWIVES 9. MAID 10. NURSE
11. GOODLY 12. HEBREW 13. SISTER 14. RIVER 15. BRINK

Enough's Enough
CONCUBINE
In the Old Testament times, some men had one or more of these.
1. PRECIOUS 2. FOUNTAIN 3. UNRULY 4. SCRIPTURE
5. IMPUTED 6. BRIDLE 7. FRIEND 8. WANTON 9. MEMBERS

Favorable Hospitality
MARY and MARTHA
They were always ready to have Jesus as their guest.
1. MEEKNESS 2. PECULIAR 3. SAVIOR 4. GAINSAYER
5. MAGISTRATES 6. GRACE 7. LOVER 8. EXHORT 9. HAND
10. APPEARED

No Way to Treat a Guest
RHODA
She left an important guest at the door.
1. PRISON 2. HOUSE 3. VOICE 4. DAMSEL 5. GATE

Sharing the News
ELISABETH
Her husband returned home excited but speechless.
1. RIGHTEOUS 2. ALTAR 3. INCENSE 4. CUSTOM 5. ANGEL
6. BLAMELESS 7. PRIEST 8. LOT 9. CHILD

Anagrams

Bad Guys
PONTIUS PILATE, JUDAS ISCARIOT, NEBUCHADNEZZAR

Improper Names
ANTICHRIST, GOOD SAMARITAN, PRODIGAL SON

It's a Miracle!
EUTYCHUS, BARTIMAEUS, MALCHUS

Join the Club
SANHEDRIN, PHARISEES, PHILISTINES

New Testament Names
NICODEMUS, SIMON PETER, ONESIMUS

Mary's Amazing Job
HANDMAIDEN, SWADDLING CLOTHES, HEAVENLY HOST

Old Testament Names
REBEKAH, PHARAOH'S DAUGHTER, DELILAH

Widows
ZAREPHATH, TWO MITES, RUTH AND NAOMI

New Testament Names
MARTHA, ELISABETH, MARY MAGDALENE

Esther's Story
MORDECAI, CHAMBERLAINS, ADVERSARY

Spotty Headlines

Do Something Amazing
PETER, PHILIP, PAUL

Old Testament Prophets
JEREMIAH, DANIEL, HOSEA

Lesser-Known Men of the New Testament
ONESIMUS, DIOTREPHES, TERTIUS

Drop Me a Line
LUKE, PAUL, JOHN

Serving Jesus
JOSEPH, NICODEMUS, SIMON OF CYRENE

Not an Easy Road
STEPHEN, TIMOTHY, JAMES

Strong Women
LYDIA, ESTHER, DEBORAH

Wives of David
ABIGAIL, BATHSHEBA, MICHAL

Terrific Troublemakers
HERODIAS, JEZEBEL, SAPPHIRA

Women Who Suffered
NAOMI, MARY, HAGAR

Old Testament Mothers
SARAH, REBEKAH, HANNAH

Close to Jesus
ANNA, ELISABETH, MARTHA

Telephone Scrambles

Those Who Judged
MOSES, JOEL, OTHNIEL, SHAMGAR, GIDEON, JEPHTHAH, SAMSON, ELON

Unexpected Good Guys
BALAAM, AHIKAM, ZACCHAEUS, AHASUERUS, GAMALIEL, CORNELIUS, TIRHAKAH

Old Testament Deceit
POTIPHAR, JACOB, ACHAN, EHUD, DAVID, SANBALLAT, DARIUS, LABAN

Knowing David
SHIMEI, MIGHTY MEN, JONATHAN, JOAB, NATHAN, GOLIATH, AHIMELECH, ACHISH

Prisoners
HOSHEA, JOSEPH, PAUL, PETER, SAMSON, SILAS, SIMEON

Deacons
NICANOR, NICOLAS, PARMENAS, PHILIP, PROCHORUS, STEPHEN, TIMON

Ahead of Her Time
DEBORAH, RUTH, JOANNA, ABIGAIL, PRISCILLA, DAMARIS, CHLOE

Bad Girls
HERODIAS, ATHALIAH, DELILAH, JEZEBEL, SAPPHIRA, MAACAH, COZBI

Regarding Dorcas
TABITHA, JOPPA, DISCIPLE, GENEROUS, PETER, MIRACLE, ALIVE

Regarding Lydia
PURPLE, THYATIRA, MERCHANT, BELIEVER, PAUL, BAPTIZED, CLOTH

Mothers
EUNICE, ZILLAH, RACHEL, ELISABETH, TAMAR, BATHSHEBA, JOCHEBED

Heroines
MIRIAM, RAHAB, MICHAL, JAEL, JEHOSHEBA, ESTHER

Bible Quotations

Follow Him
"Jesus saith unto him, I am the way, the truth, and the life: no man cometh unto the Father, but by me." John 14:6

Finding Someone Special
"He raised up unto them David to be their king; to whom also he gave. . .testimony, and said, I have found David the son of Jesse, a man after mine own heart." Acts 13:22

Visiting with God
"Noah was a just man and perfect in his generations, and Noah walked with God." Genesis 6:9

An Engaging Man
"Joseph her husband, being a just man, and not willing to make her a publick example, was minded to put her away privily." Matthew 1:19

A Worthy Helper
"Take Mark, and bring him with thee: for he is profitable to me for the ministry." 2 Timothy 4:11

Recognizing the Call
"And the LORD came, and stood, and called as at other times, Samuel, Samuel. Then Samuel answered, Speak; for thy servant heareth." 1 Samuel 3:10

Serve the Servant
"I commend unto you Phebe our sister, which is a servant of the church which is at Cenchrea: That ye receive her in the Lord, as becometh saints." Romans 16:1–2

Testing the King

"When the queen of Sheba heard of the fame of Solomon concerning the name of the Lord, she came to prove him with hard questions." 1 Kings 10:1

All Things Are Possible

"Through faith also Sara herself received strength to conceive seed, and was delivered of a child when she was past age, because she judged him faithful who had promised." Hebrews 11:11

A Bitter Woman

"And she said unto them, Call me not Naomi, call me Mara: for the Almighty hath dealt very bitterly with me." Ruth 1:20

Given to Moses

"And Moses was content to dwell with the man: and he gave Moses Zipporah his daughter. And she bare him a son." Exodus 2:21–22

The First Lady

"And Adam called his wife's name Eve; because she was the mother of all living." Genesis 3:20